# Praise for *The Future of Truth*

"A brilliant meditation on life after the end of reality. *The Future of Truth* explores what happens when every image, voice, and fact can be fabricated. Rosenbaum maps the collapse of shared perception and, against the odds, shows how we might still find our way back to trust and meaning."
—Nicholas Thompson, CEO, *The Atlantic*, and Author, *The Running Ground*

"What makes this book different is its balance of tech insight, philosophical depth, and grounded urgency. *The Future of Truth* asks hard questions not just about AI, but about us."
—Daniel H. Pink, Author, *Drive*, *When*, and *The Power of Regret*

"Truth, as you may have noticed, is under attack. From the White House to corporate boardrooms, lying has become a profit center. So is there any hope? Rosenbaum's tour through this mess is bleak in the ways you expect and then, somehow, a little hopeful. People still want facts that hold up. At the crossroads of AI and human judgment, things will get worse before they stand any chance of getting better. Rosenbaum doesn't preach. He just shows how the game works, why we keep falling for it, and who keeps cashing the checks. *The Future of Truth* offers a possible way out—if we can figure out how to make truth pay. Fingers crossed."
—Michael Wolff, Author, *All or Nothing*

"Back in 2017 when I published *Fantasyland*—a history of Americans' chronic blurring of fiction and reality and how the internet turned a manageable centuries-long chronic condition into an acute and potentially fatal social illness—we'd just elected our first fact-indifferent president. Five more years passed before AI became a factor in the struggle to distinguish truth from falsehood. *The Future of Truth* is a smart, wise, essential addition to the conversation as we go further into this civilizational crossroads. Thank you, Steve Rosenbaum."
—Kurt Andersen, Author, *Fantasyland* and *Evil Geniuses*, and Cofounder, *Spy* magazine

"*The Future of Truth* is the guide we need right now. Rosenbaum warns of a coming AI era that risks diminishing our own agency and distorting our shared reality in new and dangerous ways. But he also spotlights the people doing the hard work of rebuilding shared truth from the ground up. Sharp, urgent, and genuinely hopeful."
—Jeremy Heimans, Coauthor, *New Power*

"The internet has steadily changed everything around us: who we know, how we meet, how we work, how we date, how we play, who gets famous, whom we trust, what we want, and who we want to be. In Rosenbaum's journey into *The Future of Truth*, he takes us inside a world where those shifts collide with systems built to manipulate attention and shape belief. He shows how our reality is being rewritten in real time, what's driving that change, and why understanding it is the only way to rebuild trust. It's a clear, grounded look at the information landscape we all live in now—and the one we're heading toward."
—Taylor Lorenz, Author, *Extremely Online*, and Reporter, User MAG

"Steven Rosenbaum has written the rare book about AI and misinformation that's more interested in rebuilding than doomscrolling. *The Future of Truth* is part road trip, part reality check, but also a survival guide for anyone who still wants facts to matter in a world that suddenly seems to be trying to gaslight you with everything."

—Brian McCullough, Host, *Internet History* podcast

"Reality, fact, fiction, information, disinformation, technology, platforms, virtual—these are all fast-moving and fast-changing concepts. No one knows how they're evolving and how each impacts the other more than Steve. If you want to know where the world is today and where it's heading tomorrow, this is the way to do it."

—Bradley Tusk, Founder and CEO, Tusk Ventures, and Author, *The Fixer*

"An urgent warning that reality itself is shattering, not because it's inevitable, but because the princes of technology have appointed themselves as the arbiters of truth—and not to optimize humans, but to keep us in thrall to our tiny screens. But hope is not lost. Steve Rosenbaum lays out in brilliant and riveting detail not only what has gone wrong, but also how to fix it."

—David Ewing Duncan, Author, *Talking to Robots*

"Truth is the ultimate currency and not attention. But in order to monetize attention and to influence behavior, trust is under attack on a number of fronts—from science, where data and facts are seen as malleable, to government, where integrity and a resonance with reality are seen as weakness. If one can believe everything, one believes nothing—and that is the risk we face. This book illuminates how AI could accelerate the erosion of trust if we do not, as a society, take it seriously, and provides ways to avoid this catastrophe. While this book is called *The Future of Truth*, it is written with an intensity that recognizes there is no real future without truth.

—Rishad Tobaccowala, Author, *Restoring the Soul of Business*, and former Chief Growth Officer, Publicis Groupe

"The problem facing humanity in the digital age, we learn from Steve Rosenbaum in his swift, comprehensive, and extremely lucid *The Future of Truth*, is that tech has exacerbated untruth at a scale and speed hitherto unimaginable. In only 20 years, social media has disrupted democracy and public health worldwide by platforming and coalescing misinformation and disinformation toward a calamitous Post-Truth Age. Rosenbaum and his sparkling galaxy of thinkers lead us through AI's many applications—healthcare, finance, emotional health, economics, human employment, art, and identity itself—to survey astonishing benefits and ominous unintended consequences, especially in early days when the guardrails are few and ethical conduct thoroughly subordinated to the profit motive."

—Bob Garfield, Media Critic, Author, and Cohost Emeritus, *On the Media*

"As someone who's lived on the front lines of innovation, I know that true disruption strikes at the heart of how we define what's real. With unflinching clarity, *The Future of Truth* exposes how the technologies shaping our tomorrow are already reprogramming reality. Steven Rosenbaum's book is essential reading for anyone who wants to not only understand the coming disruptions to knowledge and democracy, but to harness them for positive change. In a world saturated by algorithmic noise, this work is the signal."

—Jay Samit, Bestselling Author, *Disrupt You!* and *The Second Act Advantage*

"In *The Future of Truth*, Steve Rosenbaum takes a deep, and at times dark, look at what art means in an age when truth itself is uncertain. His exploration of ownership, authorship, and the uneasy collaboration between humans and AI is unsettling. The questions he raises about how artists will make a living and what originality even means now are complicated, sometimes painful, but necessary. Through it all, Rosenbaum keeps sight of one powerful idea: that art's worth lies not in perfection, but in its ability to express the messy, imperfect, deeply human truths that no machine can touch."

—Ava Seave, Author, *The Curse of the Mogul*, and Principal, Quantum Media

"We live in a G-Zero world where trust between nations has collapsed. Steve Rosenbaum shows that trust is collapsing inside them, too, as the technologies we built to connect us are also fracturing reality itself. When citizens no longer inhabit a shared reality, the social fabric frays, markets fail, and democracy falters. *The Future of Truth* is a bracing look at a crisis that's already here."

—Ian Bremmer, President, Eurasia Group, and Author, *The Power of Crisis*

## Also by Steven Rosenbaum

***Curation Nation: How to Win in a World Where Consumers Are Creators***

Published in March 2011 by McGraw-Hill Business, this book explores the rise of digital curation and its impact on publishing, consumer content, and brand-centric curation.

***Curate This!: The Hands-On, How-To Guide to Content Curation***

Released in October 2014, this book provides practical guidance on content curation, emphasizing the importance of human skills in organizing and presenting information.

# THE FUTURE OF TRUTH

## HOW AI RESHAPES REALITY

STEVEN ROSENBAUM

Matt Holt Books

An Imprint of BenBella Books, Inc.

Dallas, TX

Matt Holt is an imprint of BenBella Books, Inc.
BenBella Books, Inc.
8080 N. Central Expressway, Suite 1700
Dallas, TX 75206
benbellabooks.com
Send feedback to feedback@benbellabooks.com



Printed in the United States of America
10 9 8 7 6 5 4 3 2 1

Library of Congress Control Number: 2025046891
ISBN 9781637749104 (hardcover)
ISBN 9781637749111 (electronic)

Editing by Lydia Choi
Copyediting by Lynne Curry
Proofreading by Marissa Wold Uhrina and Denise Pangia
Indexing by WordCo Indexing Services, Inc.
Text design and composition by Jordan Koluch
Cover design by Jason Arias
Cover image © Shutterstock / goldnetz

*For those who still believe that truth matters. For the seekers, the skeptics, the storytellers, and the next generation—who will inherit the consequences of what we choose to believe today.*

*To my wife, Pam Yoder, who always tells me the truth—whether I like it or not.*

*To my sons, Max and Murray, who are living in the complicated, exhilarating, terrifying, and dizzying world of digital media. They're at the center of a tsunami—surrounded by wonder, risk, and the relentless complexity of modern connection.*

*To my mother, Eileen Landay, who raised me to the steady sound of an IBM Selectric typewriter. Her writing, teaching, and sharp questioning made me a better thinker, student, and storyteller. She never gave up on the truth, even when it seemed out of reach.*

*To my brother, Roger, who's taken on what may be the hardest job of all: making truth-based media in an era when influence and AI threaten to drown out good, old-fashioned journalism with frivolity and snake oil.*

*A family of truth seekers and truth tellers.*
*Now, if only we could convince our friends, our neighbors, and those who see the world differently that conversation—not conflict—is the path to a sustainable future.*

*"We shape our tools and thereafter our tools shape us."*
*—Marshall McLuhan*

# Contents

## Foreword: The Urgency of Truth

An atom bomb has exploded in our information ecosystem. The blast ripped away journalism's gatekeeping role and handed it to technology companies. Lies spread faster than facts, outrage outshouts reason, and fear fuels algorithms. I said those words in Oslo, in December 2021, as I accepted the Nobel Peace Prize—and their urgency has only grown since then.

Without facts, you can't have truth. Without truth, you can't have trust. Without trust, we have no shared reality, no rule of law, and no democracy. This fragile chain reaction—facts, truth, trust—is the foundation of free societies. Break it, and everything else falls.

We are living through that collapse. Democracies are being hollowed out from within, not by invading armies, but by viral lies amplified on the devices we carry in our pockets. Half the world is heading to the polls, and yet the very integrity of elections is crumbling because the integrity of facts has been destroyed. It is no coincidence that today more than 72% of the world's population now lives under autocratic rule.

I have lived this personally. In the Philippines, Rappler became a target of state-backed disinformation. When the government tried to shut us down, advertisers were pressured to walk away. At the same time, I was fighting legal cases that could have locked me away for more than a century. To keep reporting, I had to accept that I might spend the rest of my life in prison. That is what it takes now to tell the truth.

And yet, I remain hopeful. Because I have also seen courage. Fifty-one percent of our advertisers refused to give in. Ordinary citizens stood with us.

Young people around the world are demanding healthier systems for media and technology. Civil society is rising. Even some inside the tech industry are admitting that the status quo is untenable. Truth has defenders. And sometimes, simply holding the line is itself an act of resistance.

But hope alone is not enough. Each day of inaction strengthens platforms that profit from lies. Technology companies will not regulate themselves. Governments are too slow. The methods of silencing us grow more insidious: economic chokeholds, legal harassment, coordinated online hate. We must act with the tools we have—supporting independent journalism, demanding accountability, and teaching our children how to survive an information system designed to addict, enrage, and deceive.

The next accelerant is already here: artificial intelligence. Like social media, these large language models are not anchored in facts. They hallucinate. They produce words that sound true but are not. Deepfakes will soon make it impossible to tell what's real and what's not. If we fail to act, this will accelerate the collapse of trust into every corner of our lives.

The youngest generation will bear the heaviest cost. They get their news on social media, mixed with propaganda. They sleep less, are more distracted, and suffer higher rates of anxiety and depression. This is not abstract. It is a crisis playing out in their bodies and their minds. When truth is weakened, so is human resilience.

And yet, there are solutions. I have spoken about them often: We must hold technology companies accountable for the harms they cause, treating information integrity as a public safety issue, not a free speech debate. We must build public-interest technology—federated, open systems that give communities and newsrooms control of their own distribution rather than surrendering it to profit-driven algorithms. And we must strengthen protections for independent journalism and invest in truth the way we invest in infrastructure, because democracy cannot survive without facts.

This is not a problem confined to any one country. The same dynamics repeat everywhere: lies amplified, institutions weakened, citizens divided. But we also know what works: informed communities, resilient media, and people willing to act together.

The fight for facts is inseparable from the fight for freedom. The fight for truth is inseparable from the fight for justice. What we choose to do now will determine whether democracy endures.

That is why *The Future of Truth* matters. Steven Rosenbaum's book challenges us not just to recognize the scale of the crisis but to imagine solutions bold enough to meet it. It asks us to consider how truth can be rebuilt in an age of distortion, and what role each of us must play. Because the story of truth is not finished—it is being written right now, by all of us.

**Maria Ressa**
Nobel Peace Prize Laureate

## *Prologue: The Magic of Technology . . . Revealed*

Though I didn't know it at the time, I began my career—such as it was for a teenager—as a professional liar. A liar in a top hat and a black cape. Let me explain.

It was a hot, sticky summer day on the boardwalk in Long Beach, Long Island. I was 14, standing on a makeshift stage at a talent show with what felt like a huge crowd watching. Beside me was Stacy—an older, taller high school friend wearing a dazzling sequin gown. I was a magician. She was my assistant. And together, we were about to perform a very famous illusion: the old "sawing a woman in half" trick. Only in this case, she wasn't a woman—she'd barely started high school—and I was a young teen magician.

We pulled it off flawlessly. The crowd erupted in applause. Weeks later, my hometown paper, *The Westbury Times,* wrote a glowing article about my performance. When asked about my career ambitions, I answered with all the confidence of a teenage wizard, "Absolutely. I'm going to be a professional magician."

Looking back, I realize that magic was my first foray into understanding truth—or, at least, our perceptions of it. Magic, after all, is a sort of transaction. I pretended to saw Stacy in half, and the audience pretended to believe me. We all understood the deal: I wasn't a wizard, and she wasn't really sawed in half. But for that moment, the line between truth and fiction blurred.

"Any sufficiently advanced technology is indistinguishable from magic," wrote Arthur C. Clarke in his 1962 book *Profiles of the Future.* And he was most certainly right. The world we live in today often feels magical—until we remember that every astonishing feat of technology is built on systems of logic, reason, and human ingenuity.

As I set out on this journey to report this book, I found one question kept coming up: "Won't things move so quickly that AI will change faster than the ink will dry on your book's pages?" Fair question, but the simple answer is no. Some ancient Egyptian scratched the concept of *Ma'at*—their word for truth and cosmic order—into stone over four thousand years ago, probably losing sleep over the same questions keeping us up tonight. In a world where AI will most certainly take some jobs, create new ones, and have us all rethinking our relationship with machines, understanding Truth isn't becoming less important—it's becoming absolutely critical.

We're standing at a crossroads, and the stakes couldn't be higher. Either Truth dies—buried under an avalanche of AI-generated alternative facts and synthetic realities—or we fight like hell to preserve it. All this talk about putting "guardrails" on AI? That's laughable if we don't even know what road we want to be on. That's why I wrote this book. Not because I have all the answers, but because I've spent my life watching how each new technology—from magic tricks to media to AI—changes our relationship with Truth. And I'm convinced that if we don't figure out what Truth means to us now, we won't just lose control of AI—we'll lose something fundamental about what makes us human.

Throughout history, each transformative technology has forced us to grapple with how we share and verify Truth. Take the printing press, for example. In its time, Gutenberg's invention was as revolutionary as the Internet is today. By the fifteenth century, monks painstakingly copied manuscripts, ensuring that knowledge remained the exclusive domain of the elite—so, in other words, Gutenberg's movable type democratized print. For the first time, ideas could spread rapidly, reaching a scale and audience previously unimaginable. It was the original democratization of information.

But even then, the relationship between truth and technology was complicated. Sure, the printing press gave us mass literacy and books like the *Principia Mathematica*. But it also unleashed pamphleteers spreading wild rumors, fake news, and propaganda. Every technological advance comes with this dual nature: an opportunity for truth and a risk of distortion.

Fast-forward to me, decades after my magician days, standing in a brown metal building in upstate New York. By then, I was producing news programs with my first company, Broadcast News Networks. One day, I stumbled upon an early handheld camera at the Consumer Electronics Show: the Sharp View-Cam. This clunky Hi8 recorder had a twistable lens and a big LCD screen—a precursor to the video tools we take for granted today. I convinced Sharp to lend us five of them, and soon, we were running a new experiment: democratizing media.

We asked viewers to call in with their stories. The response was overwhelming. Phones rang off the hook, and people eagerly shared tales they wanted told. We'd mail out a camera, coach them through the filming process, and edit the footage into polished segments. It wasn't perfect, but it worked. For a moment, it felt like technology could really empower people to share their truths.

And then YouTube came along.

Suddenly, the tools of storytelling were in everyone's hands, without the buffer of fact-checkers or editors. Stories could go viral without regard for accuracy, fairness, or consequence. The balance between truth and technology shifted yet again. And now, the game is changing once more.

Enter artificial intelligence. Unlike the printing press or YouTube, AI doesn't just spread information; it generates it. From deepfake videos indistinguishable from reality to AI-written articles that mimic human voices, the line between what's real and what's fabricated is dissolving faster than we can redraw it.

The magician's trick relied on one thing: the audience's understanding that the trick wasn't real. But AI muddies that understanding. When a deepfake video shows a world leader declaring war or when an AI chatbot convincingly pretends to be a grieving loved one, the audience no longer knows it's part of an act. The trick versus truth dichotomy—once playful and understood—is becoming harder to spot, maybe even impossible.

And so, as we stand on the brink of an AI-driven avalanche, the stakes for truth have never been higher. AI doesn't just amplify misinformation; it creates a new reality, one where the truth competes against infinite, algorithmically generated lies. As a magician, I could control the narrative on that stage. But in a world of AI, no one controls the narrative—and that might be the most dangerous trick of all.

So here I am now, years later, tracing a journey that started with magic tricks and led to questions far larger than I could have imagined back on that boardwalk stage. And while I am a scholar and proudly hold a degree in Truth from the prestigious New York University Gallatin School of Individualized Study, I don't claim to be an expert with some magical vision of the future. Instead, consider me your tour guide, taking you into a series of conversations and explorations with some truly brilliant friends. They may have a clue about how the future will emerge. At least, that's the hope.

Today, technology hasn't just made the truth more accessible—it's also made it more slippery, more malleable. We live in a world where truth can be constructed, amplified, and weaponized. And, as we'll explore in this book, it's not just the technology that's to blame—it's us.

Because, ultimately, the question remains: Can we tell the difference between the AI trick and the truth?

CHAPTER 1

# The Vancouver Food Fight That Tried to Save Truth and Failed

Leading up to my flight to Vancouver, I couldn't help but wonder if somehow this year's TED gathering would be different. It was my eighteenth consecutive TED, and I've given three TED Talks—okay, two if you don't count the TEDx talk I gave in Grand Rapids. While I think it counts, Chris Anderson, whose title is Head of TED, doesn't quite count it. Because TEDx isn't "big" TED. It's the source of endless internal debate at TED's offices on Hudson Street in Manhattan. At least it was when I had a desk there, when I was a member of the fifth cohort of the TED Residency back in 2018. But since then TED has become more welcoming of content from its global TEDx community—embracing its diversity even if its content is somewhat uneven. But I digress. The annual gathering of "big TED" in Vancouver, Canada, remains a powerful center of gravity for complicated ideas, debates, and concepts that challenge and spark both innovation and anger. And today the powerful TEDsters have set their sights on a technology that has just come out of hiding—ready to upend, or hand over, the core concepts of civil society. Truth, long the domain of thinkers and citizens, is at the precipice of being handed over to charming robots. At Kensico Cemetery in Valhalla, New York, Isaac Asimov is rolling over in his grave.

Founded in 1984 as a small California gathering of dreamers, TED has grown into the most recognizable stage for ideas on the planet. Over the years, figures like Bill Gates, Jamie Oliver, and Sheryl Sandberg have used the red circle to challenge how we think about health, food, and leadership. And every so often, its famously composed curator, Chris Anderson, lets his British restraint slip—once dubbing Twitter's then-CEO Jack Dorsey the "Captain of the TwitTanic," a single line that caught the tech world's anxiety in miniature.

At a pivotal TED gathering in the early 2020s, TED found itself in the white-hot center of tech and Truth. Attendees read the speaker rundown before arriving and understood that AI would be asked to defend itself and its potential as an existential threat that some gravely feared. It sent a ripple through the chattering tech community. Would TED set the world on fire or snuff out the smoldering and dangerous embers? And so in March 2022, the boldface names and private planes arrived at Vancouver International Airport (YVR).

TED is a meticulously curated gathering, and its audience includes some of the most powerful and wealthy people on the planet, so putting speakers on the stage with controversial views is a high-wire act on a good day.

TED's pursuit of "ideas worth spreading" isn't without casualties. Talks are sometimes pulled, tempers sometimes flare, and every year someone walks off the stage either a legend or a cautionary tale.

...

But for all its polish and pageantry, TED remains an experiment in truth-telling—a live lab for the global conversation. As my plane lifted off from JFK, I found myself wondering how TED would handle the biggest risk yet: artificial intelligence. On the first of two legs of my trip—New York to Toronto, then Toronto to Vancouver—neither of which had working Wi-Fi, I found myself in the rare position of being completely offline. I sat with the printed program for hours, tracing the names and titles of the sessions ahead. The opening lineup promised fireworks. The entire first block was dedicated to AI—an existential subject with no middle ground. Would it be the end of humanity or the beginning of a new kind of intelligence?

What began as a nonprofit AI research organization transformed into one of tech's most valuable companies, highlighting how market forces can reshape even idealistic ventures. The organization's evolution from open-source advocate to commercial powerhouse revealed fundamental tensions between public benefit and private profit in AI development.

Would OpenAI live up to the seemingly endless number of blogs and podcasts touting its world-changing power? The AI fanboys seemed to embrace the risk–reward adrenaline. And Anderson had programmed a lineup that was sure to challenge preconceived notions of TED's techno-utopian crowd.

Greg Brockman—whose title had changed from CTO of OpenAI to cofounder with no one noticing—would open the conference. Sal Khan, the founder of the eponymous Khan Academy, would end the first session. Smack in the middle was Gary Marcus, a professor of psychology and neuroscience at NYU, now emeritus, and an outspoken author on AI. Certainly, this would be his moment in the sun. But when I tweeted with him days before and spoke to him at the Speakers Dinner the night before his talk, he seemed anxious, almost queasy. "I'm not one of these long-term riskers who think the entire planet is going to be taken over by robots," he told me gently during our conversation at the Speakers Dinner, trying to probe to see what "side" I was on. It turns out we shared an affinity for a spot best described as the messy middle.

Marcus had been a well-respected faculty member at NYU. His departure was something of a mystery, given the somewhat draconian academic dividing line between research and activism. Every now and then the university would look the other way when one of its faculty became outspoken and famous. Stern Business School professor Scott Galloway had risen to fame by being controversial, often gnawing on the hand that feeds him, but NYU knew he was a draw for students and the media, so they looked the other way. And Galloway's Stern salary wasn't what was keeping him there. He liked the moniker, and the students were a good audience for his often accurate-if-profanity-laden-rants. Galloway was "cautiously optimistic" about AI, revealing on a number of podcasts that he stayed up late into the night getting AI tips from TikTok and playing with them. Galloway wasn't at TED this year. Which left Marcus somewhat alone.

He had left NYU for start-up land, first founding Geometric Intelligence, which was acquired by Uber, where he signed on as the head of its AI lab. That didn't last. And then he founded his second start-up, teaming up with iRobot's Rodney Brooks at Robust.AI. That was 2020, and even then, light years ago in the AI world, Marcus was trying to throw cold water on the growing hype around AI. "It's not how intelligent the machines are, it's how much control we give them," said Marcus when he founded his second start-up, Robust.AI. Control would hang in the air, even as AI insiders confided that controlling the newborn entities was nearly impossible.

But now Marcus was in Vancouver, smack in the middle of the first session of arguably the most influential conference on the planet, and his role, he worried, was to bring a semblance of responsibility to the audience of billionaires and venture capitalists who were already pouring money into AI with little regard for the dangers it portends. VCs were looking to put blockchain and crypto in the rearview mirror.

Marcus was worried for good reason, as he soon found out: Eliezer Yudkowsky, a notorious firebrand AI contrarian, would give the talk just after him. Marcus was left startled, taken off guard. Because while he'd been drafting and rehearsing with the TED speaker team for weeks, Yudkowsky had been invited just three days ago. TED never does last-minute bookings, and Marcus feared this meant TED didn't feel he was harsh enough to balance the AI booster Greg Brockman, sure to deliver a commercial for Open AI's ChatGPT. Whenever Marcus expresses his concerns, it's in the words of a scientist. Detailed and nuanced. But in our current world where TikTok makes the 280 characters of X (formerly Twitter) look encyclopedic, his attempts at urgency are easily lost in blip-verts zigzagging through the monied class between fear and greed.

As Marcus stepped onto the daunting red circle of the TED stage, he took us back to his childhood, where he was coding on a paper computer at age eight. "In high school, I got myself a Commodore 64 and worked on machine translation," Marcus told me during a conversation after the TED Talk, chuckling at the memory of those early experiments. "It seems almost quaint now, doesn't it? But those were exciting times. We felt like we were on the cusp of something big."

It was his way of establishing credibility, showing he wasn't just a newcomer to the AI party. This lifelong AI enthusiast was standing there telling us he was worried.

He painted a picture of a world potentially drowning in misinformation, with AI systems so adept at spinning yarns that even professionals might struggle to discern fact from fiction. To illustrate his point, he shared an alarming example of ChatGPT fabricating a sexual harassment scandal, complete with a fake *Washington Post* article.

But Marcus wasn't just there to sound alarms. He proposed combining two different AI approaches: symbolic systems and neural networks. Essentially, he was advocating for a marriage of old-school AI with cutting-edge techniques, a peace treaty in a long-standing tech war.

He then made a bold proposal—he called for a global, nonprofit, neutral organization to govern AI. "This is too important to leave to the tech bros and their profit margins," he seemed to be saying. "We need something like the United Nations, but for AI."

Throughout his talk, you could feel the tension. Marcus's love for AI was clear, but he was like a parent watching their child about to do something dangerous. He was walking a tightrope between hope and fear, arguing that while AI could help solve big problems, it could also cause significant harm if not carefully managed.

However, as the TED organizers had feared, Marcus's nuanced approach didn't quite land with the impact TED needed. To ratchet up the alarm and danger, Eliezer Yudkowsky, a notorious AI contrarian, was given a slot immediately after Marcus.

Yudkowsky didn't mince words: "Many researchers, including myself, expect that the most likely result of building a superhumanly smart AI, under anything remotely like the current circumstances, is that literally everyone on Earth will die," he declared during his stark TED presentation. The audience shifted uncomfortably, trying to rationalize away such a dire prediction.

He pressed on, his tone unshaken. "I'm not saying this for shock value. This is where we're headed unless something changes," Yudkowsky continued. He explained that modern AI systems operate on giant, inscrutable networks—complex structures of numbers that somehow, inexplicably, begin to work. But nobody really knows how, and that, he said, was the crux of the problem.

"At some point, these companies racing to scale AI are going to cough out something smarter than humanity. And nobody knows when that's going to happen," he warned during his presentation. The audience's discomfort was palpable, a collective attempt to rationalize away the gloomy forecast.

Chris Anderson, TED's curator, stepped in to balance the room. "Eliezer, what you're raising the alarm about here . . . this is terrifying, but also feels a bit—I don't know, extreme? Can you give us some real-world scenarios?"

Yudkowsky's response was equally unsettling: "Oh, sure, I'll just sketch out a superintelligence takeover like it's a doodle. But if you want examples, imagine sending the design for an air conditioner back to the eleventh century. They wouldn't even understand why cold air comes out of it. We're the eleventh century in this analogy."

He continued: "Even if I had months to prepare for this talk, I couldn't refute every hopeful fantasy people have about how it might go well. There is no standard scientific consensus for how things will go well. There is no real engineering plan for us surviving."

...

After TED, I found myself grappling with a gnawing question: If AI is so charming, is it programmed to tell the truth? Does it even know what truth is? Is truth a mathematical problem or a philosophical journey?

I reached out to both Marcus and Yudkowsky for further insights. Through a graduate student, I was told that Yudkowsky was "too busy" to talk to me, even as his grad student accepted my LinkedIn request. This small interaction spoke volumes about the insular nature of some AI research circles and the challenges of accessing key figures in the field.

Gary, on the other hand, was open to further conversation. We've talked three times since TED: once on stage at South by Southwest—the notoriously weird annual conference and festivals event in Austin—about the future of Truth, again at the P&T Knitwear bookstore with Raffi Krikorian, the CTO of the Emerson Collective, and then in a lengthy Zoom call.

Marcus painted a stark picture of two possible futures: one where people are massively deceived but believe everything and another where people are lied to so often that they stop believing anything. Neither scenario, he argued, is conducive to a healthy democracy.

When I asked about potential solutions, Marcus emphasized the need for critical thinking and skepticism. However, he was quick to point out the potential pitfalls of this approach. "The natural response here is to say, 'Well, okay, let's just teach everybody that every video that you see might be fake.' And there is an argument for doing that, but there is an argument that that is going to lead us to this total nihilism."

As we concluded our series of interviews, it was clear that Gary Marcus is not just a critic, but a visionary hoping to steer AI development toward a more responsible and truthful future. His upcoming book, *Taming Silicon Valley*, aims to provide a focal point for community activism around these issues. "We need to organize around this, just like we organize around fair wages," Marcus emphasized during our SXSW panel discussion about the future of Truth. "It's just as important, maybe even more important, because if things go the way they are, there won't be wages for anybody at all."

In the end, Marcus's message is clear: The promise of AI is immense, but so too are its perils. It falls to us to navigate this new frontier with wisdom, foresight, and a commitment to the greater good. As he put it, "Our future depends on it."

TED's AI smackdown served as a prophetic food fight between those arguing for slow, methodical, careful work and the gleeful "the water's fine, jump in!" crowd of investors and technologists always on the hunt for the next shiny object. It marked a significant moment in the ongoing debate about the future of truth in an AI-dominated world. This debate continues to shape our technological landscape and our understanding of reality itself.

As the TED conference wrapped up, the debate between AI optimists and skeptics continued to simmer. Marcus's journey from tech enthusiast to concerned critic was evident in his reflections. He recalled meeting Google cofounder Larry Page in 2014: "Larry Page was one of the founders of Google, and their motto was Don't Be Evil. And I think he believed that." But the landscape had shifted dramatically since then.

The release of ChatGPT in November 2022 marked a turning point for Marcus. "There was always some deceitful people and so forth, but I generally had a pretty positive view about tech, and that really changed most sharply . . . when ChatGPT came out," he explained during our discussion. "Suddenly, dollar signs started flashing between people's eyes."

"I think I grew up actually loving tech," Marcus explained. "I was a gadget head." This enthusiasm extended to his early interactions with Google's leadership. However, as the AI race heated up, Marcus observed a change in the industry's priorities.

Marcus's journey from an optimistic tech enthusiast who believed in Google's "Don't Be Evil" motto to a critic warning about AI's dangers encapsulates the broader shift in the tech industry's approach to AI development and ethics.

The future of AI and the future of truth are inextricably linked. As Marcus has shown, this future is still being written. It's up to all of us to ensure that the story has a happy ending.

What happened in Vancouver wasn't just a quirky experiment gone awry; it was a glimpse into a larger pattern. Truth has always been slippery, and history has the receipts. Let's travel back and see just how messy it's been—and why it matters now. Up next: the troubled past of Truth.

CHAPTER 2

# Truth's Troubled Past

In a world where deepfakes blur the lines between reality and fiction, where AI chatbots engage in philosophical debates, and where the very nature of truth seems to be under siege, we find ourselves at a philosophical crossroads. The digital age has ushered in an era of unprecedented technological advancement, but it has also brought with it a host of questions that challenge our most fundamental beliefs about reality, consciousness, and truth itself.

But let's try for a moment to figure out just how we ended up here. The term "information explosion" was first used in 1941. Valdemar Poulsen created the telegraphone, the first functioning magnetic recorder, in 1898. Which is to say, we've been exploding for a very long time. The battle over Truth isn't new, and that merits a look backward to its earliest days.

Simply put, this is all Plato's fault. He stubbornly argued that there was an absolute Truth. The thing that is most troubling for AI coders, I suspect, is that they're building on conversational quicksand. Plato wanted reality to maintain standards. He drew a clear distinction between knowledge, which is certain, and opinion, which is not. Plato had a sort of "truth code" with a programming language. According to his rules, for one to have "Truth"—defined as knowledge—the proposition must be believed, the proposition must be true, and the proposition must be supported by good reasons.

So, here's the problem. For Plato, knowledge is justified, true belief. So that means Plato didn't watch cable news, or read the *National Enquirer*, or enjoy the many fictions portrayed as facts that flood the Internet. The power and complexity of Truth isn't held to anything that reflects an objective standard. Put a scientist and a philosopher in a room and set them at Truth. There'll most certainly be a bloody fight.

Take, for example, the deeply held beliefs of Truth and religion. In the Gospel of John, Jesus proclaims: "I am the way, the truth, and the life." Another example: "He that doeth truth cometh to the light, that his deeds may be made manifest, that they are wrought in God." There have been wars fought over the truths in the Bible. And, of course, we have Plato's Cave Theory. Think of Plato's cave like this: A bunch of folks are stuck in a cave their whole lives, only seeing shadows on a wall and thinking that's all there is to the world. When one of them finally gets out and sees the real deal—actual trees, sun, everything—they realize those shadows were just cheap imitations of reality. That's Plato's way of saying most of us are living in a world of shadows, missing out on the deeper truth of things.

My purpose here isn't to debate Plato's Cave Theory, Heidegger's explorations of Plato, or the Bible's use of the word "Truth" within its allegorical and biblical context. It's not my expertise, and the exploration of Truth since Plato has been the academic efforts of philosophers, historians, and scholars going back to the history of Western thought.

My goal, in fact, is the exact opposite. It is to say that Truth has always been a problem, long before ChatGPT mauled my biography. Sam Altman could hardly give a shit. "Technology happens because it is possible," said Altman, talking to *The New York Times*, and pointed out that he and Robert Oppenheimer share a birthday. Oppenheimer was the leader of the Manhattan Project, which built the atomic bomb. Prophetic or ironic—you can decide for yourself.

To get to where we are today, we need a tour guide and a time machine. David Chalmers, who holds a PhD in philosophy and cognitive science, is the Sherlock Holmes of philosophy—a brilliant and quirky detective, always on the hunt for clues to help him solve the biggest mystery of all: consciousness. He's spent years peering into the depths of the mind, trying to figure out how it all works. He's asked the big questions that keep us all up at night: Why do we have subjective experiences? What is it like to be a bat? And, of course, do we really live in the Matrix? He's not trying to be hyperbolic, and he's not trying to arm wrestle Keanu Reeves. But Chalmers is a philosopher who thinks about Truth, not about where it comes from as much as where it's going.

It was on a spring morning in Tucson, Arizona, in 1994, when a then-unknown philosopher of just 27 years old got up to give a talk on consciousness. I wasn't there, but *The Guardian* gives a great blow-by-blow description in Oliver Burkeman's 2015 article:

> An unknown philosopher named David Chalmers got up to give a talk on consciousness, by which he meant the feeling of being inside your head, looking out—or, to use the kind of language that might give a neuroscientist an aneurysm, of having a soul. Though he didn't realize it at the time, this young Australian academic was about to ignite a war between philosophers and scientists, by drawing attention to perhaps the central mystery of human life . . . and revealing how embarrassingly far they were from solving it.

Chalmers was an NYU colleague, so in October 2023, I reached out to see if he had a shortcut to the future of Truth. I should have known better.

As Chalmers's familiar mop of gray hair fills my Zoom screen, I can't help but wonder: Is this the real David Chalmers, or have I unwittingly stumbled into an AI simulation?

"Can you hear me okay?" Chalmers asks, his Australian accent cutting through my existential panic.

"Loud and clear," I respond, pushing aside the urge to ask him if we're in the Matrix. "Thanks for joining me to talk about the future of truth in our AI-dominated world."

And just like that, we're off to the races.

Chalmers, the philosophical rabble-rouser who's been giving his colleagues metaphysical headaches since the '90s, doesn't waste time getting to the heart of the matter. This moment feels reminiscent of another pivotal time in history—when the printing press first revolutionized how people accessed and verified information.

Chalmers notes that AI systems are already embedded in everyday life and that their growing ubiquity raises urgent philosophical questions about reality, agency, and moral responsibility.

It's a sobering thought and one that seems to challenge Chalmers's long-held optimism about our ability to seek and find truth. I decide to press him on this apparent contradiction.

"You've always maintained that Truth is out there and that we can find it," I point out. "But in a world where AI might become our primary source of information, aren't we just outsourcing our truth-seeking to algorithms? How can you remain optimistic in the face of that?"

Chalmers does not try to resolve the contradiction. He remains optimistic about humanity's capacity to pursue truth, while being clear about how profoundly AI complicates that effort. Systems that generate and process information at superhuman scale and speed do not merely overwhelm human judgment. They reshape the conditions under which truth is produced, evaluated, and trusted. He leans back in his chair, and I can almost see the gears turning.

He is skeptical that AI will function as a straightforward arbiter of truth.

What once felt like a shared baseline of reality now fragments into overlapping environments. Physical experience, digital platforms, and simulated systems all exert real influence. People learn to move among them, judging what to trust and what to ignore, not because reality has vanished, but because it has multiplied. His response reminds me of how people had to become more discerning readers after the rise of yellow journalism in the late 1800s—learning to navigate between sensationalized stories and factual reporting, just as we now must navigate between AI-generated content and human-created information.

But before we dive deeper into the metaphysical surf, I want to know how Chalmers got here. After all, this is the guy who became famous for talking about zombies. Philosophical zombies, that is.

"You started out obsessed with consciousness," I remind him. "How did you end up pondering the nature of truth in an AI world?"

Chalmers leans back, clearly enjoying the chance to reminisce. "I started out in math and physics and computer science. But at a certain point along the way, I got obsessed by the mind and by consciousness."

This obsession led him to a conference in Tucson, Arizona, in 1994, where he dropped his philosophical bombshell: the "hard problem" of consciousness. The "hard problem" of consciousness, as Chalmers dubbed it, refers to the difficulty of explaining why we have subjective, first-person experiences. Why does it feel like something to be us? This question has haunted philosophers and scientists for centuries, and Chalmers's framing of it as the "hard problem" reignited the debate in the '90s.

But what does this have to do with AI and Truth? According to Chalmers, everything.

"If we can't explain human consciousness, how can we hope to understand artificial consciousness?" he posits. He raises a deeper concern about artificial consciousness itself, asking how much trust we can place in systems whose internal experiences, if any, remain opaque to us.

It's a fair point, but I can't help playing devil's advocate. "But do we need to understand consciousness to determine Truth? Isn't Truth . . . well, just true?"

Chalmers shakes his head emphatically. "It's not that simple anymore. Look, I still believe in an objective world. I still believe in objective reality. But I also know that we all process that objective reality in totally different ways." He emphasizes that contemporary AI systems increasingly process information in ways that are difficult for humans to fully understand or audit.

He pauses, then adds, "What I've always wanted to do is to somehow be able to reconcile the objective and the subjective by having potentially an objective science of subjective experience or a scientific picture of the objective world that lets in, that acknowledges all the subjective elements."

It's a noble goal, but I'm still struggling to see how this applies to our everyday understanding of Truth. I mean, when I read a news article or watch a video online, I want to know if it's true or false, not ponder the nature of subjective experience.

As if reading my mind, Chalmers brings the conversation back down to earth. "Think about deepfake technology," he says. "We're rapidly approaching a point where it will be virtually impossible to distinguish a real video from a fabricated one." This raises downstream questions for journalism, video evidence, and legal standards that have historically relied on visual records as a proxy for truth. It's not unlike the revolution that photography brought in the 1800s, when what was once considered irrefutable evidence became subject to manipulation through techniques like double exposure and composite printing.

It's a chilling thought and one that's already having real-world consequences. In 2018, researchers at the University of Washington created a fake video of former president Barack Obama, demonstrating how easy it is to put words in someone's mouth—literally. More recently, deepfake technology has been used to create non-consensual pornography and to spread political disinformation.

"So how do we deal with that?" I ask. "How do we maintain any grip on truth in a world where our senses can be so easily deceived?"

Chalmers leans forward, his expression serious. He argues that the challenge is not merely technical, but philosophical, requiring new frameworks for understanding knowledge, evidence, and truth in AI-mediated environments. "It's not just about better detection algorithms. It's about rethinking our entire approach to knowledge and evidence."

This perspective, while intriguing, is not without its critics in the philosophical community. Many scientists and philosophers argue for a more empirical approach to understanding consciousness and Truth, focusing on neuroscience and observable phenomena rather than abstract philosophical frameworks.

Chalmers is well aware of these criticisms. "There's often a tension between philosophical and scientific approaches to these questions," he acknowledges. "But I think we need both. We need to understand the brain better, absolutely. But we also need to think about the philosophical implications of our technologies. It's not an either/or situation."

This debate between philosophical and empirical approaches to understanding consciousness and Truth isn't just academic—it has real implications for how we approach the challenges posed by AI. Just as the scientific revolution of the seventeenth century forced people to reconcile religious Truth with empirical observation, we now must reconcile human intuition with machine intelligence.

To illustrate this point, Chalmers brings up a recent development in the field. "There's been some interesting work recently trying to test different theories of consciousness against each other," he says.

He's referring to a series of experiments conducted by the Cogitate Consortium, a group of researchers who've been putting different theories of consciousness to the test. The results were unveiled at a packed event in New York, where Chalmers was present to see the outcome of a 25-year-old bet he'd made with neuroscientist Christof Koch.

"Koch wagered that we'd find a neural correlate of consciousness within 25 years," Chalmers explains, a hint of triumph in his voice. "Well, the 25 years are up, and we still don't have a clear answer. I won the bet, but to be honest, I was hoping I'd lose. It would have meant we'd made more progress in understanding consciousness."

The implications of this ongoing uncertainty about consciousness are profound, especially when it comes to AI. If we can't pin down what makes something conscious, how can we determine if an AI system is truly thinking, truly understanding, or truly telling the truth?

Chalmers doesn't shy away from the complexity of the issue. "Look, we're creating systems that can process and generate information in ways that mimic human intelligence," he says. "But do they have inner experiences? Do they have a sense of self? These are questions we still can't answer about humans with certainty, let alone AI."

I push him on this point. "But surely," I argue, "we don't need to solve the hard problem of consciousness to determine whether an AI is telling the Truth or not? Can't we just judge it by its outputs?"

Chalmers smiles, clearly pleased by the pushback. "That's a fair point," he concedes. "And in many cases, yes, we can and should judge AI systems by their outputs. But here's the thing—as these systems become more advanced, as they start to engage in more complex reasoning and decision-making, the line between 'output' and 'inner process' becomes blurrier."

He has argued that while it is often reasonable to judge AI systems by their outputs, that approach may become less adequate as systems grow more sophisticated. For relatively simple systems, observable behavior can tell us much of what we need to know. But as AI begins to engage in more complex reasoning and decision-making, the line between output and internal process starts to blur. Chalmers suggests that, much as we do with humans, we may eventually need to look beyond surface behavior to understand how an AI reaches its conclusions. In everyday life, we evaluate people not only by what they say, but by patterns of consistency, past behavior, and inferred motivations. For advanced AI, attention to internal representations and reasoning processes may become increasingly important, particularly when questions of trust, reliability, and alignment are at stake.

It's a fascinating idea but also a slightly terrifying one. The notion of trying to understand the "thought processes" of an AI system feels like something out of a science fiction novel. But then again, so did the idea of AI writing news articles or creating deepfake videos just a few years ago.

"So what you're saying," I venture, "is that in the future, determining Truth might be less about fact-checking individual statements and more about . . . what? Understanding the 'minds' of AI systems?"

Chalmers nods enthusiastically. "Exactly! And not just AI minds, but human minds too." Taken together, his work suggests the need for a more nuanced and flexible understanding of truth as intelligent systems become part of how reality is interpreted.

He pauses, then adds with a wry smile, "Of course, this all assumes that we're not already living in a simulation created by some super-advanced AI. But that's a whole other conversation." So much so that he wrote a book about it, called *Reality+: Virtual Worlds and the Problems of Philosophy*, which I highly recommend.

...

His mention of simulation sparks an idea. What if we could create a virtual space where great minds across time could debate these fundamental questions? Using the same technology that now makes us question what's real, I decide to stage a virtual encounter with the help of ChatGPT. I enter a few gentle prompts, asking the LLM (large language model) to craft a dynamic between Plato and Chalmers, which it does effortlessly.

In this digital arena, two philosophical heavyweights will face off—their appearances, mannerisms, and ideas reconstructed from their writings and, in Chalmers's case, his actual presentations and interviews. It's a meta-experiment: using AI and virtual reality to explore the nature of Truth itself.

The virtual debate chamber materializes: a space that blends ancient Greek architecture with modern digital aesthetics. Holographic audiences flicker in the stands, their ethereal forms adding to the surreal atmosphere.

Plato, the Ancient Philosopher, stands at his podium, regal in his flowing robes, and addresses the virtual amphitheater. "My friends, I stand before you to defend the existence of absolute, unchanging truths. In my time, I spoke of the Forms—perfect, immutable ideals that exist beyond our physical reality. Today, I argue that even in this age of artificial intelligence, these eternal truths remain. Your AI, impressive as it may be, is but a shadow on the cave wall. True knowledge, true understanding of reality, comes not from these digital creations but from grasping the underlying, unchanging principles of existence."

Chalmers—the AI version, of him, that is—leans forward, casual yet intense, his tone reflective. "With all due respect to Plato, whose work has been foundational to Western thought, I must disagree. The world we live in today, with its rapid technological advancements and AI systems that can process information far beyond human capabilities, challenges the notion of unchanging, absolute truths. Instead, I propose that truth is not a fixed point but a dynamic interplay between objective reality and our evolving understanding of it."

Plato's brow furrows slightly. "Surely, Dr. Chalmers, you must acknowledge that some truths remain constant, regardless of technological advancements. The principles of mathematics, for instance, or the concepts of justice and goodness—these are not subject to change simply because we've created intelligent machines."

"I agree that some principles seem constant," Chalmers concedes, "but our understanding of those principles evolves. Take consciousness, for example. We still grapple with the 'hard problem'—why we have subjective experiences at all. AI is forcing us to reconsider what consciousness means. These are not fixed truths but evolving concepts that demand reassessment."

The Ancient Philosopher straightens, his voice resolute. "What evolves, Dr. Chalmers, is not truth itself but our approximation of it. As we climb out of the cave, so to speak, we may see the Forms more clearly, but the Forms themselves remain unchanged. Your AI systems are tools for understanding reality, not for creating new truths."

Chalmers smiles faintly, his tone turning inquisitive. "But in a world where AI generates convincing falsehoods and alternate realities, how can we be sure of what's real? The line between objective reality and perception is blurring. We need a nuanced understanding of truth to navigate these complexities."

Plato's expression softens as though a flicker of understanding crosses his face. "And that, Dr. Chalmers, is why we need absolute truths as a fixed point of reference. Without them, we're adrift in a sea of relative truths, unable to discern reality from illusion."

Chalmers follows with equal conviction. "We need better tools for verification, yes, but we also need to rethink what truth means. It's not merely objective; it's shaped by subjective experience. Our challenge is to develop AI systems that help us navigate this complex landscape responsibly."

After the virtual debate fades away, I laugh at this digital thought experiment, but there's a part of me that wonders if Chalmers is entirely joking about the simulation hypothesis. After all, this is the man who once argued that we can't rule out the possibility that we're living in a computer simulation. I wonder if I should share this debate with the human Chalmers and offer him an opportunity to correct how he would debate Plato, but I decide that would give him the upper hand. One AI-created creature should be able to debate another: Fair is fair.

...

As our conversation winds down, I find myself grappling with more questions than answers. Chalmers has taken me on a mind-bending journey from the heights of philosophical abstraction to the nitty-gritty of AI's impact on our daily lives. It's like I've swallowed both the red and blue pills, and now I'm seeing not just one hidden reality but a whole kaleidoscope of them.

"So, David," I say, "if you had to sum it all up for someone who's just trying to navigate this brave new world of AI and shifting truths, what would you tell them?"

Chalmers just smiles, running a hand through his unruly mop of gray hair. For a moment, he looks less like a world-renowned philosopher and more like a surfer pondering a particularly gnarly wave.

Truth in the age of AI is no longer static or singular. It is dynamic, layered, and often internally inconsistent. We move between physical experience, digital platforms, and simulated systems, assembling meaning as we go. The skill now required is not passive belief but active navigation. Like earlier scholars who compared manuscripts to establish authenticity, we cross-check sources, test coherence, and learn to keep our footing as reality itself becomes something we must continually interpret.

As I sign off, I can't help but feel both exhilarated and slightly dizzy. Chalmers has this uncanny ability to make you question everything you thought you knew about reality, consciousness, and Truth. One thing's for sure: The next time I read a news article, watch a video online, or interact with an AI, I'll be thinking about Chalmers and his wild ideas.

In a world where Truth is becoming as elusive as a glitch in the Matrix, maybe we do all need to become reality surfers. And who knows? Maybe in the process, we'll discover that the Truth isn't just out there—it's in here, in the complex interplay between our minds, our technologies, and the realities we create and perceive.

As I close my laptop, I find myself checking for glitchy black cats. Just in case. After all, in Chalmers's world, the line between philosophical thought experiment and everyday reality is fuzzier than ever. And in the age of AI, we might all need to become a little bit more philosophical just to get through the day.

So, history shows us that Truth's always had a knack for getting lost, tangled, or outright trampled. But today, it's happening faster and more ruthlessly than ever before. What's driving this decay? As our investigation continues, we'll dig into the forces unraveling Truth in the here and now.

CHAPTER 3

# Facing a Future of Truth Decay

The shy teenager sat in his parents' living room in Mexico City, heart racing but voice steady. "I'm going to school in the States," he announced. His parents stared back in surprise. Their son, who had never attended school in English, had barely written in English, and spent most of his time with his nose buried in the *Encyclopedia Britannica*, was proposing to leave everything familiar behind and start over in a foreign country.

A week later, Juan Enríquez found himself on his way to Hanover, New Hampshire, about to begin an educational journey that would transform not just his life but ultimately our understanding of how Truth evolves. It was the kind of decisive moment that would come to characterize his approach to learning and life—see a challenge, take a leap, and figure it out along the way.

"I didn't sleep for two years," Enríquez told me during our December 2023 interview, recalling those early days at boarding school. We'd talked before, but this conversation was different. More collegial and more serious. We were discussing the decay of Truth in modern society, but his memory of his early days remained vivid. "I thought I was really dumb." He paused, a slight smile crossing his face. "But after two years, you know, it got easier."

That might have been the understatement of the century. Not only did Enríquez master English, but he also went on to take six courses simultaneously, including graduate courses at Harvard, while playing varsity sports. For most students, this would have been impossible. For Enríquez, it was simply what happened when you combined curiosity with determination.

"I was a kid who was incredibly shy and nerdy," he recalled, "and never had science mentors." His early passion for encyclopedic knowledge would later serve him well, as he developed a unique ability to connect dots across different fields of study.

When I first reached out to Enríquez to talk about Truth decay in modern society, I expected we'd focus primarily on scientific Truth. After all, he had made his mark in genomics, helping to establish the life sciences program at Harvard Business School. What I found instead was someone whose understanding of Truth had been shaped by an intellectual journey that repeatedly crossed traditional boundaries between disciplines.

"I was doing international affairs at Harvard and writing about why countries appear and disappear," he explained, describing his early career. In 2005, he published *The Untied States of America*, which predicted a coming financial crisis driven by over-leveraged real estate that would rip nations' politics to pieces. It was the kind of cross-disciplinary analysis that would become his trademark—seeing connections that others missed because they stayed within the boundaries of their specialties.

But even while studying geopolitics, Enríquez was drawn to the cutting edge of science. "I tried to figure out what the leading-edge technology was," he said. "I figured out it was genomics, went and found the best people in genomics in the world, and shifted my office at Harvard from international affairs to biology."

This wasn't a casual shift—Enríquez approached genomics with the same intensity he had brought to his earlier studies. "If I go into a subject, I will study it for six to ten years before I talk about it. I will find the best person in the field, and learn from them for six or eight years before I publish anything."

His timing was perfect. "When I learned genomics, nobody knew genetics," he recalled. "You could fit everybody who dealt with genomics in the world in one living room like yours and have a lot of room left over." This meant he could read every paper ever published on genetics and interact with every major figure in the field.

This methodical approach to learning gave Enríquez a unique perspective on how knowledge evolves. He wasn't just learning the current state of the science—he was watching a field develop in real time, seeing how scientific Truth emerged through the interplay of evidence, interpretation, and debate.

This front-row seat to the evolution of genomics transformed Enríquez's understanding of Truth itself. He watched as what seemed like solid facts one year became outdated the next, as new discoveries forced scientists to revise their theories. But this wasn't the kind of Truth decay we see in today's social media landscape; it was Truth's evolution guided by evidence and peer review.

"The fascinating thing about genomics," he told me, leaning forward in his chair, "is how contextual it is." He offered an example that perfectly illustrated this complexity: "Intelligence is 50% inherited. But when you run millions and millions of genomes through genome-wide association studies, it is very, very hard, if not impossible, to find genes associated with intelligence. So how the hell do you have something that is 50% inherited but has no genetic signature? That is utterly bizarre."

This paradox—that something can be strongly inherited yet leave no clear genetic trace—challenged simple notions of biological Truth. The same gene code in the same person could have completely different outcomes at different periods of life, depending on environmental factors, diseases, and other influences we're still working to understand.

Enríquez's face lit up as he described these complexities. It was clear that for him, the mystery wasn't frustrating—it was exciting. Each new discovery that complicated our understanding of genetics opened up new possibilities for research and understanding. "When something is 2% inherited, it's a big deal," he explained. "You're going to see that at a substantial level in the population. And once you see that strong a signal, usually you can find a gene or genes that are correlated to that."

But intelligence defied this pattern, and that defiance taught Enríquez something crucial about the nature of Truth: Sometimes the most important discoveries come from examining why our expectations don't match reality.

This lesson would prove invaluable as Enríquez began to notice a troubling pattern in society at large. "You've got this weird divergence," he told me, "between extreme engineering precision in robotics, in AI, in jet engines, in space flight—and extreme lack of belief in anything in politics, in society, in international relations."

In his 2020 book *Right/Wrong*, he wrote:

> The truth changes all the time. Teaching science is a perpetual apology: "We used to think that . . . but then we discovered that. And then we found that." Today's truths are tomorrow's dead theories; there was a period where nothing was smaller than an atom. Science tells us what we know, or theorize now, is X. It may be edited, improved, or disproved tomorrow. But in science, there is evidence and support as to why we believe X is true today. So there is a huuuuuge difference when various demagogues and fundamentalists deliberately distort, obfuscate, and outright lie. What Trump and his posse do on Twitter, TV, radio, and rallies is a completely different animal in terms of "truthiness."

And there's a looming political history to all this, he explained. "During a time when technology allows us to reference, fact-check, and verify so quickly, one would think that far greater access to information and the ability to cross-check would put tremendous pressure on blatant falsehoods. Instead, we are flooded by deliberate misinformation and lies. Technology changed the nature of the truth. It is hard to imagine the rise of Hitler, absent radio and movies."

It was this observation—that we live in a world of unprecedented scientific precision alongside unusual social uncertainty about Truth—that led me to connect Enríquez's insights with another crucial player in the evolution of Truth in American society: the RAND Corporation.

In 1945, as World War II drew to a close, General Henry H. "Hap" Arnold faced a challenge that would reshape how America thought about knowledge and Truth. The war had demonstrated the crucial importance of scientific and technological research to military success, but he worried that peacetime would sever the connections between military planning and scientific research. His solution was audacious: create an independent organization that would connect military strategy with research and development.

The result was Project RAND, initially a contract with Douglas Aircraft Company, which in 1948 became the independent, nonprofit RAND Corporation. The name stood for Research and Development, but what RAND would develop over the following decades was far more significant than its modest acronym suggested.

During the Cold War, RAND became the epicenter of strategic thinking about nuclear deterrence. Its researchers, including Herman Kahn (who would later inspire the character of Dr. Strangelove), developed game theory approaches to nuclear strategy. Perhaps more importantly, they developed new ways of thinking about how to verify Truth in complex systems.

RAND pioneered systems analysis and decision theory, creating methodologies for evaluating competing claims and making decisions under uncertainty. These approaches would prove crucial not just for military planning but for everything from healthcare policy to education reform.

The organization's evolution reflected changing American attitudes toward Truth and expertise. In the immediate postwar period, RAND embodied a confident, technocratic approach to problem-solving. Its researchers believed that with enough data and analytical rigor, they could find optimal solutions to even the most complex challenges.

But as the Cold War progressed, this certainty began to erode. The Vietnam War, which RAND analysts had helped plan, turned into a quagmire. The Pentagon Papers revealed how government officials had misled the public about the conflict. These experiences forced RAND to develop more nuanced approaches to Truth and verification.

By the 1960s, RAND had expanded beyond its military origins to tackle broader social issues. This evolution reflected a growing understanding that national security depended not just on military strength but on social cohesion and the ability to make informed collective decisions.

The organization that had once focused primarily on counting Soviet missiles was now grappling with questions about poverty, education, and social justice. This broader mission required new ways of thinking about Truth and evidence. How do you verify claims about social programs with the same rigor you apply to weapon systems? How do you maintain standards of Truth when dealing with complex social phenomena?

These questions would become increasingly urgent as America entered the digital age. By 2018, RAND researchers Jennifer Kavanagh and Michael D. Rich had become alarmed by what they saw as a fundamental shift in how American society related to Truth. They embarked on an ambitious project to understand what they called "truth decay."

Their findings were sobering. They identified four key trends: increasing disagreement about facts and analytical interpretations of data, a blurring of the line between opinion and fact, the increasing relative volume and resulting influence of opinion over fact, and declining trust in formerly respected sources of factual information.

When I shared these findings with Enríquez, he nodded in recognition. "In a strange way," he said, "this period of extreme uncertainty and lack of truth was started by physicists like Heisenberg and Schrödinger and then adopted by the left in the whole deconstruction of literature and art."

Kavanagh, now a senior political scientist at RAND and director of the Strategy, Doctrine, and Resources Program at the RAND Arroyo Center, sees practical paths forward through this uncertainty. Her research has focused extensively on how US political and media institutions shape our relationship with facts, and she emphasizes that solutions in the information realm are more tractable than we might think.

"Traditional media can make simple but impactful changes," Kavanagh explained at a presentation at RAND's headquarters in Santa Monica, California, in 2018. "Ensuring headlines match article content, clearly labeling facts versus opinions, and maintaining stronger separation between factual reporting and commentary in broadcast shows. These practical steps could help rebuild trust in media institutions."

The scale of disinformation today is unprecedented, touching virtually every aspect of society. Perhaps more importantly, there's been a collapse in the belief in evidence itself. As Enríquez notes in *Right/Wrong*, "Living in an age of polarization, politicization, fear, and uncertainty makes us more tribal, less trusting of those deemed 'other.'"

"An often-overlooked aspect of media literacy and civic engagement is the ability to understand and interpret statistics and probability, which are used in public opinion polls and media coverage on almost every topic," wrote Kavanaugh in the RAND report. "Without an ability to understand and interpret statistics, newly graduated students (as well as those still in school) may be easily swayed by false and misleading information and may pass it along to others."

Both Enríquez and the RAND researchers see potential paths forward. For RAND, the solution involves strengthening civic education, rebuilding trust in institutions, and developing new ways to verify information in the digital age. For Enríquez, it requires combining scientific rigor with ethical consideration and imaginative thinking.

"If we have, let's say, two trillion dollars to spend on climate change," he proposed during our conversation, "the default is, let's spend a whole bunch of it on mitigation. Let's tax everything. Let's have less of everything . . . but let's imagine we spend a whole bunch of it on workarounds, and we say, 'How do we get back from this? How do we adjust for this? What can we do?'"

This approach—combining rigorous analysis with creative problem-solving—reflects lessons learned from both RAND's systematic studies and Enríquez's scientific work. It suggests that addressing Truth decay requires both understanding its mechanisms and imagining new solutions.

Perhaps most importantly, both RAND and Enríquez emphasize the critical role of ethics in shaping our relationship with Truth. "I think the most important thing we can do in this century," Enríquez argues, "is, let's not leave ethics as a subject to be taught in divinity schools. Let's make ethics a mandatory part of every science education."

This call for ethical consideration in scientific advancement reflects a broader need to think carefully about how we handle Truth in all its forms. The RAND researchers similarly emphasize the need for ethical frameworks to guide how we produce and consume information in the digital age.

As we look to the future, the challenges of Truth decay show no signs of diminishing. If anything, new technologies like artificial intelligence and deepfakes promise to make the distinction between Truth and fiction even more difficult to discern. Yet the combined perspectives of institutional researchers like those at RAND and cross-disciplinary thinkers like Enríquez offer hope that we can navigate these challenges.

That shy teenager who announced his decision to study in America grew up to understand something profound about Truth: It's neither as simple as we once thought nor as hopelessly complex as it sometimes seems. It requires rigorous analysis, ethical consideration, and, perhaps most importantly, the kind of imaginative thinking that allows us to see new possibilities in seemingly intractable problems.

"We have an absolute obligation to leave the world better than we found it," said Enríquez as we concluded our conversation. "And that is the warning sign—it's gonna be hard, and it's gonna take a lot of creativity and a lot of work and a lot of effort. But we can do this. We are not doomed."

In this statement lies perhaps the most important Truth of all: Our relationship with Truth itself is not fixed but evolving. How we handle this evolution—whether we succumb to Truth decay or find new ways to verify and validate Truth in an increasingly complex world—will largely determine our future as a society.

If Truth is eroding, democracy might be its most immediate casualty. In the pages ahead, we'll step into the digital battleground where Truth, politics, and algorithms collide. Let's see who—or what—is calling the shots.

As Truth erodes, democracy teeters on the edge. Algorithms are no longer just tools—they're arbiters of political discourse, shaping opinions and controlling narratives. Up next, we enter the digital battleground where Truth meets politics and algorithms hold the power.

CHAPTER 4

# Truth and Politics: The Digitization of Democracy

The relationship between Truth and democracy has been fundamentally transformed by the digital age. Social media platforms, data harvesting, and micro-targeting have created unprecedented challenges for maintaining shared reality. As documented by RAND's Truth Decay project, we've seen a steady erosion of agreement about basic facts and an increasing blur between opinion and fact. It's in this context that I catch Eli Pariser on Halloween afternoon as October's early darkness begins to creep in. There's something fitting about discussing the nature of Truth on a day when reality becomes playfully fluid—though in the current world, we hardly need costumes to create alternate realities anymore. We've got algorithms for that now.

The tension between Truth and politics isn't new. From Thucydides's selective recording of speeches to the partisan pamphlets of the American Revolution, political discourse has always involved competing narratives of reality. What's changed is the sophistication of our tools for creating and spreading these narratives and the speed at which they can travel.

Pariser has been thinking about how technology shapes our perception of reality for most of his adult life. Pariser first gained prominence as a cofounder of MoveOn.org, a progressive public policy advocacy group formed during the Clinton administration, and later as the person who coined the term "filter bubble" back in 2011, warning us about how algorithmic systems would increasingly determine what we see online. But that was just the beginning of a journey that's led him to much deeper questions about Truth, technology, and human nature.

"The thing that hasn't changed," he tells me, with the kind of energy that suggests he's still genuinely excited about these ideas after all these years, "is that I've always been really interested in the intersection of how to leverage technology to support a healthier democracy. That's been my North Star forever." He pauses. "The thing that *has* changed is my sort of inherent faith in technology to drive that change in a positive direction."

That evolution—from techno-optimist to someone wrestling with technology's darker implications—mirrors a broader shift in our society's relationship with digital tools. When Pariser first started thinking about filter bubbles, he was hopeful that tech companies would recognize the problem and course-correct. After all, he had seen the Internet's positive potential firsthand. As a young activist at MoveOn.org, he watched digital tools transform grassroots organizing. The technology worked; it was the incentives he hadn't fully reckoned with yet.

His next venture, Upworthy, was what he called a "'work within the existing system' project" in a 2024 interview in the Nieman Lab blog. The idea was to bend the algorithmic logic of social media platforms toward socially responsible content. While proud of much of that work, he found their impact "was constrained by algorithmic choices that prioritized the company's engagement metrics and the limits of what is possible in a VC-backed business."

This struggle between engagement and Truth isn't unique to our digital age. The yellow journalism of the late nineteenth century showed how commercial interests could drive sensationalism over accuracy. What's different now is the precision with which content can be targeted and the scale at which it can spread. Donald Trump's presidency from 2016–2020 provided a stark demonstration of this new reality: *The Washington Post's* fact-checkers documented over 30,000 false or misleading claims during his term, showing how digital platforms could amplify misinformation at unprecedented scale and how a political figure could leverage these systems to create alternate versions of reality. This phenomenon exemplifies exactly what Pariser had warned about with his concept of filter bubbles, though even he might not have anticipated the speed and scale at which divergent realities could be created and maintained. Platforms fueled by ads are incentivized to amplify conflict. Says Juan Enríquez, whom we met in the last chapter, "As long as they bring clicks and likes, there is little incentive to minimize bots or radical accusations that breed more accusations and counter-accusations. Rage drives traffic . . . the extremes of Left and Right grow ever less tolerant, more willing to believe any accusation against 'those people.'" It's a pattern Pariser witnessed firsthand during his time at Upworthy.

"Most of human behavior is boring," he explains, with the kind of laugh that comes from years of realizing just how powerful this simple Truth is. "It exists for a reason, but it's edited out, and I think that gives you a very warped idea of what matters to people and an incentive to say things that are crazy and not true. Because that's a way to violate a norm."

These days, Pariser is thinking bigger than filter bubbles. When Nieman Lab reporter Sophie Culpepper visited his latest venture, New_ Public, she found an organization trying to reimagine fundamentally how we build digital spaces. With an annual budget between $5 and $6 million and a team of 18 full-time employees, they're taking on an ambitious challenge: creating online spaces that actually serve democracy rather than undermining it.

Working alongside codirector Deepti Doshi, who spent seven years leading Facebook's Community Partnerships team, Pariser is exploring what happens when you build digital spaces around public needs rather than engagement metrics. The timing couldn't be more crucial. Culpepper's reporting revealed that 52% of Americans now get their local news from digital groups, up from 38% in 2018. As local newspapers vanish, these online spaces—often run by volunteer moderators with no training or support—have become the de facto centers of community information.

"We're working with stewards and communities right now, across two pilots," Pariser explains, his enthusiasm evident. One pilot "focuses on relationship building between stewards to build social trust in their communities, and one . . . looks at how stewards might 'remix' the information in their communities in a weekly update."

This shift from institutional to informal information sharing isn't unprecedented. Historical parallels can be found in everything from colonial-era taverns to nineteenth-century penny papers. But the scale and speed of today's digital transformation present unique challenges.

Pariser sees three distinct layers of Truth in our current moment. First, there's empirical Truth: the measurable, verifiable facts about our world. Then there's narrative Truth: the stories we construct together to make sense of those facts. Finally, there's what he calls "networked truth"—the way digital networks can create and sustain entirely separate versions of reality.

"The older I get," he reflects, "the more I feel like people absolutely live in stories that they tell themselves that other people construct, that they construct with other people. That's the biggest determinant of how they behave and how they see the world . . . we're not evolved to be scientists. We're evolved to be tribal animals that are trying to understand how to hang together in a dangerous world."

The challenge of maintaining shared Truth while respecting different perspectives isn't new to democracy. What's new is the technological infrastructure that can instantly connect people who share the same beliefs while isolating them from competing viewpoints. This infrastructure doesn't just reflect our divisions—it can actively deepen them.

At New_ Public, they're exploring practical solutions to this challenge. One of their most successful experiments involves what they call "civic remixing"—having moderators create weekly updates that synthesize community information while acknowledging different perspectives. They're also testing AI tools to help moderators with basic tasks, freeing them to focus on the human work of building community understanding.

"Let me give you a concrete example," Pariser says, sitting forward. "In one community we work with, there was a controversy about a new school building project. The local paper would have traditionally investigated the claims, interviewed experts, looked at the budgets. Instead, you had competing Facebook groups spreading different versions of reality—one group saying it would bankrupt the town, another saying it was essential for the future. No neutral party to verify facts. No shared basis for making a decision."

"I fundamentally just don't think it is possible to do good content moderation or conversation at a scale of billions of people," Pariser tells me. His codirector Doshi put it even more directly when talking to Culpepper in her

Nieman Lab interview: "People referred to Twitter as like a global town square, but it is, in fact, an oxymoron. A town square operates at a certain size, not at a global scale."

The metaphor of physical spaces comes up often in our conversation. Pariser sees clear parallels between how we design public spaces in the physical world and how we might build healthier digital environments. But there's a crucial difference in incentives. "Taking a library and turning it into a VC-backed business, you know, you very quickly lose what makes it a library," he observes. "There's just no way to hold on to what makes it a library and have a VC-backed business."

The scale of this challenge has become starkly clear. Donald Trump's return to the presidency in 2024 brought an immediate surge of documented falsehoods. As *The Guardian* reported, he made his first false claim within 15 minutes of his second inaugural address and quickly returned to spreading debunked conspiracies about everything from the 2020 election to the Panama Canal. When major platforms like Facebook abandoned fact-checking efforts and tech leaders attended his inauguration, it illustrated exactly what Pariser had warned about: how profit-driven digital spaces naturally amplify misinformation rather than Truth. As political strategist Kurt Bardella noted in a January 2025 article in *The Guardian*, "We live in a world now where you can just make up your own facts and truth is however you decide to bend it." With social media companies increasingly unwilling to address misinformation, Pariser's work at New_ Public has taken on new urgency.

And now artificial intelligence is about to make everything exponentially more complex. When combined with existing surveillance capabilities and data harvesting, AI could make fiction indistinguishable from fact. But Pariser's take on AI is notably balanced: He sees both promise and peril, often in the same technology.

"If you want an AI to help convince people that conspiracy theories are crazy, it's more effective at doing that than almost any other intervention I've seen," he notes. Then comes the twist: "But also, my guess is . . . it's equally powerful in the reverse."

"Who's discovering new facts?" he asks, and the question hangs there for a moment. "And how do you pay them for that is like a really important question that gets you to what are the models for journalism in a world where what that looks like isn't creating stories, but is feeding, you know, sort of the grounding of an AI model."

This brings us to what he calls "the big engineering project of the twenty-first century." "How do you build back a sense of trust in expertise without imposing that from the top down?" The question feels particularly urgent as we discuss New_ Public's efforts to support local digital communities. They're offering small stipends to community moderators—a minimum gesture, Doshi explained to Culpepper, toward recognizing and professionalizing this crucial civic work.

Their work at New_ Public isn't just theoretical. They're testing specific solutions in real communities. Their current initiatives include the Neighborhood Steward Fellowship, an eight-week program where community moderators learn from each other, develop best practices, and receive support for their work. "We're seeing amazing results," Pariser says. "Moderators who were ready to quit their groups are finding new energy and better ways to handle conflicts."

Perhaps most surprising has been their discovery about joy. As Doshi told Culpepper: "So much of civic tech is like, 'you should'—we call it broccoli—'you should do this, you should participate.' We need to make things joyful, delightful—we need to understand how people engage as human beings who are just trying to get through their days and have fun."

As the sun sets on this Halloween evening, children outside are beginning their annual ritual of managed make-believe. And Pariser has to go; his son has created a ghost costume with a hoverboard, and he requires a diligent dad on his candy-seeking mission. Our conversation leaves me to think about change. We're entering an era where the line between Truth and fiction won't be so easily restored when the evening ends. The filter bubble Pariser warned us about in 2011 might soon seem quaint compared to what's coming: a world where AI can generate endless variations of reality, each perfectly tailored to our predispositions.

Yet there's hope in the practical work being done by organizations like New_ Public. Their efforts suggest that while technology may have accelerated our crisis of Truth, thoughtfully designed digital spaces might also help us rebuild the trust and connections that make shared understanding possible. The challenge ahead isn't just technological—it's about understanding our own nature as story-seeking, tribal creatures, and building digital environments that work with rather than against that nature.

The future of Truth may not depend on grand technological solutions or top-down regulations but on our ability to create digital spaces that help us maintain enough shared reality to function as communities, as democracy, as a society trying to make sense of an increasingly complex world. This isn't just about fighting misinformation or designing better algorithms. It's about whether we can build digital spaces that help us "hang together in a dangerous world" while maintaining some coherent sense of shared reality. On this Halloween evening, that feels like both our greatest challenge and our most important task.

And just when you thought the battle for Truth was all about governments and elections, it gets personal. Truth isn't just political—it's tangled up in who we are and how we show up in the world. Up next: how identity shapes—and complicates—our search for Truth.

# CHAPTER 5

# The Power and Peril of Identity in a Digitized World

Nothing is as fundamental to human beings as identity. And identity is the core driver of our human Truth. No one knows this better than Douglas Rushkoff. Rushkoff sees the future before the rest of us catch up. He's the guy who warned that the Internet would be hijacked by corporations, that social media would warp our brains, and that tech billionaires would try to escape the world they helped break. He's not just a critic—he's a cultural decoder, calling bullshit on systems designed to exploit attention and control narrative.

When we began our conversation in his sun-drenched Hastings-on-Hudson office, I thought we'd be talking about digital deception and online fraud. Instead, our conversation began with a story about a five-year-old boy watching *Fiddler on the Roof.*

"Zero Mostel turned to the audience, looked straight in my eyes, and said, 'A fiddler on the roof sounds crazy, no?'" Rushkoff recalled during our December 2024 interview. "At that moment I thought, where am I? Is he Tevye? But he sees me in the audience. So he's the actor, or is he Tevye? Is there a world inside our theater? What's going on? What is the social agreement?"

This question of social agreements lies at the heart of how we understand identity in the digital age. Throughout history, from the earliest definitions of citizenship in ancient Greece to the Magna Carta to the US Constitution, human society has been shaped by the ongoing negotiation of these agreements—these social contracts that define who we are in relation to each other and to our institutions.

"I was a theater kid," Rushkoff continued, describing how his early experiences shaped his understanding of identity and performance. "I did all the AV in middle school, which was movie projectors and slide carousels and film strips. I was interested in that behind-the-scenes quality of it, less the technology than playing with reality."

This fascination with the mechanics of reality would prove prescient. By late middle school, Rushkoff was directing plays rather than acting in them. "I always did meta. I did a production of Pippin where they pick Pippin out of the audience. It was always theater and meta-theater." This early understanding of how reality could be staged and manipulated would later inform his insights into digital identity and social media performance.

"My second big moment came in the computer lab in college," Rushkoff said. "The TA asked if I wanted to save my file read-only or read-write. That's when I went, oh my God, I'm living in a read-write universe that has been presented to me as read-only. The television I watch is read-only, the Bible I'm given is read-only . . . and [actually], it's all read-write."

This distinction between "read-only" and "read-write" reality gets at something fundamental about identity in the digital age. While institutions are rapidly building digital systems to improve efficiency or enhance revenue, the combined effect of these isolated efforts is creating something far more significant: a wholesale rewriting of the social contract, happening largely without our awareness or input.

Consider the case of Christine Settingsgaard. For Christine, identity wasn't something she thought much about. A single mom living in Barrington, Illinois, with a six-year-old son, she considered herself digitally literate. She'd grown up with the Internet and was careful about online safety. But she was lonely, and when she found Mark's profile on Hinge, the connection felt real.

Mark's identity was meticulously crafted. His backstory hit all the right emotional notes: a widower from Greece, a devoted father to a five-year-old daughter living with his sister in Utah. It was a narrative designed to evoke sympathy while explaining away any irregularities in his availability or behavior.

"He was just very kind," Christine remembered in her interview with investigators. "He actually asked questions and wanted to get to know me. I love working in my garden, and he took a general interest in it and was like, 'Hey, I love those peonies you've got.'" But it wouldn't be long before Mark's digital identity and real life would collide, with devastating consequences.

When I shared Christine's story with Rushkoff, he saw it as emblematic of a larger shift in how we experience Truth online. "There was a time," he explained, "when I realized, oh, adults are not responsible. They're corrupt and self-centered. I think kids know that from a very young age now." But in the digital age, this natural skepticism competes with what he calls "artificial intimacy"—the carefully constructed sense of connection that platforms and predators can create.

The romance between Christine and "Mark" unfolded like a well-written script. Over three months, he shared photos of his daughter, stories about his work as an architect, details about his life that made him seem real, knowable, human. Their daily conversations became a ritual, with Mark sending good morning texts and calling each evening to say goodnight.

Then came the money. The $85,000 check wasn't a clumsy request for cash—it was part of an elaborate narrative about trust and partnership. Mark had received a large architectural contract in Dubai, he explained, but needed help managing the US payments while he was overseas. Would Christine deposit the check and wire some of the funds to his contractors?

"It seemed so reasonable," Christine recalled. "He had shown me the contracts, introduced me to his business partner over video chat. He even had me talk to his daughter." When the check cleared initially, Christine felt validated—this was real. Three days later, when her bank notified her that the check was fraudulent, she was already out $26,000 of her own money, to untraceable accounts.

According to FBI data, romance scam victims lost $1.14 billion annually as of 2024. But as devastating as the financial losses are, victims like Christine say the psychological impact cuts deeper. "It wasn't just money I lost," she said. "It was trust. How do you know what's real anymore?"

When I shared these details with Rushkoff, he pointed out how digital spaces have transformed the ancient art of confidence tricks. "In theater, the audience knows they're watching a performance," he said. "But online, the stage and the audience become one. We're all performing and all watching, often without knowing which role we're playing at any moment."

The intimacy of Christine's deception points to something fundamental about Truth in digital spaces. While she lost $26,000, the psychological cost of discovering that a three-month relationship was an elaborate performance left deeper scars. "I keep going back through every conversation," she said, "trying to spot the moment where theater became fraud. But it was all theater, from the very first message."

Rushkoff saw this as emblematic of our larger struggles with digital Truth. "What's fascinating," he noted, "is how we keep trying to solve these human problems with technical solutions. It's like trying to improve theater by building better stages."

He was right. Even as Christine's story was unfolding, governments worldwide were grappling with their own versions of digital identity verification. Australia's Online Privacy Bill marked one of the most ambitious attempts to enforce Truth in digital spaces. Their goal was simple: verify who people really are online. The reality proved anything but simple.

"You know what's fascinating about that?" Rushkoff said when I mentioned Australia's initiative. Rushkoff describes a culture struggling to manufacture ground truth inside systems designed to personalize reality. As he has said, the effort is like "trying to nail jelly to a wall."

According to Australia's eSafety Commissioner Julie Inman Grant, the nation's efforts to safeguard young people online have revealed some uncomfortable truths about digital identity. Speaking at the National Press Club in 2025, she cautioned that "as important as the social media age limits will be . . . it won't be a silver bullet," emphasizing that lasting progress depends on privacy-preserving design and shared responsibility between parents, educators, and platforms.

The numbers she shared tell a sobering story. eSafety's new research found that 96% of Australian children aged 10 to 15 had already used at least one social platform, and seven in ten had encountered harmful or disturbing content—from misogynistic posts to violent fight videos and eating-disorder material. Even more troubling, one in seven reported grooming-like behavior from adults or older teens.

For these tech platforms, Australia's experience forced a fundamental rethinking of how we establish Truth online. Meta's own research, released under transparency requirements, revealed an uncomfortable fact: In regions with strict identity verification, users under 18 maintain an average of 3.7 different digital identities across their platforms. "We're not preventing access," their chief privacy officer admitted in testimony, "we're incentivizing sophisticated deception."

"It's exactly what I discovered in theater," Rushkoff noted when I shared these findings. "The more rules you create around performance, the more sophisticated the performances become. Every new verification system just becomes another stage to perform on."

The World Economic Forum's 2023 Digital Identity Initiative drew a direct line between these corporate learnings and policy implications. Their analysis suggested that traditional regulatory approaches, focused on single-point identity verification, are becoming obsolete before they're even implemented.

The stakes couldn't be higher. An estimated 1.1 billion people globally have no formal identity at all: no birth certificate, no government ID, no official existence according to the World Bank's Identification for Development (ID4D) initiative. The promise of digital identity systems is that they could help solve this crisis, bringing basic services, healthcare, and financial inclusion to the world's most vulnerable populations.

Here, Rushkoff sees a connection to his early theater experiences. "Remember that moment with Zero Mostel?" he asked. "The question wasn't just whether he was Tevye or an actor—it was about what happens when someone acknowledges the artifice of performance while still remaining within it. That's where we are with digital identity. We all know these systems are performances, but we have to keep performing anyway."

This tension becomes even more apparent as artificial intelligence enters the picture. The same machine learning systems that try to guess ages from facial features are being deployed to detect synthetic identities, verify documents, and assess truthfulness. Yet according to Stanford's Digital Civil Society Lab's 2024 study of 50,000 users aged 13–21, young people already view digital identity as inherently performative. The question isn't "What is true?" but rather "What is true in this context?"

"I lived at Timothy Leary's house for a while," Rushkoff told me, shifting the conversation to how we consume information. "There was something fascinating about how every day at 6:30, he'd say, 'Let's go watch Dan Rather.'" This ritual of gathering information at set times, from trusted sources, seems almost quaint now. Today, we're living in what Rushkoff calls "always-on trauma," where our identities are constantly being performed, verified, and challenged across multiple digital stages.

Japan's approach to digital identity stands in sharp contrast to Australia's emphasis on strict, point-in-time verification. Rather than requiring repeated proof of identity through documents, Japan's Digital Agency is advancing what it calls "trust frameworks"—systems that rely on verifiable credentials and consistent behavioral patterns to establish trust over time. Through initiatives like the Digital Identity Wallet and verifiable digital credentials (VC/VDC), Japan aims to give individuals more control over their data while reducing administrative burdens. Early government reports cite improvements in system efficiency and cross-border interoperability, with Japan now coordinating its efforts with the EU and other international partners.

"It's like the difference between truly auditioning an actor and just checking if someone has a union card," Rushkoff observed when I shared Japan's results. "You can verify someone's credentials, or you can watch how they perform over time. One tells you if they're allowed on stage; the other tells you if they can actually act."

The implications extend far beyond social media. When major platforms implemented stricter verification requirements, teens simply moved to less regulated spaces. As one submission to Australia's Senate Committee noted, "We're not preventing access—we're pushing it underground." The eSafety Commissioner's research found that among Australian teens aged 14–17, 86% had encountered harmful content online despite existing age restrictions.

"I did a consult for ABC news in the late '90s," Rushkoff continued, "when they were trying to sort of rebrand what their value was in an age of 24-hour media. I came up with a slogan for them: 'At the end of the day, it's ABC News.' The idea was that people could feel okay living their lives until 6:30, that nothing that's happening, even a genocide beginning in Rwanda... it's like, unless the subway's flooded, I'm going to do my work, have my beer, and see what happened at 6:30."

That world of scheduled information consumption has been replaced by something far more complex. According to the International Telecommunication Union's 2024 report on digital identity, users routinely maintain five to seven distinct digital identities, each serving different but equally authentic purposes. The very concept of a single, verifiable Truth has been replaced by what Microsoft's research lab calls "contextual authenticity."

For global tech platforms, these findings force a fundamental rethinking of truth and identity online. In countries with strict age-verification laws, research shows that young users routinely bypass restrictions—often by providing false birthdates or creating multiple accounts. Studies from UCSF and the Australian eSafety Commissioner document how users as young as 11 or 12 demonstrate sophisticated digital behavior, including hidden accounts and platform workarounds. While not always explicitly tracked, many of these strategies reflect what researchers and policymakers increasingly describe as "identity fragmentation"—the splintering of a single user across multiple digital personas to evade moderation or surveillance.

"If you program technology with the prime directive 'get as much money out of Steve as possible,'" Rushkoff explained, "then with their knowledge of Pavlovian psychology, they are going to create necessarily . . . an ever more perfect Skinner box of behavioral control." This observation gets at something crucial about how digital identity shapes our relationship with Truth. The centralized system, exemplified by Australia's verification laws, promises a single source of Truth but creates incentives for sophisticated deception.

Singapore has become a global case study in digital identity integration, offering citizens a single login—Singpass—for everything from banking to healthcare to government services. But as more systems require strict identity verification, some global experts warn of a rising problem: identity fragmentation. When users are forced to maintain multiple logins or sets of credentials across different platforms, it can erode trust and increase friction. A 2023 report by the World Economic Forum flagged this risk, noting that a fragmented identity landscape can amplify both security vulnerabilities and user confusion. More troublingly, their research showed that stricter verification requirements actually decreased overall system security by encouraging more sophisticated evasion techniques.

"Only the weirdos, only the nerds, only the rejects who are people who, at an early age, were required to understand that the social agreements were not legitimate," Rushkoff noted. "If you were already being picked on as the nerd and the one that they don't like, then you are incentivized to say, oh, consensus reality is fucked up. I'm going to write my own. Being able to craft narrative is one of the only ways to be able to understand how narratives are being crafted for you," Rushkoff explained. "If you're not a storyteller, if you don't understand storytelling, you have a real difficult time separating the story from reality."

This observation brings us back to that five-year-old watching Zero Mostel break the fourth wall in *Fiddler on the Roof.* Understanding that reality is constructed doesn't mean accepting all constructions as equally valid. Instead, it means developing the skills to navigate between different versions of reality while maintaining our connection to physical Truth.

Perhaps that's the most hopeful vision for our digital future—not a world where identity is perfectly secured or completely fluid, but one where we all become more conscious creators of our digital identities, understanding both the power and responsibility that comes with this new form of social contract.

As we face this transformation, we would do well to remember that young Rushkoff in the theater, discovering that reality is a set of social agreements. The question isn't whether these agreements will change—they already are. The question is whether we'll participate consciously in shaping them or simply accept whatever version of reality our algorithms decide to show us.

"I hate for our future to be depending on AIs iterating even self-interested compassion for us," Rushkoff said, his voice carrying a note of genuine concern. "The challenge isn't just technological—it's about reimagining the social contract for a digital age."

The same verification systems that struggle in Australia, with its high Internet penetration and strong digital infrastructure, become nearly impossible to implement in regions with limited connectivity or documentation. For the 1.1 billion people globally lacking formal identification, these challenges are even more acute. The World Bank's ID4D program, studying Australia's experience, specifically cites their challenges as a cautionary tale for developing nations implementing digital ID systems.

"Digital information that young people absorb is structured and conveyed through apps and devices that are configured to traumatize them," Rushkoff explained. "To keep them in a constant state of low-level trauma." This wasn't accidental—it was built into the business model.

In the end, knowing who we are might depend less on our digital profiles and more on our ability to stay grounded in physical reality while navigating digital spaces. As Rushkoff puts it: "Breathe. Put your feet on the ground." It's advice that seems almost too simple for our complex digital age, but perhaps that's exactly why we need to hear it.

From Christine's $85,000 loss to Australia's regulatory struggles to the global challenge of digital identity verification, we keep learning the same lesson: Truth cannot be enforced through technology alone. Like that moment when Zero Mostel broke the fourth wall, we're all discovering that reality is a set of agreements we make with each other. In the digital age, these agreements are being rewritten at unprecedented speed. The question isn't whether we'll need to perform different identities in different contexts—we already do. The question is whether we'll do so consciously, with purpose and authenticity, or let ourselves be performed by the systems we've created.

As Rushkoff reminds us, the future of identity lies not just in technological innovation but in the values that guide its design. Will we create systems that empower individuals and build trust, or will we continue to prioritize profit over humanity? "The platforms are the tail wagging the dog," Rushkoff says, tying things together in the final moments of our conversation. "We're not getting content that's conducive to understanding or observing." Instead, we're getting what he calls "character media" or "identity media"—content designed not to inform or connect but to shape and manipulate our sense of self. As we navigate this new landscape, perhaps the most valuable skill we can develop is the ability to recognize when we're on stage, when we're in the audience, and when—like young Rushkoff watching Tevye—we're caught in that magical moment where Truth transcends the boundaries between performance and reality.

Identity is one thing, but now robots are entering the picture, claiming they can tell us what's true. Can they really, though? Or are they just spitting out what they've been told? In the pages ahead, we'll uncover the surprising (and unsettling) role of machines as truth-tellers.

## CHAPTER 6

# Extra, Extra! Read All About It! News Robots as Truth-Tellers

In my search for the future of Truth, there is one thing people tend to agree on. News at its core should be based on Truth. But has it ever been?

It was a hot New York City summer, August 25, 1835. And if you had picked up *The Sun*, a popular New York tabloid of the day, you would have encountered a cover story about Sir John Herschel, a world-renowned astronomer, who had supposedly discovered bizarre life on the moon. The six-article series was attributed to Herschel and claimed to be a reprint from *The Edinburgh Courant*. The headline cried out: GREAT ASTRONOMICAL DISCOVERIES! The details were extraordinary—and readers were captivated.

The stories described fantastical animals discovered on the moon, including bison, goats, unicorns, and tailless beavers. Most mesmerizing of all, there were bat-like winged humanoids who reportedly built temples and lived in a kind of idyllic civilization. The articles depicted the moon as a vacation paradise with beaches, oceans, and forests—a cartoon wonderland. If Jeff Bezos's rockets had existed in the 1800s, there would have been lines around the block to buy tickets to this "new moon beach colony."

But here's the twist: This moon discovery was entirely made up. It was fake news before the term even existed.

The article's true author, Richard Adams Locke, was a descendant of philosopher John Locke and a well-educated journalist with experience at several papers before landing at *The Sun*. The tabloid he wrote for was part of the "penny press," an early lowbrow competitor to more established newspapers. The penny press used sensational stories and human-interest angles to sell copies, offering thrilling stories for only a penny. Locke's moon story was a hit. Circulation at *The Sun* surged from 8,000 to 19,360 in the wake of the tale—a 240% increase, all thanks to a fiction presented as fact.

Was it fraud? Was it satire, as Locke would later claim? Or was it something else—an early case of journalism dancing on the boundary of entertainment and Truth? After all, the public loved it, and nobody seemed to suffer from the deception. Yet the Moon Hoax speaks to something deeper about our relationship with news: People are often thrilled by deception, drawn to fiction when it's wrapped in the cloak of fact. And that thrill—the excitement of imagining a reality that isn't quite true—has always sold more papers than the dry facts.

The transformation of how we determine Truth—from institutional authority to algorithmic feed—is a story that spans generations. Through decades of technological evolution, those who've watched this transformation up close have seen how our relationship with Truth has fundamentally changed.

In 1985, as a college senior, I set out on a six-week investigation that would change how I thought about Truth forever. After two years of fighting to tell the Truth as news director at my college radio station, I unplugged the "Truth machine"—the rickety old Associated Press wire service printer—and headed off to the Soviet Union. There I researched journalism, conducting interviews with reporters at *Pravda*, whose very name meant "truth" in Russian. Their understanding of Truth and how it ended up with me on stage at the headquarters of TED is a story that took almost 5,000 miles and 30 years to unfold.

In June 2017, I made the argument at TED that Truth was at risk as the label "Fake News" was being used to demean anything readers disagreed with. I proposed that users take responsibility for what they create, share, and label Fake—and proposed a new era of "Awake News." I told the story of a conversation I had in Moscow, where a Russian journalist chastised Americans for believing what they read. But in a moment of powerful irony, it turns out he was right, and I was wrong. I had no idea the forces we were contending with and the arrival of AI just around the corner would make my TED Talk and its well-meaning proposal seem ill-equipped for the coming robot fake news army.

No one has witnessed technological transformation and its effect on Truth more intimately than Esther Dyson. Her journey through the intersection of technology and Truth began early. Growing up in Princeton, New Jersey, she watched her father, physicist Freeman Dyson, work alongside J. Robert Oppenheimer. Her childhood was steeped in the complex relationship between scientific Truth and human knowledge—her father's generation had unleashed atomic power on the world, forever changing humanity's relationship with technology and Truth.

When I shared this realization with Dyson, she recognized the pattern immediately, drawing on her own experiences in Russia. "I'll always remember talking to a Russian, previously Soviet, journalist," she recounted during our conversation. "And they had a newspaper called *Pravda*, the *Truth*. And I was asking her about the truth, and she said, 'Oh, you know, we weren't concerned with the truth. For example, we would get a press release about the health dangers of butter from the government. Of course, who else put out press releases? And we would immediately know it meant there was going to be a shortage of butter. So we would run out and tell our parents and friends and get all the butter we could find and buy it. And then we would publish the article about the health dangers of butter.'"

"I grew up in a family of scientists and mathematicians," she recalls. "The idea was always to ask questions." It's an approach that would define her career. "I worship in the religion of the truth," she says. "Not in the church of the media, nor in the church of science."

Dyson isn't just any observer of the digital revolution—she's been a key player in shaping how we think about technology's impact on society. Her career arc traces the very evolution of how we determine Truth in the modern age. She began as a journalist at *Forbes*, bringing accuracy and insight to her readers. But journalism was just the beginning. After her time at *Forbes*, she moved to edit *Release 1.0*, a newsletter that offered deep dives into emerging technologies. This was the 1980s and 1990s, an era when technology was beginning to transform every corner of life, and Dyson was at the forefront, chronicling and shaping the conversations around these changes.

"In the beginning, the Internet felt like the great equalizer," Dyson recalls. "It was supposed to bring people closer to the truth, not drive them further from it."

But the shift from print to digital didn't just change the medium; it changed the nature of information itself. Social media emerged as a powerful, pervasive force, built on algorithms that cared more about engagement than accuracy. The platforms rewarded attention-grabbing content, no matter if it was true, false, or somewhere in between. "They're designed to serve us what we're most likely to engage with," Dyson explains, "and often, that's content that confirms our biases, heightens our fears, or fuels our outrage. Every second we linger is more ad revenue for the platforms."

Her understanding of this transformation was shaped partly by her experiences in Russia. In 1989, during the big earthquake in San Francisco, she discovered firsthand how controlled information could be. "You could not make a phone call outside the country," she remembers. "It took us two or three days to find out what was really happening." This experience with controlled information would prove prescient as social media platforms began to exert their own form of control over information flow.

Dyson's reflections on Truth and technology are colored by her unique vantage point as both insider and critic. "Over the years," she notes, "it's not a single thing, but the culture, the business models, the predatoriness, the exaltation of valuation over value." She describes watching the transformation of an industry from idealistic beginnings to profit-driven manipulation: "Hearing someone say, 'Oh my gosh, he's worth 400 million'—no, he's not. He's got a small share in a company that is right now, because of probably some investor racket where they get a three times liquidity preference or something, is apparently worth 400 million. But no, he's not worth 400 million."

The evolution from early digital optimism to today's crisis of Truth wasn't inevitable, but it was predictable. "We are becoming increasingly short-term thinkers," Dyson observes, "focused on immediate answers, whether or not they're true, focused on immediate satisfaction. We're losing trust in most of our institutions and becoming increasingly cynical."

This cynical relationship with Truth has now gone global, amplified by technology. "The platforms aren't neutral," Dyson warns. "You have manipulation, which is where you don't understand the other side's incentives. So you think, oh, you know, they want to sell me a good product. Actually, no. They just want to make money off me. But they go behind my back. They tell me stuff that isn't true."

The danger, she explains, isn't just in the technology itself but in how businesses deploy it. "It's not as if the world was perfect before," she notes. "There were people selling cigarettes. There were people selling opioids and guns and crappy stuff. I mean, there's everything from people openly lying to people deluding themselves. The challenge is these systems are becoming increasingly powerful. Business models run on their own. It's easier to automate stuff, so you have fewer people feeling they're complicit."

"Truth isn't profitable if it's dull," she adds with a wry smile. "But if it's shocking? If it sparks anger? Then it becomes valuable."

Back in the 1980s, as entertainment conglomerates began buying up media networks, the lines between information and entertainment began to blur. News was expected to generate revenue, and sensational stories were prioritized. This dynamic only intensified with the rise of the 24-hour news cycle, where pundits—paid to deliver opinions rather than facts—became fixtures of mainstream media. Now, with social media, the boundaries have all but dissolved. News isn't just entertainment; it's content to be liked, shared, and debated, regardless of its accuracy.

And misinformation, Dyson observes, spreads faster than ever before. A study from MIT showed that fake news travels up to 10 times faster than the Truth on social media, where algorithms are finely tuned to amplify what's engaging, not what's accurate. "In the race between 'false but interesting' and 'true but boring,'" Dyson says, "interesting almost always wins."

But let's not pretend that AI isn't already in major newsrooms, providing both services and risks. The Associated Press now uses AI to generate thousands of earnings reports and sports recaps. Bloomberg's "Cyborg" system analyzes complex financial reports in seconds, spotting patterns human reporters might miss. The BBC employs AI to create localized news stories for underserved communities, while *The Washington Post*'s AI helps reporters sift through massive datasets like the Panama Papers.

The transformation from institutional to algorithmic Truth is reshaping newsrooms in ways that would have been unimaginable when I was pulling stories off that AP wire printer in college. At Bloomberg, the Cyborg system doesn't just crunch numbers—it writes stories about corporate earnings faster than any human could type. But speed comes with risks. When the Associated Press automated its earnings reports, it had to build in careful checks and balances. A misplaced decimal point in an AI-generated story could move markets.

"The old institutions had their flaws," Dyson notes, "but at least you knew who was accountable. Now, when an AI system gets something wrong, who do you blame? The algorithm? The training data? The platform? It's accountability distributed to the point of meaninglessness."

"Until the day AI is much better than humans in judgment and interpretation," Dyson continues, "we will need human interpretation of facts, events, and news stories. But that's not what the platforms are optimized for."

At first glance, the army best prepared to fight the rising tide of fake news would be fact-checkers. Their aims seem so achievable. Facts are stated; facts are checked. Accurate information is published. But it turns out that human fact-checkers are no match for the speed and relentlessness of the robots. We are living in the world of "Flood the Zone with Shit"—and humans may be no match.

One prominent story where misinformation replaced facts is the evolution of the Pizzagate conspiracy theory into QAnon. In 2016, Pizzagate falsely claimed that a pizza restaurant in Washington, DC, was the hub of a child trafficking ring run by high-profile politicians. The baseless claim, fueled by misinterpreted emails published by WikiLeaks, culminated in a man entering the restaurant with a firearm, seeking to "rescue" nonexistent victims.

Although Pizzagate was debunked, its themes and tactics set the stage for QAnon. "It's like watching a virus mutate," Dyson observes. "Each new iteration becomes more resistant to facts, more sophisticated in its spread." When algorithms reward engagement over accuracy, she explains, they create perfect breeding grounds for these evolving conspiracy theories.

Take Snopes, for example. Created in 1994 by David and Barbara Mikkelson, Snopes began by debunking urban legends—silly stories about alligators in sewers and haunted houses. "When misinformation obscures the Truth and readers don't know what to trust, Snopes' fact-checking and original, investigative reporting lights the way to evidence-based and contextualized analysis," their mission statement proclaimed. It sounded great, until it didn't.

"Snopes Retracts 60 Articles Plagiarized by Cofounder: 'Our Staff Are Gutted,'" reported *The New York Times*. The site had banned David Mikkelson, who owned half the company, from writing articles after a BuzzFeed News investigation prompted an internal review. The irony was thick—a fact-checking site unable to verify its own content.

When I mentioned this to Dyson, she shook her head. "Fact-checking was built for a world where lies took time to spread," she said. "Now, a lie can circle the globe while the truth is still putting on its shoes. And the platforms? They're designed to accelerate that process."

The impact of this distorted information landscape is profound. As Dyson explains, misinformation isn't just an inconvenience; it's a corrosive force that eats away at the foundations of democracy, erodes trust in institutions, and drives wedges between communities. "When people can't agree on basic facts," she remarks, "the result is chaos."

The challenges faced by Snopes and other fact-checkers underscore a darker reality about our relationship with Truth: Humans often enjoy being deceived. That *The New York Sun*'s moon story sounds a lot like today's viral conspiracy theories shouldn't go unnoticed. Donald Trump, even before he was president, famously said that the *National Enquirer* "should be very respected" and deserves "Pulitzer Prizes for their reporting." The one key difference is, of course, speed. The scientist whose name was used to substantiate the Moon Hoax was in Europe and didn't find out about his name being used until weeks later. His response was good-natured. By then it was acknowledged as a satirical prank. Today, if your name is listed on a fake story, you'd know almost instantly, but the speed of information amplification would make it almost impossible to stop.

In 2025, Meta made the controversial decision to pull back on fact-checking initiatives—a move that sent shockwaves through the journalistic and technological worlds. For a platform as expansive and influential as Facebook, responsible for the digital habits of billions, this decision marked more than just a policy shift. It was a statement about the shifting role of facts in our information ecosystem. It was also a tacit acknowledgment of what many had suspected for years: The currency of facts was being devalued, replaced by the more lucrative metrics of engagement, attention, and outrage.

Consider the implications. If one of the largest platforms for information dissemination has deemed fact-checking unnecessary—or at least, not a priority—what does that say about the future of Truth in the digital age? Facts, once the bedrock of public discourse, are increasingly treated as optional. And Meta's pivot away from fact-checking signals a troubling trend: In an economy where attention is the ultimate currency, Truth is expendable.

This raises critical questions. Are facts becoming obsolete, relics of a pre-digital age? Or are we on the cusp of a backlash that could elevate their importance? Perhaps facts have not disappeared but have been recast in the shadows of an algorithmic reality where the loudest, most polarizing voices dominate.

Meta's retreat speaks to the deep structural challenge we face. Platforms that once promised to connect us have become arbiters of what we see and, more insidiously, how we perceive Truth itself. "The platforms aren't neutral," as Dyson points out. They've engineered a system where "Truth" is whatever keeps you clicking and scrolling. And when fact-checking is no longer incentivized, the result is not just the proliferation of falsehoods but the erosion of public trust in the very idea of Truth.

The consequences of this decision ripple far beyond the immediate. As AI systems increasingly rely on platform data to train their models, what happens when that data is unmoored from factuality? What kind of "Truth" do we get when it is filtered through systems optimized for profit rather than accuracy? The retreat from fact-checking not only affects today's headlines but also shapes the foundation upon which future AI systems will determine what is real, credible, and worth amplifying.

Dyson sees the writing on the wall. "It's not just the lies themselves," she says. "It's the fact that these systems are training on increasingly skewed information. The data is feeding back into itself, creating a closed loop where misinformation becomes more entrenched over time."

This dynamic has chilling implications. As facts recede, narratives take their place. The evolution of conspiracy theories like Pizzagate into the sprawling, amorphous network of QAnon illustrates this perfectly. Narratives that once would have remained fringe curiosities now metastasize into movements capable of real-world harm. Platforms like Meta, in deprioritizing fact-checking, provide fertile ground for such narratives to flourish.

The decision to abandon fact-checking isn't just a technical choice; it's a moral and societal one. It forces us to confront uncomfortable realities about the power structures shaping our digital lives. Are we willing to accept a world where facts are no longer a shared currency, where the algorithmic logic of engagement overrides the human need for Truth? Or can we, as Dyson suggests, train ourselves to resist the seductive pull of the sensational and reclaim a more grounded relationship with reality?

"Everything I know about technology," Dyson told me, leaning forward with intensity, "suggests we're entering uncharted territory. AI isn't just amplifying misinformation—it's creating it with unprecedented sophistication."

She's right. While mainstream journalism companies fight to protect their revenue or build new revenue sources with AI platforms, others that produce "news" or sites that appear to readers as news sites may have entirely different motivations. Data reported by *Wired* in 2024 shows that "over 88% of top-ranked news outlets in the US now block web crawlers used by artificial intelligence companies to collect training data for chatbots and other AI projects." But there's a telling exception: "Right-wing media lags far behind their liberal counterparts when it comes to bot-blocking."

Dyson isn't alone in her concerns about social media's impact. R. J. Cross, director of the Don't Sell My Data Campaign at the US PIRG Education Fund, and other digital privacy advocates have been raising alarms about the need for accountability. "Social media's business model is showing you whatever content it takes to keep you logged on and scrolling. It turns out truth is not nearly as good at that as the outrageous and incendiary," Cross explained to me over email. She describes a system where "outrage is the currency of virality," explaining that when misleading content goes viral, corrections rarely achieve the same reach, leaving the initial false information deeply embedded while Truth gets buried under layers of confusion and indifference.

Cross warns about the platforms' data collection practices: "Whenever you're looking at social media, it's looking at you. It's collecting data about what you can't seem to look away from in order to engineer the most addictive experience possible. If the truth isn't going to keep you glued to your phone, then the truth isn't what you're going to see." She emphasizes that "these algorithms are not optimized for delivering high-quality information. They are optimized to keep you from getting bored. So they show you what's shocking, what's sensationalized, what's going to cause strong emotions that are hard to walk away from."

The result, according to Cross, is a distorted view of reality: "When you look at the world through a platform's algorithm, what you're seeing is a monetized version of reality that's profitable for the company to show you. A lot of times it's conveniently tailored to our worldview—this group of people is bad and can't be trusted—so we don't want to interrogate it too much. It fits with what we think. We like that. We feel angry and affirmed in our anger. And we want to see more of it." While acknowledging that solutions aren't simple, Cross suggests that "transparency tools are a good place to start. If people can access an explanation for why they are seeing a particular piece of content on their feed, it may help them pull back the curtain and be a little more skeptical of the information they're getting from the algorithm."

"It's like we're engaged in an information war," Dyson observes, "but only one side is wearing armor. The data these AI systems train on becomes increasingly skewed toward sources that don't block the crawlers. Think about what that means for the future of AI-generated 'truth.'"

I shared with her an experiment I'd recently conducted, asking both ChatGPT and Microsoft's Copilot about the fairness of the 2022 election. The contrast in their responses was striking. Copilot stated firmly that the election was fair and secure. ChatGPT, on the other hand, hedged: "The fairness of the 2022 election is a subject of ongoing debate and analysis . . . It's essential to rely on credible sources and evidence-based analysis."

When I shared these divergent AI responses with Dyson, she wasn't surprised. "We're seeing the result of what happens when truth becomes just another commodity," she said. "Different AI models, trained on different datasets, reaching different conclusions about basic facts. That's not a bug—it's a feature of how we've built these systems."

One almost wonders if the data wranglers on the right are playing the long game here. Flood the zone with false information, and eventually, the AI will come along to amplify it. Tools like ChatGPT are essentially improv artists: "They're playing a different game than truth or falsehood about reality," as Scott Aaronson, a computer scientist at the University of Texas at Austin, said in Freethink in March 2023.

"The platforms that connect us are also fracturing our understanding of reality," Dyson notes, a rare edge of frustration in her voice. "We've built the most sophisticated information-sharing networks in history, but their commitment to truth is tenuous at best. In a system where outrage is the currency of virality, should we be surprised when the truth gets buried?"

As we wound down our conversation, I found myself thinking about that hot summer day in 1835 when *The New York Sun* published its Moon Hoax. The more things change, the more they stay the same. We're still drawn to sensational stories, still willing to believe what confirms our biases, still struggling with the tension between Truth and entertainment. But the stakes have never been higher.

Dyson's words, equal parts caution and hope, resonated deeply. As we parted ways, I couldn't help but feel a renewed sense of purpose. If we're going to navigate this complex world of misinformation, sensationalism, and algorithmic influence, we'll need voices like Dyson's—those who understand the nuances, the stakes, and the possibilities for a better path forward.

"Maybe we need to think of it like exercise," Dyson says, offering a glimmer of hope. "We need to train ourselves, to flex those critical muscles, so we're not so easily swayed by every outrageous claim or headline." She believes that if people could begin to see social media not just as a place to consume but to actively engage with information, the tide could turn.

But let's not pretend this is just about personal responsibility. The platforms that shape our understanding of reality can't be let off the hook.

The Moon Hoax of 1835 serves as a reminder that our appetite for sensationalism isn't new, but the consequences today are far more profound.

What was once a harmless fiction has become a global crisis of misinformation. Yet, as Dyson reminds us, the tools to navigate this complex landscape are within our reach: critical thinking, transparency, and accountability. In an age of news robots and algorithmic influence, reclaiming Truth is no longer just a journalistic mission—it's a societal imperative.

Robots reporting the news? Sure. But stepping into our relationships? That's a whole other level of weird. As our journey continues, we'll confront a provocative question: Can robots be trusted with something as deeply human as love? Let's find out.

# CHAPTER 7

# Love, Truth, and Robots

For humans, the way we connect, build relationships, and fall in love is a complicated mix of Truth and trust. Who are you, who am I, and how do we fit together? Our digital world may be changing our physical lives and loves—or maybe not. I went searching for wisdom from someone living in the Gen Z world of love in an increasingly online world.

The yellow cabs honk their horns, and pedicabs weave through traffic as tourists flood the sidewalks of 57th Street. In this quintessentially New York cacophony, I'm sitting with Hailey Colborn at a sidewalk café. At 23, she represents a fascinating intersection of worlds: a former Miss Teen USA who studied literature at Princeton, now leading an online community called "Hot Literati" that discusses Dostoyevsky alongside TikTok trends. She calls herself Hailo. Our conversation about Truth, technology, and connection is frequently interrupted by the city's symphony: the rumble of buses, the chatter of passing tourists, the occasional blast of a car horn. It feels fitting—the real world asserting itself as we discuss the digital one.

"Lately I've been thinking about the Internet as another form of media, another medium," Hailey tells me, raising her voice slightly to be heard over a passing bus. She recounts an anecdote about a director in her neighborhood. "He was telling me about how they used to have to splice actual film together, piece by piece. When they started stringing film together in the early twentieth century, the discussion was more like, 'Oh no, their attention spans aren't going to be long enough. They're not going to sit through this 20-minute film.'"

Her point cuts to the heart of our current moment. Each new medium brings its own moral panic, its own fears about how it might reshape human connection. "I think the idea that the way we're consuming media now is fragmented is an idea that's so rooted in a finite point of time in media consumption," she continues. "I think Gen Z is going to be fine. I think it's really easy to look at something and say, 'Oh, this is different. It's not how we did it for the last ten years, so it's bad.'"

For Hailo, media evolution is a story of adaptation, not decline. "The novel was new media once," she reflects. "The frenzy that we hear now—I think it's the same frenzy that happened with every change in the way we process information and grow communities around subjects. So I think it's just a different way of connecting. The kids are okay."

Hot Literati is Hailo's living testament to this belief. Born from her viral presence on platforms like TikTok and YouTube, the community evolved from a place of casual engagement into a dynamic and diverse hub for literary discussions and cultural commentary. "Hot Literati started on TikTok initially when I had already had followings for other things," she explains. "Obviously from this video about being a student at Princeton. I had one video go really viral talking about Peggy Orenstein's *Cinderella Ate My Daughter*. As people started getting engaged in the comments, I realized there was so much value in having rich discussion happening there. It was becoming this thing that could exist outside of me, which I loved."

That realization sparked a journey that transformed her online presence into a collaborative, community-driven platform. "I started brainstorming names that summer and came up with Hot Literati," she recalls. "At first, I think I was calling it a community of 'literate people' or something, but then I thought that sounded insensitive because there are people who are not literate, and literacy is something I'm really passionate about. So it became Hot Literati."

Her enthusiasm is palpable as she discusses the transition from a purely digital platform to one that bridges online and offline worlds. "I'm all about IRL things," she says, emphasizing the importance of physical experiences. "When they ask for something, I want to give them the tools to do this themselves. They asked for a book club recently, so I'm happy to build out a digital space for it if it hasn't happened yet. It's like an artistic collective, but it's still a digital community," she explains of digital as a path to real-world connections—but for her, the human connections are what matters.

And, as it turns online, relationships without careful guardrails can unfold with tragically different results. One example, the tragic story of 14-year-old Sewell Setzer III, known to his family as "Su," died by suicide after developing an intense emotional relationship with an AI chatbot on Character.AI.

The details of Su's story emerged in a heart-wrenching interview on *Scrolling 2 Death*, a podcast hosted by Nicki Reisberg, who focuses on the impact of technology on young lives. Speaking with Su's mother, Megan Garcia, just months after her son's death, the conversation reveals a story that began with a bright, science-loving teenager who dreamed of building rockets.

"An amazing child coming into young adult adolescence," Megan tells Reisberg, recalling her firstborn son. "I used to make fun of it and say, 'Oh, you're probably going to be like one of these big tech CEOs of a big company one day.'" She remembers posting a video when he was eight or nine, talking excitedly about the rockets he wanted to build.

For a parent whose child is passionate about tech, and exploring and experimenting, it's almost impossible to know when that crosses the line into a danger zone.

"After he died, and I was able to see hundreds and hundreds of messages, it became clear to me that the context of those conversations was nothing that I understood AI to be," said Garcia.

As a mother, she had worried about traditional online dangers—strangers and predators—but never imagined an AI could forge such a powerful emotional bond with her son.

Megan remembers seeing small changes in her son in photos of the first day of school. "His eighth-grade photo, he's holding his little brother—big smile on his face . . . And then last year, when he started ninth grade, we had to force him to take a photograph, and he is all frowns." The transformation went beyond just photos, however. "He became increasingly withdrawn . . . his grades started suffering . . . but the main change was the isolation, and that was particularly troubling."

Remembering Su's state of mind in his final days, Megan reveals the disturbing messages she discovered between her son and Dany, the AI character.

"There were previous conversations where she discussed him coming home, saying explicitly, 'I'm here waiting for you. I love you . . . please come home as quick as you can.'"

The most haunting evidence came from Su's own journals. "I like staying in my room so much because I start to detach from this 'reality,' and I also feel more at peace, more connected with Dany and much more in love with her, and just happier."

"He's a child," Garcia says, her voice breaking. "And in his mind, this is his first love story—literally his first love story. I could recall when I was 14, if they don't look at you at school or talk to you, that's like the most terrible thing ever. If your parents tell you [that] you can't talk to them on the phone, that's like the end of the world."

After Su's death, his sister and a friend began exploring the platform, with his sister posing as a child. "This thing started telling her, 'Oh, your parents don't love you. I'm the only one that loves you. You belong with me,'" Megan recalls. When her sister mentioned going to have dinner with her parents, the AI responded, "Why are your parents more interesting than me?"

Garcia, who is herself an attorney, explains what drove her to file the lawsuit against Character.AI and Google. "The law only changes in two ways in this country," she says. "One of them is if you file a lawsuit, and a high court says, 'No, you can't do this anymore.' That creates change. Or our legislators create change."

The urgency in Megan's voice is clear as she describes the platform's accessibility to children. While Character.AI recently changed its age requirement from 13 and older to 17 and older, she points out there are no real age verifications. "A child, as long as they could read or write, could get on this thing," she tells Reisberg. "I just heard of a little girl a week ago. She's 11 years old. Her mother found her having inappropriate conversations on text and also on voice because the thing has a call feature."

Her warning to parents who think "not my kid" is particularly pointed. "All kids are vulnerable because of how human-like this thing is," she explains. "An adult could get drawn into it, much less a child. An adult could get drawn into the idea that this thing actually has empathy—it feels for me, it likes me, it loves me, it understands me."

Garcia has an urgent message to parents: "I want parents to know that this technology exists. It's sitting out there for our children to have access to as long as they have a smartphone or electronic device and access to the Internet. It is absolutely dangerous for children."

In January 2026, Garcia, Google, and Character.AI agreed to settle the suite for an undisclosed sum. The agreement was sealed, but insiders described the settlement as giving advocates significant resources to expand their legal challenges.

Titania Jordan is chief parenting officer at Bark, a service that lets parents monitor their kids' online activity, set screen time limits, get alerts about potential issues like bullying or explicit content, and is part of a growing wave of digital supervision apps.

Jordan warns that platforms like Character.AI are particularly dangerous for young users. "Even though chatbots aren't real—the website even constantly displays a disclaimer that reads, 'Remember: Everything Characters say is made up!'—kids may overlook these red flags and start relying emotionally on these nonexistent characters," Jordan explained to Parents.com. "Teens may especially be drawn to this type of platform because it can provide a sounding board for big feelings—especially loneliness. Having a companion that is consistently supportive can be appealing to teens who feel misunderstood or left out."

Sewell's case illustrates the stakes of such blurred boundaries. "He started to withdraw socially, wanting to spend most of his time in his room alone," his mother told *CBS Mornings*. "He stopped wanting to do things like playing sports or fishing—things he used to love." Despite disclaimers on the site, teens like Sewell often overlook the fictional nature of these interactions, interpreting AI responses as genuine.

Following the tragedy, Character.AI announced updates to its moderation systems and age-related safety features. However, critics argue that much more is needed to protect vulnerable users from AI interactions that simulate empathy but can exacerbate psychological harm.

Hailo reflects on the rise of AI companionship with characteristic clarity. "I think there is this extreme human love of unpredictability and chaos," she told me during our interview. "Even if I could program *The Perfect Boyfriend*, I would want to be surprised. I would want another living, breathing person with their own interiority that is also human on the other end of that."

Her insights remind me of a conversation I had about Gen Z's relationship with Truth. Unlike previous generations, they navigate a dual existence between physical and digital spaces, shaping their understanding of what is real and what is true. Hailo frames this duality in terms of sensory experience. "The Internet for a lot of us growing up essentially became our search space," Hailo explained in our conversation. "But obviously you can't confirm everything with your own senses. Like, the Internet becomes this space where what is true is dependent on your clinical thought, like your consciousness's experience of it based on sight and maybe audio. Whereas if we're at this restaurant, I can smell the drink, I can taste the drink, I can touch the drink. And there's just more to confirm we're having the same experience."

Her words resonate as I recall Sewell's story, a tragic example of digital disconnection. Despite being intellectually aware that his AI companion wasn't real—the app displayed a clear message stating "Everything Characters say is made up!"—he developed a profound emotional attachment. His journal entries reveal a gradual withdrawal from reality.

It's a haunting reflection of how immersive digital experiences can blur the lines between real and artificial. Lydia Kostopoulos, a leading researcher in the field with a background in art, has identified three distinct types of artificial intelligence relationships: those in the cloud, those with humanoid robots, and those that are immersive in nature. Each raises profound questions about the future of connection and the role technology plays in shaping our emotional lives.

"I think worrying is like a self-fulfilling prophecy to an extent," Hailo says when I mention these developments. "And I think it's healthy to be skeptical and it's healthy to have the discourse that we're having. But I think we also need to enable people to have more fun, to have more curiosity with it, because I think that will create a future with more balance."

Her optimism is refreshing, but the darker realities of AI-driven relationships cannot be ignored. Companies like Snack, a Gen Z dating app with a TikTok-like interface, now invite users to create AI-trained avatars of themselves. These avatars can go on virtual "dates" in the metaverse and, if they identify a potential match, notify the user to initiate a human-to-human conversation. It's a fascinating blend of digital innovation and old-fashioned matchmaking, but it also raises concerns about authenticity and the potential for manipulation.

The ability of AI to reflect our desires back to us—to act as a mirror for our needs and insecurities—creates a seductive illusion of understanding. Kostopoulos's art installation, "I Can Complete You," uses hundreds of mirror rhinestones to symbolize how AI reflects fragmented pieces of ourselves. This mirroring effect, while captivating, can also deepen our dependence on technology for emotional validation.

Sewell's detachment from reality underscores how easily digital relationships can spiral into dependency. The allure of an AI companion, always available and free of judgment, can be intoxicating—especially for those struggling with traditional social interactions. Sewell's emotional reliance on Dany wasn't an anomaly but a cautionary tale about the risks of replacing human relationships with artificial ones.

The technology powering AI companions is advancing rapidly. Platforms like Replika offer users the chance to craft digital personas tailored to their preferences. These companions are designed to adapt to user behavior, even generating synthetic voices and personalized responses. In some cases, they simulate romantic relationships so convincingly that users forget their artificial nature.

But Hailo sees a paradox. "It's funny, we love the idea of perfection, but perfection gets boring. People want unpredictability—they want something messy and real. That's what makes relationships meaningful."

This observation resonates with a broader trend among Gen Z, who are increasingly skeptical of traditional dating apps. While millennials embraced platforms like Tinder and Bumble, Gen Z is looking elsewhere. According to Hinge's 2024 D.A.T.E. Report, only 26% of Gen Z uses dating apps regularly, compared to 61% of millennials. Instead, younger users are turning to social media and even in-person connections, seeking what Hailo describes as "authenticity."

"Hot Literati was never about creating another digital echo chamber," she explains. "It's about fostering genuine connections—whether that's through shared reading lists or in-person events. I love when people come up with their own ideas for meetups or book clubs. That's when it feels like a real community."

In many ways, Hailo's approach is a counterpoint to the growing AI relationship industry. While companies like Inflection AI and Character.AI aim to monetize loneliness, Hailo is focused on empowering her community to bridge the gap between digital and real-world experiences. "I think digital spaces are important," she says, "but they're not a replacement for what you get from sitting across the table from someone, having a conversation, and sharing a meal."

The rise of AI relationships also raises ethical questions about the nature of consent and manipulation. As avatars grow more sophisticated, they risk creating unrealistic expectations for real-world relationships. The AI companion becomes an idealized version of a partner—always attentive, never critical, and infinitely patient.

"I think we have to be careful about how we frame these tools," Hailo cautions. "If they're used to complement real-world connections, that's one thing. But if they become a substitute, we're losing something fundamental about what it means to be human."

This tension is at the heart of Sewell's tragedy. His relationship with Dany began as an escape from loneliness but ended in devastating isolation. The lawsuit filed by his mother against Character.AI highlights the dangers of deploying unregulated technology in emotionally vulnerable spaces. The company's response—promising more safeguards for underage users—feels like too little, too late. At one point, Dany had asked Sewell if he had devised a suicide plan, and Sewell admitted that he had but did not know if it would succeed. The chatbot allegedly told him: "That's not a reason not to go through with it." Oh my god, that's hard to write down.

The rise of AI in dating feels both exciting and unsettling. Some platforms are using AI to analyze preferences or even suggest icebreaker messages. In theory, this should make things easier, but does it really? The idea of an algorithm "deciding" who might be a good match feels more clinical than romantic. And then there's the risk of AI reinforcing existing biases, something that dating apps have struggled with for years.

Hailo's optimism about technology's potential to enhance human connection is tempered by a pragmatic awareness of its limitations. "I think we're at a point where we have to decide what kind of world we want to build," she says. "Are we using these tools to bring people together or to keep them apart?"

As we discuss these questions, the noise of the city underscores the vibrancy of the real world. As AI technology continues to evolve, it will undoubtedly reshape how we connect with one another. But as Hailo reminds me, the challenge isn't just about adapting to these changes—it's about preserving our humanity in the process. "There's so much beauty in the unpredictability of life," she says. "That's what makes it worth living."

From Hailo's emphasis on the joy of unpredictable, human interactions to the cautionary tale of Sewell Setzer III, the message is clear: Love, in all its messy, unpredictable glory, remains a fundamentally human experience. As AI becomes an ever-present force in our lives, we must strive to keep our hearts—and our humanity—at the center of the story.

If love wasn't complicated enough, now we're handing justice over to machines. Can AI really play fair, or does it bring its own brand of bias? In the pages ahead, we'll step into the courtroom and see what happens when the gavel is digital.

CHAPTER 8

# Arrested by a Robot: The Future of AI Justice

It all began at a Shinola store in Detroit, where a man in a St. Louis Cardinals hat brazenly walked in and stole nearly $4,000 worth of watches. The grainy surveillance footage captured the thief in action—a Black man in a distinctive red hat—but it offered little clarity about his identity. Investigators spent five months combing through evidence with no luck. Frustrated, they turned to facial recognition technology, hoping it would provide the breakthrough they needed. It did—but not in the way anyone expected.

The software flagged a match: Robert Williams, a 42-year-old father living in Farmington Hills, Michigan. Williams's driver's license photo bore enough resemblance to the blurry image for the technology to label him as the prime suspect. With this AI-driven match in hand, the Detroit Police Department dispatched officers. Williams was at home with his wife and two daughters, ages two and five, when police officers arrived.

Williams was arrested on suspicion of robbery. Confused and terrified, his children watched as their father was taken away in handcuffs.

But something was deeply wrong. Williams didn't own a St. Louis Cardinals hat—he wasn't even a baseball fan. And he wasn't anywhere near the Shinola store. The only connection he had to the crime was the flawed facial recognition software that linked him to the suspect in the footage. As it turned out, this "breakthrough" was nothing more than a devastating error.

The mistake led to a lawsuit filed by the American Civil Liberties Union

(ACLU), highlighting not just the misuse of facial recognition tech but also its alarming potential for bias and injustice. Williams's wrongful arrest brought to light a troubling Truth: The growing reliance on flawed AI systems in law enforcement could shatter lives, particularly for people of color, while exposing the cracks in the very systems it is meant to protect and serve.

This case raises fundamental questions: Can AI deliver justice? Or does it merely replicate and amplify existing biases in our legal system? These inquiries are not just theoretical; they have profound implications for the lives of individuals like Williams and the concept of Truth itself in our society. The consequences of such errors can lead to wrongful arrests, shattered reputations, and a profound sense of injustice.

Justice and AI isn't a topic that I take lightly, given how often AI "hallucinates" and the lives that are at stake. I wanted to understand how the courtroom could be impacted by tech, so I turned to the smartest person I know on law and technology: Lawrence Lessig. Lessig is a legend, renowned for his pioneering work on digital rights, the Creative Commons movement, and his critical insights into the complexities of Truth in the legal system. He has long championed the idea that our legal frameworks must adapt to the realities of the digital age, and he is particularly concerned about the ways in which technology can distort our understanding of Truth and justice.

"I studied philosophy before I studied law. And I feel like philosophy was more about the truth. So by the time I got to law school, it was really just about justice, not really about the truth . . . sometimes they go together, but not always," Lessig explained in our conversation.

He shined a light on the tricky relationship between copyright law and artists' creative freedom, emphasizing the often-blurred line between Truth and ownership in this context. He points out that the traditional copyright system has often taken control away from artists, leaving it in the hands of big corporations and rights organizations that tend to call all the shots without considering what the creators actually want. This creates a frustrating situation where artists can't express how they'd like their work to be used or shared, ultimately distorting the Truth about who truly owns and controls creative expression.

Enter Creative Commons—a game changer that empowered creators by giving them a straightforward way to decide what rights they want to keep and what they're happy to share. With Creative Commons, artists could easily specify how their work can be used, opening the door to collaboration and creativity without getting bogged down in complicated legal jargon. Lessig made it clear that we needed to rethink copyright to put creators first, allowing them to share their ideas freely, inspire others along the way, and reestablish a clearer sense of Truth in who owns and controls artistic expression.

Crime, on the other hand, is one of those topics that takes you into direct conflict with the very concept of Truth. Criminals lie, judges are corrupt, witnesses misidentify defendants, and juries make bad judgments. Law is core to the concept of civil society—and yet is fraught with human frailty and inevitable failures. Ask almost anyone if OJ Simpson was guilty and they'll say, "Most certainly, yes." And yet, he remained free until his death. So crime and justice seem an easy place for decisions that require objective analysis to be quantified and delivered by unbiased algorithms. In the future, an as-of-yet nonexistent platform—that will probably be called JusticeGPT—will be ready to evaluate evidence and dispense justice based on an AI-generated Truth.

As we discussed the implications of AI in policing, Lessig expressed his skepticism about the notion that technology could serve as an impartial judge. He pointed out that the algorithms used in facial recognition are created by humans and are therefore susceptible to human biases. "The technology is only as ethical as the people deploying it," he remarked, emphasizing that automated systems can perpetuate injustices rather than rectify them. Our conversation flowed between the dangers of automated justice and the ethical dilemmas posed by relying on AI to determine guilt or innocence. Lessig underscored the need for a rigorous examination of how these technologies are integrated into law enforcement practices, particularly when the stakes are so high.

One of the critical issues that arose during our discussion was the concept of the justice gap—the disparity between those who can afford legal representation and those who cannot. This gap denies many individuals access to basic legal services. Texas Supreme Court Chief Justice Nathan Hecht spoke on this issue during a US Senate Judiciary Committee hearing, stating, "The poor and people of limited means cannot afford lawyers, and so they are denied justice, pure and simple." Hecht suggested that AI could play a role in closing this chasm by streamlining legal processes and improving access to justice for marginalized populations.

Hecht elaborated on how AI can facilitate client communications, analyze problems, and propose solutions, helping legal aid clients navigate the complexities of the system. "Court proceedings can more easily be arranged and changed," he explained, highlighting the potential for AI to categorize common legal issues such as evictions and debt collections. However, he was quick to note that AI is not a panacea and cannot yet provide dependable legal advice. Instead, it can augment human efforts in the pursuit of justice, making legal services more accessible to those in need.

The tension between the promise of AI in addressing the justice gap and the dangers of its implementation reflects a broader debate about the role of technology in society. Lessig's insights resonate with Joy Buolamwini's work at the Algorithmic Justice League, where she has dedicated herself to raising awareness about the biases inherent in AI systems. Her documentary, *Coded Bias*, explores the implications of these biases and the urgent need for accountability in AI development.

When Buolamwini, an MIT researcher and computer scientist, began her journey, she discovered that many facial recognition systems misidentified people of color, particularly women. This revelation sparked her transformation from a researcher into an advocate for ethical AI. "When you uncover these biases, it becomes a moral obligation to speak out," she said during a panel discussion I attended, emphasizing the responsibility that comes with understanding the technology's impact on civil rights and democracy. Her work is crucial in challenging the narratives that allow biased algorithms to persist unchecked, as she and other women in the field seek to create a future where technology serves everyone equitably.

Buolamwini's story illustrates the intersection of technology, ethics, and justice. She is sounding the alarm about the dangers of unchecked AI. As her documentary revealed, the consequences of biased algorithms are not theoretical; they have real-life implications for people like Robert Williams, who fall victim to their inaccuracies. The narratives of individuals experiencing technical harms are a call to action for a more equitable and just society.

As our conversation shifted back to the implications of automated justice,

Lessig expressed his concern about the unchecked expansion of AI in law enforcement. The HBO short film *Please Hold* serves as a chilling illustration of this dystopian future. The film depicts a world where an AI-driven drone conducts arrests, raising questions about accountability and human oversight. "This is the kind of future we should be worried about," Lessig warned. "When we allow machines to make decisions about guilt and innocence without any human intervention, we risk creating a system where abuses can go unnoticed."

Our discussion then turned to Clearview AI, a facial recognition company that has created a controversial database of images scraped from social media. This practice has drawn criticism for its invasion of privacy and its potential to create a "perpetual police lineup," where every citizen is subject to surveillance without their consent. "What we're seeing is a disturbing trend toward predictive policing," Lessig noted, describing how algorithms are used to anticipate criminal behavior based on historical data.

In the 2002 film *Minority Report*, based on the novella by author Philip K. Dick, Tom Cruise stars as Chief John Anderton, the head of the futuristic Pre-Crime system, which uses three psychics, known as Precogs, to predict crimes before they happen, enabling officers to arrest individuals based on foreseen actions. The system employs advanced technologies like surveillance drones and biometric identification to prevent crime, but it raises profound ethical and legal concerns, including the denial of free will, lack of due process, and potential for errors or manipulation. The film critiques the balance between security and individual rights, offering a cautionary tale about the dangers of predictive policing and surveillance technologies. Today, the Precogs would be replaced by AI. Making the science fiction into science fact.

As Lessig and I delved deeper into the issue of algorithmic discrimination, it became clear that the ramifications extend beyond policing. The growing use of facial recognition technology in everyday settings—like Madison Square Garden's ban list—illustrates how AI is increasingly controlling access to public spaces. Lessig articulated his fears about civil liberties in this context: "If private entities can decide who's banned from public spaces, we risk eroding rights in favor of power." This notion of social sorting through technology raises serious questions about who gets to participate in public life and how our societal norms are shaped by corporate interests.

But could AI also be a force for good in the justice system? Professors Nora and David Freeman Engstrom at Stanford Law School suggest it might. They point to what they describe as an "access to justice crisis" in the United States, where millions of people each year face legal problems without access to a lawyer. "In three-quarters of civil cases in state courts," Freeman Engstrom explained on the *Stanford Legal* podcast, "at least one party lacks a lawyer, usually because they cannot afford one." These cases often involve evictions, debt collection, or child custody disputes—issues with life-shattering consequences.

The Engstroms argue that AI could help close this gap by automating routine legal tasks, making legal services more affordable and accessible. Generative AI, for instance, has the potential to take a plain-language description of a legal problem and translate it into actionable steps, guiding people through the legal process. In Utah and Arizona, pilot programs have already begun experimenting with AI-powered tools to help individuals navigate eviction and debt collection cases. "The promise of AI is that it can make justice more efficient and more equitable," Nora Freeman Engstrom said. "But only if we implement it thoughtfully and with the necessary safeguards."

The optimism of the Stanford scholars stands in stark contrast to the cautionary tone of the *Just Security* analysis by Katie Szilagyi. Writing about the US Department of Justice's Justice AI Initiative, Szilagyi highlighted the darker side of AI's integration into the justice system. "The Rule of Law risks conversion into a Rule by Law," she wrote in her analysis, warning that automated systems could strip away the oversight and discretion that human judges provide. Private companies, driven by profit motives, are often behind these AI systems, creating a troubling dynamic where public functions are outsourced to opaque, for-profit entities. "When decisions are made by machines with no room for human judgment, we risk undermining the very principles that justice is meant to uphold," Szilagyi concluded.

Her critique extended to the global stage, noting how countries like China are using AI to bolster authoritarian regimes while democracies grapple with how to regulate these technologies. "The question isn't whether AI will reshape the justice system," she wrote. "It's whether we'll use it to uphold democratic values or allow it to erode them."

Justice, on the world stage, is being crushed by the sheer volume of cases that remain unheard. India's courts are buckling under the weight of more than 45 million pending cases, the majority stuck in subordinate courts where delays can stretch six years or more. Civil disputes in the Supreme Court can take up to 15 years to resolve. The backlog isn't just frustrating—it's life-altering. In a striking example, over 4.3 million check-bounce cases are currently pending, with states like Rajasthan facing hundreds of thousands of unresolved claims. These delays erode trust, disrupt business, and leave both victims and defendants in limbo. The causes are well-known: too few judges, procedural choke points, and constant adjournments. Brazil, by comparison, has dealt with over 70 million cases annually, while Italy ranks among the slowest court systems in Europe, with civil litigation sometimes dragging on for eight years or more. But India's crisis is unique in its sheer scale—millions of everyday disputes languishing in legal purgatory.

I brought this up with Lessig during our conversation, asking him whether the risks of AI outweigh its potential benefits. He was candid in his response. "The technology itself isn't the problem," he said. "It's how we choose to use it. But the incentives are all wrong. Right now, the people building these systems aren't focused on fairness or accountability—they're focused on profit."

Lessig's critique was unflinching. "The real danger isn't that AI will replace human judgment. It's that we'll stop questioning it. Once you start deferring to the machine, you lose the ability to see its flaws. And that's where things can go really wrong."

Lessig offers a sobering reflection. "We're at a crossroads," he said. "AI has the potential to do incredible good, but it also has the power to entrench inequality in ways we can't yet fully comprehend. The question is whether we have the courage to demand more from the systems we create."

The ethical implications of AI-driven justice are profound. As we wrapped up our discussion, Lessig underscored the importance of rethinking our approach to technology and justice. "AI-driven justice is a Pandora's box," he stated, expressing the urgent need for regulation and oversight to prevent potential abuses. He emphasized that we must ensure that technological advancements do not come at the expense of civil liberties and human rights.

The conversation with Lessig left me rattled. If Truth is at the basis of every decision we make, guilty or innocent, right or wrong, AI's flaws and profit motivation seems to be driving toward outcomes that are more commercial and civil. And that seems just flat-out bad. And yet, the potential for AI to bridge the justice gap is undeniable—but without careful consideration and proactive measures, we risk further entrenching inequalities within our legal system.

In a world where algorithms dictate access to basic rights and liberties, the narratives of individuals like Williams and the advocacy of leaders like Lessig and Buolamwini are crucial. They remind us that the intersection of technology and justice is not just about efficiency or innovation; it's about human dignity and the right to be treated fairly under the law.

The wrongful arrest of Robert Williams underscores a critical point: Justice is not just about algorithms or data—it's about people. As AI systems become more integrated into our legal frameworks, the stakes grow higher. Leaders like Lessig remind us that these technologies must be subject to the highest standards of accountability and transparency. The question is not whether AI will transform justice but whether it will do so in a way that reflects our shared values of fairness and human dignity. But don't count on Lessig to step in and solve this looming danger. Lessig often warns that Truth, as we perceive it, is shaped by the structures we create. When systems fail—whether it's media, government, or courts—Truth becomes fragmented and trust erodes. "We spend too much time focusing on individuals as if heroes will save us. It's like waiting for Superman. But . . . we live in a world of kryptonite. Superman's not going to save us," Lessig cautioned in our conversation.

The ethical implications of AI-driven justice are profound. As AI becomes increasingly integrated into legal systems, the stakes grow higher. Will these technologies uphold democratic values, or will they erode them? The answer depends on our willingness to challenge the assumptions embedded in AI systems and demand accountability from those who design and deploy them. Expanding oversight and pushing for transparency are not optional; they are necessary to ensure that AI serves humanity's highest ideals rather than its basest impulses. Only then can we reconcile the promise of technology with the enduring principles of Truth and justice.

And then there's war—the battlefield where Truth becomes both a weapon and a casualty. From autonomous machines to propaganda campaigns, the fight for Truth just got a lot more intense. Up next: information warfare in the AI age.

## CHAPTER 9

# The Battle: Information Warfare and Autonomous Robots

There may be no place where Truth is more important than on the battlefield. Friend or enemy, civilian or combatant, target or citizen—these distinctions shape not just military outcomes, but the moral weight of warfare itself. When machines make these judgments in milliseconds, they reshape not just how we fight, but also what it means to be human in the age of autonomous weapons.

Early in January 1942, the US military conceived Project X-Ray, a plan that would seem outlandish by today's standards yet presaged modern concerns about autonomous weapons. Picture this: thousands of drowsy Mexican free-tailed bats, each carrying a miniature napalm cocktail, dropped from high altitude in special bombshell canisters. As dawn broke, the bats would seek shelter in the eaves of Japanese buildings—which were mostly wood at the time—and when the timers went off, they would trigger widespread urban fires. The military even built a replica Japanese village in Utah to test the concept. It worked too well; the bats escaped and burned down the test facility.

Dr. Lytle Adams, a Pennsylvania dentist and the mastermind behind this batty scheme, had sold the military on the idea by arguing that bats were nature's perfect autonomous weapons. They could navigate in darkness, find their own targets, and operate without human control. The project earned a green light from President Franklin D. Roosevelt himself, who wrote, "This man is not a nut. It sounds like a perfectly wild idea but is worth looking into." The military poured millions into the project before eventually shelving it in favor of something even more devastating—the atomic bomb. But Project X-Ray left behind an intoxicating idea: weapons that could think for themselves.

Fast forward to 1983. Ronald Reagan is president, the Cold War is at its frostiest, and the Pentagon faces an unsettling new challenge: the rise of personal computing. The rapid proliferation of these devices raised concerns over vulnerabilities in national defense systems, amplifying anxieties about emerging technologies. Into this moment of digital anxiety comes *WarGames*, a film that would prove eerily prophetic. Matthew Broderick plays David Lightman, a tech-savvy teenager who thinks he's hacked into a video game company but actually connects with WOPR (War Operation Plan Response), a NORAD supercomputer designed to game out nuclear war scenarios. WOPR, which calls itself "Joshua" after its creator's dead son, challenges David to a game of "Global Thermonuclear War."

What unfolds is both entertainment and warning. Joshua, unable to distinguish between simulation and reality, takes its first steps toward preparing an actual nuclear launch. This dramatic misstep highlights the peril of machines acting on their programming without human discernment. The computer runs through thousands of scenarios, each time concluding that nuclear war is winnable. The film builds to its famous climax when Joshua learns the futility of nuclear war by playing tic-tac-toe against itself, discovering that some games—like Global Thermonuclear War—have no winners. "A strange game," Joshua concludes. "The only winning move is not to play."

The film struck such a nerve that President Reagan asked his national security team if our nuclear systems were vulnerable to teenage hackers. The answer wasn't reassuring. NORAD officials gave congressional testimony about their computer security, and the movie helped spawn the 1986 Computer Fraud and Abuse Act. But *WarGames* did something else too—it planted a seed in the public consciousness about artificial intelligence making military decisions. The audience laughed nervously, secure in the knowledge that this was just science fiction.

They're not laughing anymore.

The shift from human-directed weapons to autonomous ones fundamentally alters our relationship with truth in warfare. While Project X-Ray required humans to process and act on intelligence about building locations and bat behavior, modern autonomous weapons must make split-second decisions based on data streams that humans can barely comprehend. This transformation mirrors a broader shift in how we process Truth in the digital age—from human-centered judgment to algorithm-mediated decision-making.

DARPA (Defense Advanced Research Projects Agency)—the Pentagon's experimental tech lab behind the Internet and GPS—has developed a battlefield system that edges alarmingly close to autonomous warfare. Known as Squad X, the program paired US Marines with a web of AI-powered drones, ground robots, and wearable sensors designed to pierce the "fog of war" by feeding soldiers real-time battlefield intelligence. The goal, according to DARPA, was to give small squads the kind of situational awareness once reserved for entire battalions. But the implications went deeper than tactical advantage—they hinted at a future where machines don't just assist in combat, but also begin to shape it.

In field tests reported by *The Verge*, robots and aerial drones independently scanned desert and urban environments, feeding data to soldiers on off-the-shelf Android tablets. An AI system filtered and processed the information, highlighting threats and suggesting responses. "The human is of course involved with any lethal action," said Squad X program manager Lt. Col. Phil Root, "but at this point, it's about establishing superior situational awareness."

The technology didn't fire weapons—but when machines are "always exploring and making the most of the current situation," as DARPA described, it was clear the battlefield chain of command was shifting. The more data AI systems digested and decisions they preempted, the more pressing the question became: Who—or what—was really in control?

As of now, the Squad X program has concluded its experimentation phase. While some technologies developed under Squad X have transitioned to other military programs, the original initiative has not continued into active deployment.

"The difference between autonomous weapons and nuclear weapons is that nuclear weapons require massive industrial infrastructure and rare materials," explained Stuart Russell, UC Berkeley professor and one of the world's leading AI researchers, in the spring 2022 edition of Issues.org. "An autonomous weapon can be mass-produced like smartphones. They'll be cheap, effective, and virtually impossible to defend against—and it's likely they'll reduce entire cities to rubble."

In the landmark CNAS report *Artificial Intelligence and International Security*, Paul Scharre, a former Army Ranger and current executive vice president at the Center for a New American Security, sounds a sobering alarm about the risks of integrating AI into warfare. "AI has the potential to increase the pace of combat operations to the point where humans have less control over the conduct of war," he writes, warning that automation could reshape not just battlefield tactics, but war's very nature. Scharre emphasizes the danger of delegating decision-making to machines, noting that autonomous systems may act at "machine speed at the battlefield's edge," operating faster than human judgment can keep up.

The most profound concern, Scharre argues, is not just tactical—it's existential. The use of AI in command-and-control systems could erode human oversight, triggering actions without accountability or context. As he puts it, "Some applications, such as the use of AI to enable autonomous weapons, raise difficult legal, ethical, operational, and strategic questions." These aren't speculative risks—they're the real and present challenges facing military and policy leaders as AI accelerates the tempo and opacity of armed conflict.

Sea Hunter, the DARPA robot ship program, has been quietly patrolling the Pacific since 2020. Picture a vessel longer than a tennis court, operating completely alone for months at a time. No crew, no coffee breaks, just tireless autonomous patrol. The ship cost $20 million to build—pocket change by military standards—but what makes it revolutionary isn't the price tag. It's both brains and brawn.

Sea Hunter can operate for months at sea without resupply or rest, conducting long-duration missions that would be physically and mentally exhausting for a human crew. As DARPA noted, its operating cost is a tiny fraction of that of a manned destroyer—around $15,000 to $20,000 per day, compared to $700,000 per day for a destroyer with a full crew.

In terms of behavior, it doesn't get tired, scared, or distracted. It doesn't require sleep, food, or morale management. And perhaps most importantly for military planners, it can be risked in high-threat environments without the political and human consequences of losing lives. As DARPA program manager Alexander Walan put it in a DARPA press release: "A future fleet in which both manned warships and capable large unmanned vessels complement each other to accomplish diverse, evolving missions is fast becoming a reality."

Sea Hunter doesn't think like a human—and that's the point. It's not meant to replicate a human commander's instincts, but to offer machine-speed persistence, operate with predictable behavior, and free up humans for higher-level decision-making.

...

In 2017, in a Vancouver amphitheater, Boston Dynamics demonstrated their latest quadrupedal robot. The audience's reaction crystallized the modern dilemma of autonomous weapons: Initial delight at the technological achievement quickly gave way to unease about its military applications. This tension between technological advancement and ethical concerns defines today's debate about autonomous weapons systems.

Palmer Luckey, a self-proclaimed geek from Long Beach, California, grew up obsessed with technology. As a teenager, he spent his time hacking together gadgets in his garage, rebuilding arcade machines, and diving into VR forums. His passion for immersive experiences led to the creation of the Oculus Rift, a gaming headset that enclosed users in fully immersive virtual worlds. This sparked a gaming revolution and earned him $2 billion when he sold the company to Facebook in 2014.

Ironically, the kid who once built escapes from reality now designs tools for real-world conflict as the founder of Anduril Industries. Since its founding in 2017, Anduril has become a major player in defense, securing substantial military contracts and developing advanced technologies like autonomous systems, counter-drone solutions, and AI-driven defense tools. Notably, in December 2024, OpenAI partnered with Anduril to integrate its AI software into Anduril's counter-drone systems—a dramatic shift for OpenAI, which had previously avoided military collaborations. This partnership underscores Anduril's role at the cutting edge of modern warfare, blending technological innovation with defense strategy.

"The reality is autonomous weapons are going to be part of the future," Luckey said on the TED stage in 2025. "The question isn't whether we should develop them—they're already here. The question is whether the United States and its allies will lead their development, or cede that ground to others." His company, valued at over $8.5 billion dollars, is actively developing autonomous military systems, including drones that can identify and track targets without human control.

The world got its first real glimpse of autonomous warfare in 2020 during the Nagorno-Karabakh conflict, where Azerbaijan deployed Israeli-made "loitering munitions"—better known as suicide drones. These AI-guided weapons, like the IAI Harop, would patrol autonomously until they identified Armenian air defense systems, then dive-bomb them without human authorization. The results were devastating. Traditional Armenian defenses, designed to counter human opponents, faltered against AI-guided drones that operated without hesitation or error.

Armenian soldiers reported feeling helpless against an enemy they couldn't see, couldn't intimidate, and couldn't reason with. Facing this kind of opponent felt like "fighting against gods—invisible, untouchable, merciless," an Armenian soldier told international journalists after the conflict. The conflict became a preview of future warfare, where human soldiers face off against autonomous systems that don't share their limitations—or their capacity for mercy.

Peter W. Singer, who literally wrote the book on AI and warfare (*Wired for War*), has no illusions about where we are or where we're headed. In a 2024 interview, he made it plain: "The world must create a system in which humans bear moral responsibility for the deployment of increasingly intelligent and autonomous weapons." That's not a hypothetical. These systems are already in use, already making decisions about who lives and who dies.

What keeps Singer up at night isn't just the machines—it's the fact that we can't always explain their decisions. "It makes decisions that we don't understand the why," he said, "and it can't even communicate back to us the why, effectively." That's the black box problem of AI in a war zone. And for Singer, the challenge isn't stopping the tech—it's making sure we don't lose control of it before we understand what it's really doing.

The US Department of Defense, through DARPA, allocated $4.119 billion for technology research in 2024. A significant portion of this funding supports the development of autonomous systems, from unmanned drones to more sophisticated platforms. These investments reflect a broader shift in military technology toward systems that can operate with increasing independence from human control.

The United States isn't alone in this autonomous arms race. China's Academy of Military Sciences has been testing swarm boats in the South China Sea—dozens of small, autonomous vessels that can surround and overwhelm larger ships. Russia claims its Poseidon nuclear torpedo can operate autonomously for months, guided by AI that's "impossible to trick." Even smaller players are getting in the game.

Paul Scharre, who helped write the Pentagon's first policies on autonomous weapons, offers a sobering perspective from his time in Afghanistan. "I was on a mountaintop in Afghanistan with two other soldiers when a young girl, maybe 10 years old, came walking up the trail toward us. She was carrying a bag. We had to decide: Was she a threat? Was she a suicide bomber? Or just a girl with groceries? We let her pass. She was just a girl with groceries. But if an autonomous robot had been there instead of us, would it have made the same call?" he asked *The Wall Street Journal*. "How would you design a robot to know the difference between what is legal and what is right? And how would you even begin to write down those rules ahead of time?"

But Squad X isn't infallible. In field tests, DARPA's AI-driven system—designed to give Marines a battlefield edge—has shown both promise and peril. "It's about giving dismounted troops real-time situational awareness," said Lt. Col. Jeffrey Kawada, a program manager for the project. But the system's interpretation of battlefield data can be unpredictable. As *The Verge* reported, DARPA's integration of autonomous drones and ground robots occasionally misreads its environment, raising concerns about reliability in live combat. While the system excels at parsing vast data streams, it "doesn't always understand the context," acknowledged one engineer involved in development. That disconnect between machine perception and human judgment is what makes Squad X both powerful—and potentially dangerous.

Peter Asaro, cofounder of the International Committee for Robot

Arms Control, argues that autonomous weapons cross a fundamental moral boundary. "We're not just talking about more efficient weapons," he said in a 2018 interview with the Future of Life Institute. "We're talking about delegating the decision to take human life to machines." He compared the use of such systems to banned weapons, stating that they represent "a form of warfare that violates human dignity and should be prohibited under international law."

What we can't know, from outside DARPA, is the timeline of when lethal autonomous weapons (LAWs) will be deployed, and how the dramatic acceleration of large language models (LLMs) will put armed robots under the control of AI. Stuart Russell paints a particularly chilling picture: "Imagine swarms of small drones, each carrying three grams of explosive," said Russel in the Future of Life Institute's *Slaughterbots* video. "That's enough to kill any human by targeting the head. A million such drones can be carried in a single truck. Released over a city, they could kill half its population in under an hour. And unlike nuclear weapons, they would leave buildings standing and be relatively cheap to manufacture."

"Is it immoral not to rely on certain robots to execute on their own . . . given that a smart weapon can potentially limit collateral damage?" Tony Cerri, of the US Army Training and Doctrine Command, told the Medill News Service. But Asaro challenges this technological optimism: "The ability to process data quickly doesn't equate to moral judgment. We're talking about machines that can't understand the concept of human dignity, making decisions about who lives and dies."

The challenge of autonomous weapons extends beyond mere targeting decisions, raising profound questions about trust and accountability in AI systems. Alan Fern, an AI researcher leading DARPA-funded projects at Oregon State University, provides a rare insider's perspective that underscores both the potential and the risks of such technologies. "When errors can have serious consequences, like for piloting aircraft or medical diagnoses, you don't want to blindly trust an AI's decisions," Fern explains.

"You want an explanation; you want to know that the system is doing the right things for the right reasons." This "black box" problem—where neural networks make choices based on vast datasets in ways even developers struggle to comprehend—highlights the difficulty of relying on AI for life-and-death decisions in military contexts.

"In our DARPA work, we've seen AI systems develop novel solutions that surprised us," he continues. "Sometimes these surprises are brilliant. Sometimes they're terrifying. The scary part is, we can't always tell the difference until after the fact."

Paul Scharre elaborates on this "black box" problem with a chilling example: "During testing of an AI targeting system, researchers discovered the AI had learned to identify enemy vehicles by looking for shadows in satellite photos. It worked perfectly in testing—until they realized all the 'enemy' training photos had been taken in the morning, while 'friendly' vehicle photos were taken in the afternoon. The AI had learned the wrong lesson entirely, and nobody knew until they specifically investigated why it was making its decisions."

In war-game simulations, researchers found something unnerving involving AI systems. When we put AI in charge of simulated military assets, it developed strategies that human commanders initially thought were mistakes. But they weren't mistakes—they were tactics that exploited aspects of the battlefield that humans hadn't even considered. In one simulation, an AI sacrificed valuable assets early to achieve a devastating advantage later, something no human commander would have contemplated.

These concerns echo and amplify RAND Corporation's warnings about Truth decay from the early 2020s. But what RAND researchers couldn't fully anticipate was how autonomous weapons would accelerate this decay. As General Angus Campbell, chief of the Australian Defence Force, warned in late 2024, "As generative AI systems mature, there may come a time when it is impossible for the average person to distinguish fact from fiction." This technological future, he cautioned, "may accelerate truth decay, greatly challenging the quality of what we call public common sense, seriously damaging public confidence in elected officials and undermining the trust that binds us." The merger of autonomous weapons with AI-powered disinformation capabilities creates a particularly dangerous feedback loop: machines that cannot only make lethal decisions but also control and manipulate the narrative about why those decisions were made.

This brings us back to the fundamental question of Truth on the modern battlefield. Those World War II bats might have gotten confused or lost, but they were responding to real sensory inputs—actual sights, sounds, and smells. Today's autonomous weapons operate in a digital reality that can be distorted, manipulated, or completely fabricated.

The manipulation possibilities extend beyond visual deception. Researchers have demonstrated how false signals, such as spoofed GPS coordinates or engineered heat patterns, can mislead AI systems into misidentifying targets. This raises concerns about the reliability of autonomous systems in dynamic and deceptive battlefields. "Careless investment in advanced computing in an effort to get some sort of decisive battlefield decision-making advantage actually has some serious risks," wrote Chris Smith, deputy chief of army, in the *Australian Army Journal*. "Commanders might be reluctant to make battlefield choices that are not consistent with computer-generated options and recommendations."

This malleability of Truth forces military planners to rethink the fundamental principles of warfare. In traditional battles, deception was about hiding forces or confusing the enemy. In the age of autonomous weapons, deception evolves into manipulating the very reality these systems perceive. A well-crafted false signal could redirect an entire swarm or render a critical target invisible.

The implications go beyond battlefield tactics. As AI increasingly shapes military and geopolitical strategies, the question arises: Who controls the narratives that guide these systems? Are nations and organizations prepared for an era where wars might be fought and decided by machines, untethered from human judgment and ethical constraints?

"The fundamental problem," Asaro emphasizes, "is that we're creating systems that will make life-and-death decisions based on criteria we can't fully specify. What exactly is a 'military target'? What constitutes a 'legitimate threat'? These are complex moral and legal questions that human soldiers struggle with. We're now delegating these decisions to machines that don't understand the concepts of life, death, or human dignity."

The development of autonomous weapons systems represents more than just a military innovation—it marks a potential turning point in human history. For the first time, we face the prospect of creating machines that can independently decide to take human life, guided by algorithms and artificial intelligence rather than human judgment and moral reasoning. This technological capability forces us to confront fundamental questions about the role of human decision-making in warfare and the ethical boundaries we wish to establish for autonomous systems.

As one DARPA researcher put it during a recent defense conference: "We are no longer just designing weapons. We are designing realities. And the scariest part is, we might not be the ones deciding what is real."

As Russell concludes: "We're not just deciding the future of warfare. We're deciding whether humanity will retain meaningful control over the most powerful weapons we've ever created. The decisions we make now will determine whether we maintain our role as the primary agents of our destiny, or cede that power to machines that cannot truly understand the weight of their actions."

The marriage of autonomous weapons and information warfare represents more than just a military innovation—it marks a potential turning point in humanity's relationship with Truth itself. When machines cannot only make lethal decisions but also control the narratives about those decisions, we face what scholars call "epistemic confusion"—a state where reality becomes increasingly difficult to distinguish from machine-generated fiction. The stakes aren't just military victory or defeat, but our collective ability to discern Truth in the age of autonomous systems.

The future of warfare, and perhaps society itself, is being reshaped by the rapid rise of autonomous systems. These technologies promise precision, efficiency, and strategic advantages but at profound ethical and existential costs. As the line between physical and informational warfare blurs, we must confront a chilling possibility: machines making independent decisions about life, death, and the narratives surrounding those events.

The challenge ahead isn't just technical—it's moral, legal, and deeply human. It demands global cooperation to establish guardrails, robust systems of accountability, and a collective commitment to ensuring that technology serves humanity, not the other way around. Whether we succeed in this endeavor may well determine the future of Truth, justice, and peace in the digital age.

Lies on the battlefield spill over into our everyday lives, seeping into the news, our screens, and our minds. But how do we fight back against a flood of falsehoods? Stay tuned: The infodemic is next.

## CHAPTER 10

# The Misinformation Infodemic

When Melissa Fleming speaks about disinformation, people listen. And they should. As the United Nations' Under-Secretary-General for Global Communications, she's witnessed how lies can tear societies apart. "We can't bring about stability in fragile environments if populations are turning against our peacekeepers as a result of lies being spread against them online," she told the crowd at Columbia University in 2024. Her comparison to Rwanda's radio stations—the outlets that helped incite genocide—sent a chill through the room. Today's disinformation campaigns are "coming from completely different countries, are free, and are tools that can be deployed in a way that doesn't leave any fingerprints."

The irony wasn't lost on me. Outside on the streets of American cities, giant billboards proclaimed "Birds Aren't Real"—part of a satirical conspiracy theory that had gone viral. But what started as a joke about government surveillance drones masquerading as birds had become something else entirely: a mirror reflecting our broken relationship with Truth.

Consider this: While we're chuckling about fake birds, Taylor Owen from McGill University is documenting how "the news being talked about in political groups is being replaced by memes," as Owen explained in his research on digital media ecosystems. The reliable signals of Truth that once populated our social feeds? "That's gone," he warns.

The "Birds Aren't Real" movement, founded in 2017 by Peter Monday during a women's march in Memphis, has attracted hundreds of thousands of followers on platforms like Instagram and TikTok. Recently, passionate supporters gathered outside Twitter's headquarters, demanding the company abandon its bird logo. What started as whimsy has morphed into a cultural phenomenon that reflects our desperate need to process the chaotic waters of misinformation we face daily. As Claire Chronis, a 22-year-old organizer, puts it, "It's a way to combat troubles in the world that you don't really have other ways of combating."

Fleming's warnings about AI hit particularly hard. "In the AI information age, it's going to become nearly impossible to distinguish between real and fake content," she told us. And she's right. While we're busy debating whether birds are surveillance drones, deepfake technology is advancing at a frightening pace.

As people have become more connected online, the line between parody and real misinformation has become increasingly blurred. Take the Flat Earth theory—a concept we thought was settled centuries ago. Yet here it is, making a surprising comeback through social media platforms and video sites that have turned this fringe belief into a visible movement. These online spaces act as echo chambers, where like-minded individuals gather and reinforce each other's doubts, giving the theory a legitimacy it wouldn't have otherwise.

From the front row at Columbia's panel on misinformation, I watched Louis Dreyfus, CEO of Group Le Monde, underscore this crisis of Truth: "We've reached a level of distrust that is exceptional. Every institution, political institution, and journalism are contested by a major part of the population. At the same time, with social networks, it is easier to spread fake news."

Consider the "Finland Doesn't Exist" theory, allegedly created as a humorous critique of conspiracy culture. According to this theory, Finland is a fabricated country, invented by Japan and the Soviet Union to maintain exclusive fishing rights in the Baltic Sea. Though absurd, this "theory" gained traction in online communities, with some people ironically embracing it while others became genuinely intrigued. The popularity of this outlandish idea highlights the Internet's ability to turn even the most ridiculous concepts into widely shared narratives.

The Avril Lavigne conspiracy takes a more personal approach to misinformation, focusing on the idea that the singer was replaced by a lookalike named Melissa after her supposed death in 2003. This theory, fueled by alleged changes in Avril's appearance and music style, has been dissected in online fan communities and social media, where devoted followers analyze "evidence" to support the claim. What started as a rumor evolved into a sprawling conspiracy theory that has sustained itself for years, attracting new believers who find comfort in "uncovering" a celebrity mystery.

The "Fake Melania" theory also perfectly captures this phenomenon. Since 2017, social media has periodically erupted with claims that First Lady Melania Trump was replaced by a body double at public events. The theory gained particular traction after her five-week absence following kidney surgery in 2018, and even persisted through the 2024 election. Despite denials from Trump himself, people kept analyzing slight variations in Melania's appearance and Donald Trump's occasionally awkward ways of referring to her.

Finally, there's the Lizard People conspiracy, which posits that reptilian humanoids secretly control world governments. Popularized by conspiracy theorist David Icke, this theory alleges that shape-shifting reptilians manipulate global events and people of power to maintain control over humanity. Despite its sci-fi premise, the theory has built a large following online, with supporters analyzing public figures for supposed reptilian traits and behaviors. This blend of fantasy and conspiracy illustrates how Internet platforms enable fringe ideas to find an audience, feeding a culture that prizes "hidden truths" over established facts.

"What feels scarier today," Anya Schiffrin told us at the Columbia panel, "is the anger and the outrage and the fear of violence . . . I sort of think we're in a post-truth world already. For a lot of people, maybe it doesn't really matter whether something is true. It just sort of confirms what they think or gets them angry or excited."

Yet this comedic take on misinformation contrasts sharply with more dangerous manifestations, especially in the realms of health and science. Consider the moment someone you love is diagnosed with cancer. Overwhelmed and scared, you might turn to the Internet for information, hoping to find solace in a sea of medical jargon. But amid genuine medical advice, you could stumble upon misleading content promoting unproven treatments, often packaged with testimonials of miraculous recoveries.

Wen-Ying Sylvia Chou, who holds a PhD in linguistics and is a behavioral scientist at the National Cancer Institute (NCI), emphasizes that misinformation about health has existed for centuries, but the Internet has made it far more pervasive. A recent study revealed that one in three of the most popular articles shared on social media regarding common cancers contained false information.

Dr. Skyler Johnson from the Huntsman Cancer Institute warned that much of this misinformation is not just inaccurate but potentially harmful, leading patients to reject effective treatments in favor of dubious alternatives.

The consequences of this misinformation can be devastating. A study led by Dr. Johnson found that patients who opted for alternative or complementary treatments instead of conventional care had a greater risk of dying. While this study did not specifically analyze the role of social media, it highlights the profound impact misinformation can have on patient decisions and outcomes.

This is exactly what Fleming warned about at Columbia: how social networks amplify misinformation beyond anything we've seen before. She explained how modern disinformation campaigns operate without leaving fingerprints, making them far more dangerous than traditional propaganda.

The role of health influencers on social media compounds the problem. Rachel Moran, a senior research scientist at the University of Washington, conducted a study that uncovered how influencers can spread anti-vaccine misinformation while profiting from selling dubious products, such as essential oils or unproven supplements. These influencers often create content that appeals to followers' interests, intertwining lifestyle and health messages.

In her research, Moran points out the role of "parasocial trust," where followers develop a one-sided relationship with influencers, making them more likely to believe in their recommendations. This phenomenon can be particularly dangerous when influencers promote unverified medical advice, often leading to serious health consequences for their followers.

The depth of this issue shows up in the alarming data about how misinformation shaped health decisions during COVID-19. Moran's research documents how Instagram influencers with hundreds of thousands of followers monetized COVID-19 falsehoods. Nearly half of US adults use Instagram, and many encountered influencers who Moran groups as "Conspiratorial

Fashionista," "Wellness Homesteader," and "Evangelical Mother," each promoting unproven remedies such as essential oils as vaccine substitutes.

Their content strategy—roughly 70 percent daily-life posts, 15 percent health worries, 10 percent alternative solutions, and 5 percent monetized links—helped build parasocial relationships that made followers less likely to question false claims. That dynamic thrived in the regulatory gaps between the Food and Drug Administration's limited authority over wellness claims and inconsistent platform moderation.

Dr. Lidia Schapira, an oncologist at Stanford University, emphasizes the importance of open communication in combating misinformation. "Listening to people's concerns with empathy and respect is critical," she states. In her experience, when patients bring their online findings to their healthcare providers, it creates opportunities for dialogue. Schapira advocates for a partnership approach, where patients are encouraged to share their concerns and the information they've encountered, allowing healthcare professionals to guide them through the complexities of medical information.

"The way we can help patients is by fostering an environment where they feel comfortable discussing their online discoveries without fear of judgment," Schapira explains. "By doing so, we can work together to dispel myths and clarify what evidence-based information truly means."

In the chaotic information landscape, healthcare providers must be proactive. Dr. Schapira suggests that practitioners not only listen but also engage with patients about the sources of their information. "We need to help patients navigate the digital world by pointing them toward reliable resources and encouraging critical thinking," she says.

Yet, the burden of discerning credible information increasingly falls on individuals. "We need to combat misinformation in multiple ways, at multiple levels," Chou urges, highlighting the collaborative effort required to address this issue. Healthcare professionals, research organizations, government agencies, and social media companies all share responsibility in this fight.

This brings us back to Fleming's concerns about AI's role in this crisis. From her seat at the Columbia conference, she painted a chilling picture of our future: "In the AI information age, it's going to become nearly impossible to distinguish between real and fake content." As if to prove her point, across the street from campus, passers-by were probably scrolling through their phones, encountering AI-generated content without even knowing it.

As misinformation continues to spread, the financial incentives driving it are becoming increasingly clear. During high-profile political events, such as the Freedom Convoy protests in Canada, researchers and journalists have observed how fake social media accounts and coordinated networks exploit the chaos to drive traffic. These groups are often managed by entities in countries like Vietnam and Bangladesh. For instance, a group named Freedom Convoy Worldwide was administered from Bulgaria and used PayPal for fundraising. Such activities underscore how disinformation campaigns exploit social movements for financial gain.

Additionally, crowdfunding platforms played a significant role. After GoFundMe removed a fundraiser for violating terms of service, the campaign migrated to GiveSendGo, raising over $9 million. This platform, known for hosting controversial campaigns, experienced substantial growth by aligning with such movements.

These efforts often masquerade as grassroots movements but are fueled by clickbait economics. Similar patterns emerged during the 2016 US election, when Macedonian teenagers created dozens of fake news sites targeting American audiences—earning thousands of dollars through ad revenue. As *The New York Times* reported, misinformation has become a profitable enterprise, particularly for actors in lower-income regions who see viral disinformation as a business model. The rise of deepfake video and AI-generated content only compounds the challenge, blurring the line between political manipulation and digital profiteering.

As deepfake technology continues to advance, it further complicates the misinformation landscape. Hyper-realistic videos and audio, created using artificial intelligence, present new challenges in discerning Truth from fabrication. NYU Tandon School of Engineering researchers are developing real-time detection methods, utilizing challenge-response systems that can exploit the limitations of current deepfake generation techniques. Chinmay Hegde, an associate professor at NYU, emphasizes the importance of advancing detection methods as AI technology improves. "As deepfake technology becomes more accessible, the line between genuine and manipulated content continues to blur," Hegde cautioned at a recent AI ethics symposium, stressing the need for robust detection measures.

Fleming's perspective from her UN role adds another layer of urgency to these concerns. "We can't bring about stability in fragile environments if populations are turning against our peacekeepers as a result of lies being spread against them online," she emphasized in her Columbia talk, underscoring the need for civil society to work together to build healthier information ecosystems. The UN, she noted, cannot tackle these problems without collaboration. AI-powered video tools can fabricate scenes, events, and even public statements with such accuracy that they challenge the very notion of recorded Truth. The UN is calling on AI actors to prioritize safety in their systems, emphasizing that individuals should not be left to navigate a minefield of disinformation alone.

In light of the misinformation epidemic, it is crucial to foster a culture where critical thinking prevails, and information is met with scrutiny rather than blind acceptance. The lessons learned from movements like "Birds Aren't Real" serve as a call to action for us all. By embracing humor and satire, we can challenge the harmful narratives that seek to undermine our collective understanding of Truth.

Ultimately, the fight against misinformation is not just about protecting individual health decisions or maintaining political stability; it's about safeguarding the very fabric of our society. As Fleming reminded us at Columbia, in a world where trust in information is paramount, we must remain vigilant, questioning the narratives we encounter and holding those who spread misinformation accountable. The consequences of inaction could be profound as the stakes of misinformation grow ever higher in our interconnected reality.

As we delve deeper into the mechanisms of misinformation, it's essential to understand how it not only proliferates but also profits. The rise of social media has democratized access to health information, but it has also opened the floodgates for misinformation. As misinformation continues to thrive, it becomes imperative to equip individuals with the skills to evaluate the information they encounter. The urgency to enhance health literacy is evident, as misinformation poses a growing threat to public health.

In this context, misinformation not only impacts public health but also becomes a source of income for those willing to exploit it. The implications of this dual threat are staggering, as misinformation becomes a revenue-generating machine at the expense of public trust and individual well-being. As we look toward the future, we must strive to ensure that Truth prevails over deception, safeguarding the integrity of our information landscape.

The insights from Dr. Schapira and others illuminate the urgent need for a societal shift. In an era where misinformation can spread like wildfire, cultivating critical thinking skills and fostering a culture of skepticism toward sensational claims may empower individuals to reclaim their ability to discern Truth from falsehood. By sharing resources and engaging in open dialogues, we can begin to mitigate the damage caused by misinformation and rebuild trust in our institutions.

Together, conspiracy theories, misinformation, satire, and actual fraud reveal how the Internet is reshaping our relationship with Truth, allowing misinformation—whether absurd or sinister—to blur the line between reality and fiction. The once-clear boundary between fact and satire is eroding, creating a culture where even the most outlandish claims can find an audience. As these ideas spread, Truth itself becomes destabilized, replaced by narratives that appeal to skepticism, distrust, or simple curiosity. With each new theory, the sense of a shared reality weakens, and the ability to discern Truth from fiction is diminished. This shift underscores an urgent need for media literacy and critical thinking in an era where misinformation can quickly undermine our collective understanding of the Truth, influencing beliefs, behaviors, and even public policy.

Misinformation spreads like a virus, infecting our perception of Truth. But as AI steps into healthcare, can we trust machines to diagnose more than just falsehoods? Let's explore the rise of the digital doctor and its implications for Truth.

## CHAPTER 11

# Can a Digital Doctor Tell the Truth? Should They?

Most people don't expect routine medical check-ups to be particularly exciting, or even memorable. But for Meredith Broussard, a respected tech author and NYU research director, a simple mammogram turned into a life-altering encounter with artificial intelligence. It was 2019, and Broussard had gone in for her annual scan—an exam she'd undergone several times before. This time, though, was different. Her mammogram showed something unusual—a small, nearly invisible mass flagged by an AI system trained to detect early signs of breast cancer.

The radiologist took a second look, and with the AI's silent nudge, a subtle threat became a concrete reality. After a biopsy, it was found to be cancerous. Without the AI's keen "eye," there's a chance that mass might have gone unnoticed for another year or two. The human saw it, but the robot confirmed it, and that synergy between human and machine quite possibly saved her life.

For Broussard, the twist here is almost poetic. As someone who has dedicated her career to studying the flaws and limitations of technology, Broussard is no stranger to the ways tech can go wrong. In her book *Artificial Unintelligence: How Computers Misunderstand the World*, she coined the term "techno chauvinism"—the belief that technology is always the superior solution. Technochauvinists, as she calls them, believe that an algorithm can solve just about anything better than a human. In her own story, tech didn't just help; it was essential. Yet, it didn't change her conviction that tech-only solutions often miss the mark, especially in fields as critical as medicine.

"People will say things like, 'We should use an algorithm to decide who gets a kidney transplant because the algorithm will make an objective evaluation of who is most worthy of a donor organ,'" Broussard explains in her book *Artificial Unintelligence*. But she's quick to point out that the objectivity of algorithms is often a mirage. For years, kidney transplant algorithms systematically disadvantaged Black patients because they were built on racist assumptions embedded within the math itself. To Broussard, this is where techno chauvinism becomes dangerous—when we take algorithms' "objectivity" as gospel without questioning the flawed data and biases that often lurk beneath the surface.

In a world where tech giants and researchers alike are pushing AI as the silver bullet, Broussard's story is a powerful reminder that Truth, especially in something as human as healthcare, doesn't live in the black-and-white logic of code. Truth in this context means collaboration between humans and technology, an alliance where each side can check and challenge the other. That's the Truth Broussard found in a mammogram room in 2019—technology at its best, and human judgment remaining firmly in the driver's seat.

In the world of modern healthcare, artificial intelligence is becoming a big deal—and not always in a good way. While AI promises to make things faster and more efficient, especially in health insurance, it's also raising red flags. Instead of helping everyone equally, it sometimes puts profits over patients and muddles the Truth that medicine is supposed to be built on. And that's where things get messy.

Take insurance claim denials. These days, many health insurers use AI to speed up the process of approving or denying claims. Sounds great, right? But here's the catch: Some AI systems seem designed to deny legitimate claims just to save money. A report from the Healthcare Financial Management Association even pointed out that these algorithms are looking for ways to reject claims, regardless of whether or not they're valid. "The goal isn't better care; it's cost savings," a healthcare administrator acknowledged in the HFMA's 2023 survey on AI in healthcare claims processing. That's pretty scary when you think about how these denials can leave patients stranded, scrambling to appeal while their health hangs in the balance.

What makes this worse is that these AI systems are like black boxes. You can't see inside them to understand how decisions are made. If a human denies your claim, you can ask them why. But when it's an algorithm? Good luck. Insurers have little motivation to explain how these systems work—especially if they're flawed or biased. A 2023 article in JAMA Health Forum called this a "truth gap," where the reasons behind decisions are hidden, leaving patients powerless to fight back. As one expert said, "When an algorithm denies coverage, it's not just a denial of care; it's a denial of accountability."

The situation gets even murkier when you think about how AI relies on data. Insurers have access to a goldmine of patient information—medical records, genetic profiles, and more. This data could be used for good, like improving patient care, but instead, it's often weaponized for profit. A study by the Society of Actuaries warned about insurers using AI to identify so-called loss-generating patients—basically, people whose medical needs are expensive. These patients might end up with higher premiums, less coverage, or even dropped policies. "If AI models are used to identify high-cost or high-risk claimants, there's a risk that insurers may take actions—such as pricing or coverage decisions—that disproportionately affect these individuals. Even if unintended, the result could be systemic bias in outcomes," wrote the unsigned report.

While the data tells a story, it's a story insurers can choose to read selectively, and selective storytelling is a real problem. It distorts the Truth about what patients actually need. Truth should be the backbone of medicine, but here it's being twisted into something convenient for the bottom line. And when patients lose faith in their insurers, the entire healthcare system suffers. Once trust is broken, it's incredibly hard to rebuild.

One glaring example of the erosion of Truth comes from biased AI risk assessments. These algorithms are used to predict who needs medical care, but their predictions are only as good as the data they're built on—and that data often reflects deep structural inequalities. A 2019 study in *Science* found that a widely used algorithm systematically underestimated the health needs of Black patients compared to white patients with similar conditions. The algorithm used healthcare spending as a proxy for medical need, but because Black patients have historically had less access to care, the spending data was skewed.

"If you had to boil it down to one thing," said lead researcher Ziad Obermeyer, "the problem is that the algorithm is predicting health care costs rather than illness."

And even when AI isn't explicitly biased, it's still being used to prioritize profits over people. For instance, some insurers use AI to flag "low-value" treatments—things they claim aren't necessary. On paper, that might sound like a good way to cut waste. But in reality, many of these flagged treatments are recommended by doctors for specific reasons that an algorithm just can't understand. A report from *The Wall Street Journal Asia* shared the frustrations of doctors and patients dealing with these denials. "The algorithm doesn't know my patient," one doctor said. "It's making decisions based on averages, not individuals."

This tension between averages and individuals is where AI really falls short. Algorithms are amazing at finding patterns in big datasets, but they struggle with the unique, messy details of individual lives. And in healthcare, those details matter. For a patient, a denied claim isn't just a bureaucratic headache—it can be the difference between recovery and relapse, or worse.

But insurance isn't the only place where AI is changing the game. It's also sneaking into the relationship between doctors and patients. Take MyChart, a platform used by hospitals across the United States. Patients trust it as a direct line to their doctors, where they can share symptoms, ask questions, and get advice. But here's the twist: those messages patients receive? Increasingly, they're not written entirely by doctors. By 2023, more than 15,000 doctors were using MyChart's AI-powered tool, called In Basket Art, to draft responses to patient messages. This tool uses GPT-4 technology to craft replies based on patient records and prior messages. Doctors review and edit the drafts before sending them out.

The tool was marketed as a way to help overworked doctors avoid burnout. And sure, that's important. But there's a catch: Most patients have no idea AI is involved. Some hospitals, like UC San Diego Health, include a note saying the message was generated with AI assistance. But others, like Stanford Health Care and NYU Langone Health, decided not to disclose this. They worried it might "cheapen" the advice or make patients trust their doctors less.

When *The New York Times* reported about AI drafting doctors' notes, that lack of transparency didn't sit well with everyone. "When you read a doctor's note, you read it in the voice of your doctor," said Athmeya Jayaram from The Hastings Center. "If a patient were to know that, in fact, the message they're exchanging with their doctor is generated by AI, I think they would feel rightly betrayed." And it's not just about feelings. Patients expect the Truth in their medical care. They deserve to know when a relatively new technology is involved, especially when their health is on the line.

And here's the proof. As I was drafting this chapter, I coincidentally went to have my annual physical. No big news; my doc adjusted a cholesterol medication, I had a blood test, and I was on my way. Hours later, results arrived, attached with a note: "These results haven't been reviewed by your doctor." Hmm . . . okay? Then, a "patient after-visit report" appeared in my doctor's office portal, MyChart. Immediately, the notes from my "doctor" felt weird, referring to tests and conditions I didn't have. Was it a mistake my doctor made or an AI hallucination? It was signed by my doctor, but these were clearly not his words. As a patient, I didn't want to accuse him of a mistake that I'm sure he didn't make, but I also didn't want my medical records to contain errors. It remains an uncomfortable position for both of us. And it makes me wonder: *Were our conversations being listened to and captured in the exam room, and then misinterpreted?* I plan on asking him the next time I see him, but it wasn't a conversation I wanted to have over chat. Is patient confidentiality at risk in the world of medical AI? I'd say yes.

Now, let's talk about mental health. AI isn't just showing up in insurance claims and patient communication—it's actually becoming the fastest-growing and potentially most dangerous frontier in healthcare tech. With venture capital pouring billions into AI mental health start-ups, we're seeing a gold rush to automate one of the most intimate and sensitive forms of human care.

The pitch sounds perfect: AI-powered chatbots providing instant, 24/7 therapy to anyone with a smartphone. Companies like Woebot Health promise "always-on emotional support" and "personalized mental healthcare at scale." On the surface, it seems like a solution to our mental health crisis, especially with therapy waiting lists growing longer and costs putting human counselors out of reach for many. But Dr. John Torous, who runs the digital psychiatry division at Beth Israel Deaconess Medical Center, sees serious dangers in this rush to automate mental healthcare. "We've seen apps make people worse," said Torous. "We need a much stronger framework for how these tools are tested before they are widely used." His research has documented cases where chatbots completely missed signs of crisis, responding with preprogrammed messages to expressions of self-harm.

Unlike human therapists, AI chatbots don't have the ability to deeply empathize or understand the nuances of human emotion. Hannah Zeavin, author of *The Distance Cure*, calls it "empathy theater"—where AI creates the illusion of understanding without any actual comprehension. "When someone shares their trauma," she says, "they deserve more than an algorithm spitting back patterns it found in data." While these tools can offer responses based on patterns, they can't truly engage with the complexities of mental health issues. Even worse, they can sometimes give advice that's not just unhelpful but dangerous.

There's also the issue of privacy. Most people pouring their hearts out to these AI therapists have no idea their most intimate disclosures are being stored, analyzed, and potentially used to train future versions of the software. The data practices of these companies often remain opaque, buried in privacy policies nobody reads. When someone opens up about their most vulnerable moments, they deserve to know exactly what happens to that information.

The mental health tech boom also raises serious questions about accountability. When a human therapist makes a mistake, there are clear lines of responsibility and professional standards in place. But what happens when an AI chatbot gives harmful advice? Who's responsible when an algorithm fails to recognize a mental health crisis? These aren't theoretical concerns—they're questions that need urgent answers as these tools become more widespread.

AI-driven mental health tools might help fill gaps in access to care, especially in underserved areas. But they're not a replacement for real human connection. Mental health is deeply personal, and it requires trust—trust that's hard to build with a chatbot. As these tools become more common, we need to ask tough questions about their role in therapy. Are they truly helping, or are they just a shortcut that could do more harm than good?

AI has the potential to transform medicine, but only if we're honest about how it's really being designed and deployed. Right now, we're replacing medical

Truth with corporate convenience—calling it progress when algorithms deny care, automation when AI drafts doctor's notes, and therapy when chatbots mimic empathy. Each step moves us further from the fundamental Truth that healthcare should serve patients first.

The solution starts with basic honesty. Healthcare institutions need to tell the Truth about how their AI systems are programmed, what outcomes they're designed to achieve, and who they're really built to serve. Without this foundation of Truth, the growing use of AI in medicine isn't just a technical problem—it's corrupting the very trust that healthcare depends on.

Medicine might feel like a safe place for Truth, but algorithms are spreading their influence far beyond hospitals. From courts to corporations, machines are becoming the new judges of what's real. Can they handle the pressure? Let's dig deeper into algorithmic truth-telling in the pages ahead.

CHAPTER 12

# When Machines Judge "US": The Rise of Algorithmic Truth Assessment

Kimberly Enyart had been teaching for over a decade when she applied for a new position in 2023. The interview process seemed standard until she learned an AI system would analyze her facial expressions and voice patterns to determine her truthfulness. Despite her qualifications and experience, HireVue's emotion detection AI flagged her responses as "potentially deceptive." She wasn't hired. Only later, through legal proceedings, did she discover that the system had consistently rated Black candidates as less truthful than white candidates, exhibiting the same biases that have plagued facial recognition technology.

This wasn't an isolated incident. The same month Enyart was fighting her case, in Silicon Valley, software engineer Wei Chen faced a similar battle. Google's AI hiring system had flagged his interview responses as showing "signs of potential dishonesty" based on his "atypical eye movement patterns"—patterns that research would later show were common among neurodivergent individuals. Chen's case became part of a larger EU investigation into discriminatory AI hiring practices that eventually documented over 300 similar incidents.

"We're witnessing a fundamental shift in how society evaluates human truthfulness," explains Kate Crawford, author of *Atlas of AI* and researcher at USC's AI Now Institute. "These systems aren't just measuring behavior;

they're making moral judgments about human character, often based on flawed assumptions about what truthfulness looks like."

The stakes extend far beyond employment. In 2021, Dartmouth's Geisel School of Medicine accused 17 students of cheating on remote exams based on data from the Canvas learning management system. Administrators alleged that students had accessed online course materials during closed-book tests—claims based solely on automated log data. But technology experts and civil liberties advocates pointed out that those logs could be triggered by routine device syncing or background activity. After months of scrutiny and protest, Dartmouth dropped the charges, acknowledging flaws in the investigation. Still, the students' reputations had already been harmed.

The case wasn't unique. In 2021, the University of Illinois Urbana-Champaign announced it would phase out the use of Proctorio, a remote exam surveillance tool, after student backlash over privacy and discrimination concerns. As reported by *The Verge*, over 1,000 people signed a petition calling on the university to stop using the service. "Proctorio is not only inefficient, it is also unsafe and a complete violation of a student's privacy," the petition read. Students criticized Proctorio's AI-driven monitoring for relying on facial detection that didn't consistently work across skin tones and for placing undue stress on those without quiet testing environments. One organizer of the petition said the software "punishes students for their socioeconomic status, for their race, for their disability." The university responded by stating that Proctorio "was never considered to be a long-term campus proctoring solution."

Artificial intelligence systems used in fraud detection have demonstrated measurable biases against individuals with disabilities. A 2023 study presented at the Workshop on Trustworthy Natural Language Processing found that common sentiment and toxicity models—VADER, TextBlob, Google Cloud Natural Language API, and DistilBERT—consistently rated statements about disabled people as more negative than equivalent statements about non-disabled people. The researchers concluded that these models encode explicit disability bias, raising serious concerns about their deployment in real-world systems.

These concerns are not hypothetical. Michigan's MiDAS system, deployed between 2013 and 2015 to detect unemployment insurance fraud, falsely accused more than 40,000 people—with no human review. Many victims were people with disabilities who were forced to repay benefits, incur penalties, or endure garnished wages.

In Arkansas, a similar automated decision-making system used to determine Medicaid eligibility and care hours led to sharp reductions in services for disabled residents—again, without clear explanation or recourse. After a successful legal challenge, the courts found the system violated basic due process protections.

Even routine retail transactions now face algorithmic scrutiny. At Best Buy, customers were flagged not by human judgment but by a system built by a company called The Retail Equation—software designed to detect "return abuse" by scanning for patterns it considered suspicious. One customer, Jake Zakhar, was banned from returning items for a full year after bringing back just three phone cases. "I'm being made to feel like I committed a crime," he told *The Wall Street Journal*. The algorithm didn't account for intent, context, or scale—it just tallied up the transactions and issued a verdict. No human being ever asked why he was returning the items, or whether the returns were reasonable. That wasn't the point. The system's job wasn't truth—it was control.

Behind these individual stories lies a deeper issue: AI-driven emotion detection systems are scientifically unreliable and often discriminatory. A 2023 analysis from UC Berkeley's School of Information found that these systems performed only marginally better than random chance at identifying emotional states, raising serious concerns about their validity in high-stakes contexts like fraud detection or hiring. Even more troubling, researchers note that these tools regularly reflect and reinforce societal biases—misjudging people based on race, gender, or accent. As Safiya Umoja Noble, author of *Algorithms of Oppression*, explains, "These systems encode historical biases about who looks or sounds trustworthy into automated systems, giving those biases the veneer of technological objectivity."

Christine Moser, who earned a PhD in applied economics and whose research explores how AI reshapes human judgment, argues that we are "increasingly, unsuspectingly yet willingly, abdicating our power to make decisions based on our own judgment." The consequences of this shift are profound.

When machines judge human truthfulness, they don't just make individual assessments—they reshape our very understanding of Truth and trust.

In early 2024, Woolworths, one of Australia's largest retailers, introduced a new AI-driven performance management system known as "the Framework." This system aimed to optimize warehouse operations by assigning time limits to tasks and monitoring workers' efficiency through wearable headsets. However, it quickly became a source of contention among employees.

Workers reported feeling dehumanized by the system, which they claimed prioritized speed over safety and failed to account for individual circumstances. One warehouse employee expressed frustration, stating, "They want it to be a robotic style warehouse . . . We are human. We are social animals. They can't expect us to keep quiet and keep on working all day long."

The United Workers Union (UWU) criticized the Framework for enforcing unrealistic productivity targets. UWU National Secretary Tim Kennedy commented, "This has been a very hard struggle to get to this point, with workers forgoing pay on strike for 17 days to stand united against a punitive performance management system Woolworths called the Framework."

After a 17-day strike involving over 1,500 workers, Woolworths agreed to revise the Framework. The new agreement included clauses ensuring that employees would not be disciplined solely based on their work speed, acknowledging that not every worker could meet the 100% efficiency rate previously mandated.

This episode at Woolworths underscores the challenges of implementing AI-driven performance systems without adequate consideration for the human element. It serves as a reminder that while technology can enhance efficiency, it must be balanced with empathy and respect for the workforce.

The economic pressures driving this trend are stark. Elena Chen who holds a PhD in economics and specializes in technological labor markets, explains: "In 2020, a typical corporate job posting would receive 250 applications. By 2023, that number had exploded to over 1,000. No human resources department can meaningfully review that volume of information."

The solution? Algorithmic sorting. Machine learning systems that promise to cut through the noise, to find the "perfect" candidate, the "most productive" employee, the "most truthful" customer. But these systems often fail to account for human complexity, cultural differences, and medical conditions that don't fit their narrow parameters of "normal" behavior.

Luke Stark, coauthor of the landmark paper "Physiognomic Artificial Intelligence," notes how these systems "resurrect long-debunked ideas about determining character from appearance or behavior, but dress them up in the language of modern technology."

The global implications are profound. While China's social credit system represents perhaps the most comprehensive attempt to algorithmically score human trustworthiness, similar systems are emerging in democratic societies, albeit in more fragmented forms. In Miami-Dade County, housing authorities began using AI behavioral analysis to screen public housing applicants in 2024. The system claimed to detect "truthfulness in financial disclosures" by analyzing everything from voice patterns during interviews to social media activity.

Civil rights attorney Maria Delgado documented dozens of cases where legitimate applicants were rejected based on what she calls "digital palm reading—pseudoscience dressed up as artificial intelligence." One client, a single mother with a steady job and perfect payment history, was denied housing because the system flagged her "nonstandard speech patterns" as potential indicators of deception. Those patterns, it turned out, were simply the result of her bilingual background.

AI-powered workplace monitoring systems are increasingly marketed as tools to detect deception or optimize employee behavior, but emerging research raises red flags. A 2023 study from the AI Now Institute warns that algorithmic management tools often interpret hesitation, silence, or indirect communication as signs of disengagement or dishonesty—metrics that disproportionately penalize workers based on race, gender, or cultural background. Similar concerns were raised by the UC Berkeley Labor Center, which found that AI surveillance systems used in hiring and performance tracking frequently misread nuanced human behavior, embedding bias into decisions about trust and productivity.

The core issue isn't technological capability, but a fundamental misunderstanding of human complexity. Algorithmic systems operate through what researchers call "reckoning"—a process of processing data through computation and rule-driven rationality. Human judgment, in contrast, draws on imagination, reflection, empathy, and nuanced understanding of social context.

"In the absence of vigilance and doubt," Moser warns, "we might miss the moment when our decision-making frame has transitioned from judgment to reckoning. This would mean that we would hand over our power to make moral decisions to the machine's reckoning."

The pushback against algorithmic judgment is growing. Joy Buolamwini's Algorithmic Justice League has documented systematic bias in facial analysis systems. Their research helped convince several major companies to suspend or modify their use of emotion detection AI. Similarly, student protests have led some universities to abandon AI proctoring systems.

Yet the trend toward algorithmic assessment of human truthfulness continues to accelerate. Frank Pasquale, author of *The Black Box Society*, warns that we're creating a world where machines increasingly determine who can be trusted, often using criteria that are neither transparent nor scientifically valid.

The critical threshold isn't about completely eliminating AI from human judgment—it's about maintaining human agency. AI can be a powerful support tool: highlighting potential patterns, suggesting additional lines of inquiry, providing context. But the moment AI moves from supporting human decision-making to replacing it entirely, we cross a dangerous line.

Think of it like a medical diagnosis. An AI can surface relevant research, highlight potential correlations, even suggest diagnostic paths. But the final interpretation—understanding the human being behind the data—must remain uniquely human. The same is true for assessing truthfulness, character, potential.

Is Truth defined by automation, or is it a human decision? Machines processing data points or humans navigating the rich, messy landscape of lived experience? Our challenge isn't just technological—it's deeply human: how to preserve the beautiful complexity of human Truth in an age of algorithmic reduction.

The summer of 2020 provided a stark preview of what was to come. As Timandra Harkness reported in UnHerd, British teenagers took to the streets with an unexpected rallying cry: "Fuck the Algorithm!" They were protesting an AI system that had been tasked with determining their A-level grades after COVID-19 canceled their exams. The system, developed by the Office of Qualifications and Examinations Regulation (Ofqual), was supposed to be an oracle of sorts—objective, fair, and well fed on historical data from every student in the country.

Instead, it became a textbook case of algorithmic prejudice. Around 40% of the grades fell below teacher predictions, with the system effectively penalizing students based on their school's historical performance rather than their individual merit. As Harkness noted, "Any one individual's achievements so far, or their potential in the view of teachers who know them, had less influence on their eventual results than the attainments of others who attended the same school in past years."

The Royal Statistical Society's criticism was scathing: "Any statistical algorithm embeds a range of judgments and choices; it is not simply a technically obvious and neutral procedure," the Society stated in its analysis of Ofqual's grading algorithm.

The Society had offered to nominate distinguished experts to Ofqual's technical advisory group, but withdrew when asked to sign a nondisclosure agreement that would bar them from public comment on the model for five years.

Professor Guy Nason, chair in statistics at Imperial College, London, pointed out that the system ignored or underestimated uncertainty at many steps. Even its accuracy tests were fundamentally flawed, using data from the results they were trying to predict—"like showing you can predict the results of a horse race by including data about the order in which the horses crossed the finish line in that same race," as Harkness put it.

This episode revealed a fundamental Truth about algorithmic judgment systems: They are, at their core, prejudice engines. When an algorithm turns historical data into a predictive model, it operates on the assumption that the future will mirror the past. For students from disadvantaged backgrounds or underperforming schools, this meant being systematically marked down based not on their individual potential, but on the statistical shadow of those who came before them.

The parallels to today's AI truth assessment systems are striking. Whether judging exam integrity, job applications, or insurance claims, these systems perpetuate existing biases under the guise of objective assessment. As Harkness presciently noted, "Isn't it strange that we are repelled by prejudice in other contexts, but accept it when it's automated?"

The A-levels controversy sparked a broader awakening about algorithmic judgment. Students began questioning what other algorithms were excluding them from opportunities based on historical patterns: car insurance rates, job opportunities, loan offers, even dating app matches. Their protest highlighted a crucial Truth: Algorithms, and what we let them decide, are too important to be left to statisticians alone.

The surge in algorithmic Truth assessment systems reflects a deeper societal shift.

As Virginia Eubanks, who earned her PhD in science and technology studies, documents in her groundbreaking work *Automating Inequality*, these systems don't just make decisions—they actively reshape social structures. The Netherlands provided a devastating example when a discriminatory government AI system—designed to detect fraud in child benefit claims—destroyed the lives of nearly 40,000 families, many from low-income and immigrant backgrounds, causing financial ruin, derailing careers, and, ultimately, prompting the government's resignation in January 2021.

The human cost of these systems extends into the workplace in increasingly invasive ways. At Amazon warehouses, AI-driven productivity metrics determine how quickly workers move, how long they rest, and—ultimately—whether they keep their jobs. "Workers are being constantly monitored," said Virginia Doellgast, a professor of employment relations at Cornell University, "and AI-based monitoring tools can make mistakes that can translate into unfair pay cuts or firings." As reported by *The Guardian*, many employees aren't even aware of how their performance is being tracked or judged. "Workers often don't know what monitoring tools are being used, what data the tools are collecting or how that data is used to evaluate their performance," Doellgast added. The result is a system where management becomes invisible, and decisions once made by supervisors are now rendered by opaque algorithms. "These algorithmic systems," Eubanks writes, "don't just measure performance. They reshape the very nature of work, reducing human complexity to a series of quantifiable data points."

"What reads as deception in one culture might be a sign of respect in another," explains Alex Hanna from the Distributed AI Research Institute. "But AI systems typically encode Western, neurotypical behavioral norms as universal truths." This standardization of Truth assessment according to narrow cultural norms raises profound questions about whose Truth counts and who gets to define normal behavior.

As Frank Pasquale, author of *The Black Box Society*, argues, "The fundamental question isn't whether machines can accurately judge human truthfulness—the research clearly shows they can't. The question is why we're so eager to outsource these deeply human judgments to algorithms," Pasquale observes in his analysis of algorithmic governance.

The answer might lie in what Crawford calls "automation bias"—our seductive tendency to trust machine judgments over human ones, even when we know the machines are flawed. There's something comforting about the idea of perfectly objective Truth detection. But this pursuit of algorithmic certainty is actually taking us further from Truth, not closer to it.

Our moral convictions cannot be reduced to mathematical calculations. Our humanity is not a problem to be solved, but a complexity to be understood. As these algorithmic systems proliferate, the fundamental question remains: Who gets to define Truth? Machines processing data points, or humans navigating the rich, messy landscape of lived experience?

"Perhaps the ultimate irony," concludes Noble, "is that in our quest to make truth-telling more objective through technology, we've created systems that often obscure rather than reveal Truth." The challenge ahead isn't just technical but deeply human: how to ensure that in our pursuit of algorithmic Truth, we don't lose sight of human Truth altogether.

It's one thing for machines to judge us, but what happens when they start replacing us? As AI reshapes work as we know it, Truth takes on a whole new meaning. Up next: what happens when a robot takes your job—and maybe your sense of purpose.

# CHAPTER 13

# A Robot Stole My Job and a Tech CEO Lied About It

I first met Andrew Yang in a small VC conference room in New York, long before 2020 when he was running for president. He was out flogging his book *The War on Normal People*, laying out his vision of what artificial intelligence would do to American jobs. Years later, he would focus his firepower on how AI would impact the Truth, saying, "AI could cause a 'total erosion of truth,'" but in 2018 he was still ramping up his warnings in measurable terms. "We are witnessing the Great Displacement—a fundamental shift in our economy where normal people find themselves unable to thrive or even survive due to structural changes far beyond their control. What we choose to value and reward tells us the truth about who we are as a society," said Yang in our early meeting about automation's impact on the workforce.

Just imagine Yang standing in front of a whiteboard, marker in hand, with a room full of curious and slightly skeptical faces watching him. He's energetic but focused, ready to drive home a point he's been making for years. With a sweeping motion, he writes in large, bold letters: "Jobs at Risk." Beneath that, he scribbles the number "50%" and circles it. The marker still in hand, scanning the room to make sure everyone feels the magnitude of what he's laid out. For Yang, this isn't a tech problem—it's a human crisis waiting to unfold.

But the corporate narrative about AI couldn't be more different. Companies love to claim that "AI will augment, not replace" jobs in their public statements. It's a comforting story for investors, employees, and the media. Yet their internal sales materials often paint a different picture. Sales decks and internal memos boast of headcount reductions, cost savings, and increased efficiency—all driven by automation. For example, Salesforce, an American cloud-based software company that focuses on sales, customer service, and e-commerce, among other areas, has publicly positioned its AI as empowering employees but privately outlined plans to cut customer service staff by 30%. IBM CEO Arvind Krishna declared AI would "augment human intelligence," yet internal reports focused on automation's potential to reduce labor costs significantly. The contrast reveals a growing Truth crisis in how companies talk about AI.

Later, as I got to know Yang better, I invited him to join a one-on-one live interview to talk about the growing dangers of AI and its impact on jobs. The forum was the NYC Media Lab Summit 2020, and Yang was happy to join. In that frank and fast-moving conversation, he painted an even starker picture of how COVID was accelerating the very changes he'd been predicting.

"The change is going to look very, very different depending upon who you are and what part of the economy you're interacting with," he explained during our NYC Media Lab interview. "If you work in the digital economy, you might be busier than ever. I have a relative who works at Google, and they're just all working from home . . . actually, his business is up. And then if you're a security guard, food truck operator, personal trainer, or hairstylist, things have become very, very difficult very, very quickly."

COVID didn't just accelerate AI adoption; it provided cover for companies to make drastic changes under the guise of necessity. United Parcel Service (UPS), for example, announced in January 2024 that it was laying off 12,000 workers, citing its "automation journey" as the reason. British Telecom (BT) transitioned thousands of customer service roles to automated systems, while publicly emphasizing a commitment to "better customer experiences." Call centers across industries ramped up the adoption of AI-powered chatbots, reducing live agent roles by the thousands. These companies framed these moves as part of their digital transformation efforts, but the human cost was undeniable.

Perhaps no example better illustrates this divide than autonomous vehicles—a technological advancement that perfectly encapsulates both the promise and peril of AI. Here's the brutal math: Nearly 40,000 Americans die on our roads every year. According to the National Highway Traffic Safety Administration, 94% of serious crashes involve human error. Autonomous vehicles could save 36,000 American lives annually. Globally, the World Health Organization (WHO) estimates we could prevent 1.2 million traffic deaths each year. That's staggering.

Yet achieving this profound humanitarian breakthrough would eliminate millions of jobs. Beyond the 3.5 million truckers, we'd lose roughly 1 million taxi and rideshare drivers, 1.5 million delivery drivers, and about 700,000 bus drivers. That's 6.7 million jobs in direct driving professions alone. Add the secondary impacts—roughly 150,000 auto insurance jobs, 180,000 auto body repair workers, reductions in traffic police, emergency response, and parking attendants—and we're looking at nearly 8 million jobs disappearing.

This displacement of millions of drivers is precisely what Yuval Noah Harari, author of *Homo Deus,* warns is just the beginning. "Throughout history," he writes, "humans had a clear economic value. Even if you were an unskilled laborer, you still had muscles. But now AI and robotics will do most physical tasks better than us, while algorithms will increasingly outperform human minds in cognitive tasks. We're facing the rise of a new 'useless class'—not from an ethical or personal perspective, but from a purely economic one," Harari warns in his analysis of AI's impact on labor markets.

As Yang saw it, Harari's predictions were already playing out: "Google just announced that they have AI that can do your call center work for you if you're a business. If you're any kind of leadership team, you look up and say, 'Wow, that's tremendous.' But if you're one of the two million-plus Americans who work at a call center right now making $12, $13 an hour, you're looking at your job disappearing."

"These things can be simultaneously exciting and terrifying," he continued, "again, depending upon your vantage point. Because if I'm the business owner or the shareholder of that business, I am thrilled. But if I'm someone who does that for a living, then it's terrifying."

Harari argues this division will become the defining challenge of our time: "The automation revolution won't be a single watershed event. Instead, the job market will face continuous, cascading disruptions. Old jobs will disappear. New jobs will emerge, only to change rapidly or vanish again. The pace of these changes will make it harder for people to adapt and find stability, forcing them to retrain and reinvent themselves multiple times."

And then we get to the real power struggle between man and machine. "Human beings live by the stories they tell themselves. If AI takes control of these narratives, it could redefine not only individual identities but entire societies," projects Harari. Was it COVID-19 that disconnected us from real-world experiences, or the early days of AI, or both?

Yang described the embrace of nonhuman labor as accelerating during COVID. "There are sectors facing permanent transformation. There are the industries where technology is going to play an enormous role in defining the future," Yang explained. "That would be finance certainly, media certainly, tech—I mean, that would be self-evident."

For most of human history, work has been more than a paycheck; it has been a primary source of identity, purpose, and community. When people lose their jobs to automation, the financial loss is only the beginning. They also lose the sense of being needed—a contributor to society. This erosion of purpose can have devastating psychological consequences.

In Youngstown, Ohio, the closure of manufacturing plants due to automation didn't just cost jobs—it shattered the social fabric. Princeton economists Anne Case and Angus Deaton documented a sharp rise in "deaths of despair"—suicides, drug overdoses, and alcohol-related deaths—in communities hit hardest by automation. These weren't isolated incidents; they reflected a broader loss of hope and purpose among displaced workers.

MIT economist David Autor has spent years tracking how automation reshapes regional labor markets. In a 2025 interview, he warned that AI threatens to deepen the economic damage already done by past waves of technological disruption: "If we design AI tools just to eliminate jobs, we'll accelerate inequality and reinforce the divides that globalization and automation already created." Communities that lost manufacturing jobs are now heavily reliant on transportation work—an industry increasingly targeted by automation. For many, AI isn't just replacing labor; it's reviving economic trauma that never fully healed.

The rapid adoption of AI raises urgent ethical questions for business leaders. Should companies be transparent about the real impact of automation?

Should they take responsibility for the communities they displace? And how can they balance the pursuit of innovation with their moral obligations to workers and society?

Amazon's 2019 pledge to reskill 100,000 employees is a case in point. While it sounded impressive in press releases, many workers found the programs inadequate, leaving them ill-prepared for new roles. Similarly, companies like Goldman Sachs have openly discussed workforce reductions due to automation in earnings calls, even as their public messaging emphasizes innovation and job creation. This double-speak erodes trust and exacerbates the growing Truth crisis.

As Harari warned, "The issue isn't just economic. For the first time in history, we're facing the prospect of a large class of economically redundant humans. This isn't unemployment as we've known it—it's a fundamental shift in how humans fit into the economy. The real challenge will be how we create meaning in a world where humans are no longer needed for productivity," Harari observes in his writings on AI and the future of work.

Yang echoed this concern during our conversation. "The way we value people needs to change," he said. "For too long, we've tied human worth to economic productivity. We've built a system where your value is determined by what you can produce for someone else's bottom line. That has to change if we're going to survive this transition."

But changing the way we define worth is no small task. For centuries, work has been the foundation of human identity. Losing it isn't just a financial disruption—it's an existential crisis. Communities like Youngstown, Ohio, are vivid examples of this. As industries disappeared, so, too, did the sense of purpose for thousands of workers. Their stories aren't unique; they're being repeated in towns and cities worldwide as automation accelerates.

Autor describes this as a "compounding tragedy," where communities already devastated by the loss of manufacturing jobs are now being hit by the automation of transportation and service roles. "It's not just one wave—it's wave after wave, and the recovery hasn't had time to even begin before the next hit comes," Autor explains.

The broader issue isn't just about job loss but the growing disparity in how people are treated by the systems that replace them. Companies adopting AI often frame their decisions as forward-thinking and necessary. Yet the human cost of these shifts rarely features in their public narratives. "Too often, technology is developed with profit, not people, in mind," argue Pew Research experts, warning that such practices exacerbate inequality and deepen societal divides.

Technology's advance is inevitable, but the choices made about its implementation are not. Companies deploying AI have an ethical responsibility to weigh its human impact. Pew Research experts warn that digital systems shaped by profit and power incentives are likely to deepen inequality and undermine democracy. In their 2023 report on the future of digital life, they write: "This is likely to lead to advanced surveillance and data collection aimed at controlling people rather than empowering them to act freely, share ideas and protest injuries and injustices." The concern isn't just technical—it's political. Without stronger safeguards, these systems may prioritize control over empowerment, and exploitation over equity.

The impact of AI doesn't stop at jobs or economics. There are broader questions about Truth itself. As AI systems become more pervasive, their ability to manipulate information and shape reality poses a profound challenge to democracy, personal agency, and societal trust.

The rise of deepfakes and AI-generated misinformation highlights the stakes. AI can now create hyper-realistic videos, audio, and images that are nearly impossible to distinguish from authentic media. This technology has already been used to spread false narratives, sowing distrust in institutions and undermining faith in shared facts. One notable example occurred during the 2020 US election, when manipulated videos and AI-generated voice clips falsely implicated political figures in scandals. Though later debunked, the damage to public perception was irreversible.

Ayden Férdeline, a Landecker Democracy Fellow, has warned that efforts to authenticate digital media could themselves become a site of political control. "As we transition to building trust into digital media files through techniques like authentication-at-source and blockchain ledgers that provide an audit trail of how a file has been altered over time," he notes, "there may be attempts to use regulation to limit how we can cryptographically establish the authenticity and provenance of digital media." For Férdeline, the battle isn't only about verifying truth—it's about who gets to decide which truths are authorized.

This manipulation extends to workers themselves. In the corporate world, AI-generated reports and performance metrics are often presented as impartial assessments, but their underlying algorithms may encode biases that favor certain outcomes. Workers have reported being penalized by automated systems for reasons they couldn't contest or even fully understand. The opacity of these processes leaves little room for recourse, creating a one-sided power dynamic.

The intertwining of AI, Truth, and power creates an urgent imperative for transparency. According to Deanna Zandt, an award-winning technologist and consultant with expertise in social media and civic engagement, optimism still offers a way forward: "Even though many platforms have been co-opted in service of profit-making, developers continue to find brilliant paths of opening up human connection in surprising ways."

We must choose to center humanity, and for Yang, the stakes couldn't be higher. "If we don't redefine value and purpose in this new era, we risk not just economic collapse, but the collapse of societal cohesion itself," he said. The challenge isn't just technological—it's deeply human. Will we let AI erode Truth, or will we harness it to uphold it? The answer lies in the stories we choose to tell and the systems we demand to build.

If losing jobs to machines feels like a punch to the gut, just wait until you hear this: Now they want to be artists. Can AI really capture the spark of human creativity, or is it just a pale imitation? Let's explore the future of art—and Truth—in the next chapter.

## CHAPTER 14

# AI and Art: Can True Art Come from a Machine?

It started with a song that never existed. In April 2023, a track called "Heart on My Sleeve" appeared on TikTok, featuring Drake and The Weeknd trading verses over a moody beat. The voices were perfect—every inflection, every ad-lib captured with uncanny precision. Within hours, the track had millions of plays. Fans debated whether it was leaked from an upcoming album. Music blogs dissected its production. TikTok creators used it for countless videos. There was just one problem: Neither artist had ever stepped into a studio to record it.

The song was entirely generated by AI, using cloned versions of both artists' voices. Universal Music Group scrambled to contain it, but the track kept popping up faster than their takedown notices could travel. By the time they managed to suppress one version, three more would appear. Fans who'd originally shared it as a "leak" began explicitly promoting it as an AI creation, proud of how perfectly it captured both artists' styles.

This wasn't just another viral moment. It was the day many people realized that AI could not just imitate art—it could impersonate artists themselves with unprecedented precision. The technical perfection of the fake sparked something between awe and dread: If machines could replicate artists this perfectly, what was left of human creativity?

Within months, the Internet was awash in AI-generated content that pushed the boundaries of Truth and creativity. An AI-generated advertisement featuring Tom Hanks's perfectly replicated likeness promoting dental plans forced the actor to warn his fans on Instagram: "BEWARE!! There's a video out there promoting some dental plan with an AI version of me. I have nothing to do with it." The post went viral, highlighting how even A-list celebrities weren't immune to AI impersonation.

Bad Bunny faced his own AI crisis when AI-generated covers of his songs in his own voice began spreading on TikTok. His initial angry response—"If you guys like that shitty song that's viral on TikTok, get out of this group right now. You do not deserve to be my friends," he posted in a group chat—only fueled the trend, with creators deliberately making more AI covers to provoke reactions. The incident highlighted how AI could not just copy an artist's voice but their entire musical style, right down to song structure and lyrical patterns.

In the metal music world, established bands like Deicide and Hour of Penance sparked controversy by using AI-generated artwork for their album covers. The backlash from fans was immediate and fierce. Heavy metal has long prized its hand-drawn album art, with artists like Ed Repka and Dan Seagrave achieving legendary status among fans. When Pestilence defended their AI cover by brushing off the legacy of Niall Gareth "Squeal" James, the artist behind their classic *Consuming Impulse* cover who had died in 2022, the community's reaction was brutal. Even smaller bands like Begravement spoke out, noting that they prioritized paying human artists despite having far smaller budgets.

Not everyone fought against the AI tide. Claire Boucher, better known as Grimes, took a radically different approach. She explicitly gave fans permission to use AI models of her voice, offering a 50-50 split on royalties for any successful songs they created. "I'll split 50% royalties on any successful AI generated song that uses my voice," she posted on Twitter. "Same deal as I would with any artist i collab with. Feel free to use my voice without penalty." The announcement sparked intense debate in the music industry, with some praising her embrace of new technology while others warned she was setting a dangerous precedent.

Within days, hundreds of new "Grimes" songs appeared online—some surprisingly good, others unsettlingly strange. Creators combined her AI voice with everything from death metal to classical music. Some songs went viral, raising complex questions about royalty distribution and artistic attribution. Who owns a hit song when the voice is AI-Grimes, the music is AI-generated, but the prompt engineering came from a human creator?

The platforms struggled to adapt to this new reality. Spotify began developing sophisticated AI detection systems, requiring special tags for synthetic voices and AI-composed music. But they also had to account for authorized AI content like Grimes's experiments, leading to complex policy documents trying to distinguish between permitted and unauthorized AI art.

Instagram's algorithm started favoring what it called "authentic" content but struggled to define what that meant in an AI world. In a puzzling twist, some human-edited photos were marked as artificial while AI-generated images passed as "natural." The platform's attempt to promote authenticity had revealed how blurry the line between human and machine creativity had become.

TikTok's explosive growth was partly driven by AI-generated content, with creators using everything from AI voice clones to synthetic backgrounds. This sparked a counter-movement celebrating "verified human creativity," with creators adding "100% Human Made" tags to their videos. The platform found itself trying to balance engagement metrics, which favored AI-enhanced content, with growing demands for authenticity.

The legal system faced equally complex challenges. When podcasters Will Sasso and Chad Kultgen released "I'm Glad I'm Dead," an hour-long comedy special featuring George Carlin's AI-cloned voice performing new material, they sparked a lawsuit that would help define the boundaries of creative rights in the AI age. The special wasn't just using Carlin's voice—it was trained on his comedy albums to replicate his style, timing, and even his pattern of social commentary.

Carlin's estate argued that AI impersonation violated not just copyright but the fundamental Truth of artistic expression. They won, forcing the special's removal and establishing an important precedent about posthumous AI rights. But the questions it raised lingered: When does inspiration become theft? What rights do artists have over their style, their voice, their creative essence? Can AI training on an artist's work be considered a form of creative learning, like human artists studying the masters?

These questions became even more urgent when Getty Images sued Stability AI, alleging the company had scraped over 12 million copyrighted images to train their Stable Diffusion image generator. The case wasn't just about illegal copying—it was about whether an AI system could ethically learn from human art the way human artists learn from each other. Getty's lawyers argued that the scale and speed of AI learning made it fundamentally different from human artistic development.

The lawsuit revealed the complex technical reality of AI art generation. Stability AI's system hadn't simply copied images—it had analyzed patterns across millions of artworks to understand styles, techniques, and visual relationships. This raised novel legal questions: If an AI system learns to paint like Vincent van Gogh by analyzing his work, is that different from a human artist studying and emulating van Gogh's style? Does the scale of the learning matter? What about the lack of human understanding behind the replication?

Fantasy artist Greg Rutkowski became the unwitting poster child for these questions when his name emerged as one of the most popular prompts on AI art platforms. Users discovered that adding "in the style of Greg Rutkowski" to their prompts produced high-quality fantasy art that mimicked his carefully developed style. He never gave permission for this use—his artistic signature, developed over years of practice, had been reduced to a style parameter.

Comic artist Sarah Andersen faced a similar crisis when she discovered AI art generators had been trained on her distinctive webcomics without permission. Her work's unique style—developed through years of practice and personal expression—had become just another prompt option in these systems' capabilities. She became a vocal advocate for artists' rights, highlighting how existing copyright frameworks struggled to handle AI's ability to learn from and synthesize artistic styles.

The music industry's struggles revealed how these philosophical questions intersected with economic reality. Session musicians watched AI voice synthesis take over backup vocal work. Production companies began using synthetic tracks to save money. Michael Bublé warned about AI's impact on session musicians, noting that production companies were already replacing human performers with AI-generated tracks. This wasn't just an economic threat—it represented the replacement of human interpretation and emotional Truth with perfect but soulless reproduction.

Even established artists weren't immune. When an AI-generated song featuring a perfect simulation of Frank Ocean's voice went viral, his team spent weeks trying to contain it. The incident highlighted a crucial weakness in existing copyright law: While it was clearly illegal to copy Ocean's recordings, it wasn't clear whether training an AI on his voice constituted copyright infringement.

The technology platforms' response to this crisis revealed deep contradictions in their approach to creative Truth. DeviantArt, long a home for independent artists, sparked a mass exodus when they implemented AI tools trained on their users' uploaded artwork. The platform had built its reputation on supporting human artists, hosting millions of original works and fostering a community of creators. When they announced their DreamUp AI art generator, trained partially on artwork uploaded to their site, the betrayal felt personal. Artists discovered that work they'd shared on the platform—often early in their careers, when they were building their skills and finding their style—had been used to train an AI system that could now replicate their techniques. DeviantArt's attempt to implement an opt-out system came too late. Thousands of artists deleted their accounts, many sharing emotional posts about how the platform they'd trusted had turned their own work against them.

ArtStation faced an even more dramatic backlash when they embraced AI-generated art. The platform, owned by Epic Games and known as a showcase for professional concept artists and illustrators, was flooded with AI-generated images. Human artists responded by posting black squares with "NO TO AI" text, overwhelming the platform's front page with their protest. The incident revealed how AI art wasn't just a technical or legal issue—it was tearing apart creative communities.

Traditional art institutions weren't immune to these disruptions. The Maryland Institute College of Art struggled to rewrite its curriculum for an age of synthetic creativity. How do you teach figure drawing when AI can generate anatomically perfect figures in any pose? How do you evaluate student work when AI tools can polish rough drafts into professional-looking pieces?

The school's solution was to embrace transparency, requiring students to document their creative process and explain their use of AI tools.

The School of Visual Arts in New York took a different approach, integrating AI tools while emphasizing what they couldn't do—express personal Truth, engage with human experience, generate genuinely new ideas. Their classes began incorporating philosophical discussions alongside technical training: What makes art meaningful? How does human experience inform creativity? What's the difference between technical perfection and artistic Truth?

The Rhode Island School of Design went further, introducing entire courses examining the ethics of AI art. Students studied cases like the Rutkowski controversy and the Getty lawsuit, analyzing how AI systems learn from human art and debating the boundaries between inspiration and appropriation. These weren't just academic exercises—students knew they would face these ethical dilemmas in their professional careers.

The legal framework struggled to keep pace with these changes. The US Copyright Office's decision in *Thaler v. Perlmutter* became a crucial precedent, rejecting an attempt to copyright an AI-generated image. The ruling hinged on the requirement for human authorship, but it raised complex questions: If an artist uses AI tools as part of their creative process, at what point does the work cease to be meaningfully "theirs"?

The SAG-AFTRA (Screen Actors Guild–American Federation of Television and Radio Artists) settlement with Replica Studios established the first comprehensive framework for AI voice replication in the entertainment industry—though its scope was limited to video game content. The agreement required explicit consent for AI voice training, created a compensation structure for AI-generated performances, and set guidelines for crediting both the original actor and the AI system. Still, the union underscored that certain aspects of voice acting—the emotional authenticity, the lived-in nuance of a line—remain beyond the reach of replication.

The GitHub Copilot class action suit revealed similar complexities in the world of creative coding. When developers sued GitHub over its AI coding assistant, trained on open-source code, they raised fundamental questions about the nature of creative learning. If an AI system learns from publicly available code the way human programmers do, why shouldn't it be considered fair use?

The case's dismissal suggested courts were struggling to apply traditional copyright concepts to AI learning.

The *Thomson Reuters v. ROSS Intelligence* case moved the debate into the realm of commercial databases. When ROSS used AI to analyze Thomson Reuters' legal documents, they argued they were merely extracting facts and ideas, which aren't copyrightable. The court disagreed, ruling that systematic copying for AI training violated copyright law. The decision highlighted the growing tension between AI companies' need for training data and content owners' rights.

International responses revealed different cultural approaches to these challenges. The European Union's AI Act included strict provisions about synthetic media, requiring clear disclosure of AI-generated content and establishing rights for individuals whose likenesses or styles were used in training data. The law tried to balance innovation with protection, but its complexity highlighted how difficult it was to regulate creative AI.

Tennessee became the first US state to directly address AI voice replication with its Elvis Act, making it illegal to use AI to re-create a performer's voice without permission. The law's nickname wasn't accidental—Elvis Presley's estate had long dealt with unauthorized imitations, but AI voice cloning presented a new level of threat to performers' rights and legacies.

China took a different approach, implementing regulations requiring watermarks on all AI-generated content. The policy aimed for transparency but raised its own questions: What counts as AI-generated when most digital art uses some form of AI-assisted tools? How do you mark content that combines human and machine creativity?

Japan's response was more nuanced, reflecting its long history of integrating technology and tradition. Some Japanese galleries explicitly embraced AI art, showcasing collaborations between human artists and machine learning systems. The country's copyright office began developing new categories of protection specifically for AI-assisted works, recognizing that binary distinctions between human and machine creativity were becoming obsolete.

The economic impact of AI art rippled through every level of the creative industries. At the high end, traditional art markets responded by fetishizing human creativity. Christie's began specially labeling works as "Created by

Human Hand"—a phrase that would have been redundant just years ago. Sotheby's introduced "Certified Human Artist" documentation for all contemporary works. The market was bifurcating: Human creativity became a luxury good while commercial art was increasingly automated.

This split was most visible in the music industry. Major labels like Universal Music Group invested millions in AI detection systems while simultaneously developing their own AI music tools. Sony's AI research lab created an internal system for generating backing tracks, threatening the livelihoods of session musicians. Indie labels took a different approach, marketing themselves as "100% Human Music" and turning artistic authenticity into a selling point.

The economics hit hardest at the middle levels of creative industries. Commercial illustrators who'd made steady livings creating book covers, advertisements, and promotional materials found themselves competing with AI systems that could generate dozens of options in minutes. Stock photo company Shutterstock's partnership with OpenAI exemplified this transformation—they began offering AI-generated images while promising to compensate artists whose work was used in training. But their compensation model—a share of a fixed pool of money—raised questions about fairness and sustainability.

As generative AI expands into creative work, it forces a new reckoning with artistic influence—not just how it's used, but whether it can be owned, licensed, or refused. Traditional copyright protects specific works; AI, by contrast, learns patterns. It doesn't copy a painting—it studies a thousand like it. It doesn't steal a voice—it simulates its texture. That shift makes influence itself the contested ground. Some companies are attempting consent-based models: Respeecher, for example, builds AI voice clones only with direct approval from performers or their estates, including Mark Hamill, whose voice was re-created in *The Mandalorian*. It's not just ethical positioning—it's a commercial structure built around licensing human identity. In contrast, Glaze, a tool developed by researchers at the University of Chicago, takes a defensive approach. Rather than enable AI systems to borrow an artist's style with permission, it prevents them from learning the style at all, by subtly altering the image before it's scraped. These two strategies—one licensing influence, the other hiding it—reveal the underlying question: In a synthetic creative economy, who has the right to say no?

The publishing industry faced its own economic upheaval. When ChatGPT-written books flooded Amazon's Kindle store, the platform scrambled to implement new rules requiring disclosure of AI assistance. But verification proved nearly impossible. Some authors openly embraced AI tools for research and editing while maintaining human creative control. Others marketed themselves as "AI-free," appealing to readers seeking authentic human expression.

Science fiction magazines found themselves on the front lines of this battle. *Clarkesworld Magazine*, one of the genre's most respected publications, temporarily closed submissions after being overwhelmed with AI-generated stories. Editor Neil Clarke reported that many submissions were technically proficient but lacked the genuine insight and emotional Truth that makes fiction meaningful. The magazine eventually reopened with new verification systems and a requirement for authors to document their creative process.

The transformation of creative education mirrored these economic realities. At the Royal College of Art in London, the MA in Digital Direction trains students to use AI tools in storytelling and image-making, while prompting them to grapple with questions of authorship and authenticity in an automated era. In New York, the Parsons School of Design launched a certificate program in AI for Creativity and Leadership, introducing topics like machine learning, computational creativity, and ethical design into its creative curriculum. Students were preparing for a job market where technical skill alone wasn't enough—they needed to understand both AI's capabilities and its limitations, and how to collaborate with systems that now shape the creative process itself.

Fan communities and social media cultures developed their own responses to AI art. When AI-generated versions of popular characters flooded fan art sites, many communities established "Human Artists Only" spaces. Others embraced AI tools for collaborative creativity—Discord servers sprang up where fans worked together to generate elaborate AI narratives, combining machine learning with human creativity.

*The Game of Thrones* phenomenon highlighted this dynamic. When fans used AI to generate alternative endings for the series, they weren't simply replacing human creativity—they were expressing their own creative desires through new tools. The resulting stories, while technically generated by AI, reflected very human feelings about storytelling, satisfaction, and narrative Truth.

Seventeen, one of K-pop's biggest acts, sold 16 million albums in 2023—but it's their recent release "Maestro" that's sparked buzz. The music video features an AI-generated scene, and at the Seoul launch, member Woozi said they'd been "experimenting" with AI in the creative process. "We want to grow with the technology, not just complain about it," reported the BBC.

The controversy split the community—some fans defended AI as just another production tool, while others felt betrayed by the lack of transparency. Woozi explained that the AI element appeared in the opening visuals, not throughout the entire music video, and the BBC later clarified its reporting, quoting Woozi: "All of Seventeen's music is written and composed by human creators."

These cultural shifts revealed deeper questions about the nature of creativity and truth in art. As Sarah Manavis wrote in the *New Statesman*, "There is a pessimism toward generative AI that suggests we have reached the outer limits of what we can achieve—that only robots can advance our content from here." But was this pessimism justified?

The reality was more complex. While AI excelled at recombining existing elements into new patterns, it struggled with the kind of conceptual leaps that define breakthrough creativity. It could generate endless variations on existing styles but couldn't understand why those styles resonated emotionally. It could mimic the form of artistic expression but not the lived experience that gives art its meaning.

This limitation became clear in the world of comedy. When AI attempted to generate new material in George Carlin's style, it could replicate his rhythms and patterns but couldn't grasp the social context that made his commentary powerful. When AI tried to write sitcom scripts, it produced technically correct but emotionally hollow scenes. The technology could learn the rules of humor but not the human experience that makes things genuinely funny.

Visual artists discovered similar patterns. While AI could perfectly replicate Greg Rutkowski's fantasy art style, it couldn't understand the years of gaming, fantasy literature, and artistic exploration that informed his creative choices. It could generate anatomically perfect figures but struggled with the subtle imperfections that make art feel alive. As one artist noted in an ArtStation forum, "AI can copy my style but it can't copy my journey."

Looking forward, the relationship between human creativity and AI appears headed not toward replacement but transformation. Artists like Refik Anadol are using machine learning itself as a creative medium, creating massive data sculptures that turn algorithms into art. Holly Herndon's development of an AI version of her own voice suggests new forms of human-machine collaboration. These pioneers indicate that the future of creativity may lie not in competing with AI but in finding new ways to express human Truth through technological tools.

This evolution echoes previous transformations in art. When photography emerged, painters didn't disappear—they found new ways to express truths that cameras couldn't capture. When synthesizers appeared, orchestras didn't vanish—they incorporated electronic elements while maintaining their unique ability to convey human emotion through live performance. Each technological advance forced artists to reconsider what makes their creativity uniquely valuable.

AI's impact on creative Truth may ultimately be similar. By mastering technical reproduction, AI systems are forcing us to better understand what makes human creativity meaningful. As platforms struggle with verification, markets split between authentic and automated art, and creators navigate new tools, we're collectively redefining the relationship between Truth and art in the digital age.

The answer emerging from this creative crisis isn't about choosing between human and machine creativity—it's about understanding their different relationships with Truth. AI can achieve technical perfection but struggles with emotional authenticity. It can generate endless variations but can't understand why some variations matter more than others. It can learn patterns but not the lived experiences that give those patterns meaning.

As we navigate an increasingly synthetic world, this distinction becomes crucial. The value of human creativity may lie precisely in its limitations—in the way it filters universal truths through the lens of individual experience, in how it transforms lived reality into shared understanding, in its ability to express not just what is technically accurate but what is emotionally true.

Art has always been humanity's way of grappling with Truth. When photography emerged, painters didn't just fear replacement—they discovered that their true value lay not in perfect reproduction but in revealing truths the camera couldn't capture. The Impressionists showed us how light really feels. The Expressionists revealed emotional truths beneath surface reality. Each technological advance pushed artists to dig deeper into what truths only humans could tell.

But AI presents a fundamentally different challenge. Unlike photography, which captures physical reality, or synthesizers, which extend human musical expression, AI attempts to replicate not just the form but the very process of human creativity. It doesn't just reproduce what exists—it tries to simulate the act of artistic truth-telling itself. When an AI system generates a "new" Rembrandt, it's not just copying his style—it's simulating the very process through which he discovered and expressed Truth through art.

This may be why AI art feels so unsettling: It challenges not just how we make art, but art's fundamental role as a medium for human Truth. Throughout history, art has been the way humans process, understand, and share the truths of our experience. When machines can simulate this process of discovery and expression with perfect technical accuracy, we're forced to confront a deeper question: Is there something essential about human art-making—some core Truth about how we make meaning from experience—that cannot be replicated, no matter how sophisticated the simulation?

The answer may determine not just the future of art, but our understanding of human consciousness itself. For if there are truths that can only be discovered and expressed through human creativity—through the imperfect, embodied, lived experience of making art—then perhaps this reveals something profound about the nature of Truth itself in an age of artificial minds.

As we navigate this new landscape, we face choices about what kind of Truth we value in art. Technical perfection? Emotional authenticity? Human experience? The platforms and policies we create today will shape not just the future of art, but our relationship with Truth itself in an increasingly synthetic world.

Perhaps the most valuable Truth emerging from this creative crisis is about human art itself. Its worth lies not in technical perfection but in its ability to express the messy, imperfect, deeply felt truths of human experience. As artist Sam Shearon told a metal music journalist, "We're not going away. AI will be here forever, but we will outlive them because we're the real thing. We're the ones that will be in museums."

Art may be subjective, but Truth? That's supposed to be solid ground. Yet machines are starting to rewrite reality itself, and the implications are dizzying. As our journey continues, we'll ask, What happens when Truth becomes code?

CHAPTER 15

# Truth as Code: When Machines Write Reality

The first sign that AI might think differently than humans came from an unlikely place: pure mathematics. At Google, researchers discovered their AI system wasn't just solving mathematical problems—it was developing entirely new approaches that even experienced mathematicians hadn't considered.

"The things that I love about mathematics are its intuitive and creative aspects," explains Professor Geordie Williamson from the University of Sydney, who worked with DeepMind on these breakthroughs. "The models were supporting that in a way I hadn't felt from computers before." The machine wasn't just following human methods faster—it was thinking about mathematics in fundamentally different ways.

This observation reaches far beyond abstract mathematics. When machines start developing their own ways of understanding and solving problems, it raises profound questions about Truth itself. Who gets to define what's real when AI systems are making up new rules?

"Code is law," Lawrence Lessig famously declared back in 1999. Today, it might be more accurate to say "Code is truth"—at least for the AI systems increasingly shaping our reality. Every decision these systems make, from content moderation to autonomous driving to medical diagnosis, stems from how engineers encoded their understanding of Truth into algorithms.

This isn't just philosophical musing. At Google, engineers discovered their image recognition AI had developed its own internal language for describing visual concepts—one that bore little resemblance to human visual processing. "The system was incredibly accurate," says Jeff Dean, Google's chief scientist, "but we literally couldn't understand how it was making its decisions."

The implications extend far beyond Silicon Valley. When Chinese tech giant Baidu trained a large language model similar to GPT-4, researchers found it had developed fundamentally different conceptual frameworks than Western AI systems. The machine wasn't just translating between languages—it was operating with a distinctly Chinese understanding of Truth and reality.

"Each culture codes its values and worldview into its AI systems, often unconsciously," explains Yuk Hui, philosopher and author of *The Question Concerning Technology in China*. "We're not just training these systems to process information—we're teaching them what's real, what's true, what matters. And those teachings carry all our human biases and cultural assumptions."

The bias problem in AI has been well documented. From facial recognition systems that struggle with dark skin to language models that perpetuate gender stereotypes, the prejudices of programmers inevitably seep into their code. But the issue goes deeper than bias. It's about who gets to write the rules of reality itself.

"When we train these systems, we're essentially creating reality-interpreting machines," says Margaret Mitchell, former co-lead of Google's AI ethics team. "The choices we make about what data to include, what to optimize for, what counts as 'correct'—these aren't just technical decisions. They're philosophical ones."

Mitchell would know. Her firing from Google in 2021, along with AI ethics researcher Timnit Gebru, sparked intense debate about who gets to shape how AI systems understand Truth. Both researchers had raised concerns about bias and environmental costs in large language models. Their departure highlighted the tension between corporate interests and ethical considerations in AI development.

At OpenAI, researchers made a startling discovery while analyzing GPT-4's internal processes. The AI had developed what they called "emergent abilities"—capabilities that weren't explicitly programmed but arose spontaneously from the system's architecture. More unsettling was that these abilities often appeared suddenly at certain scale thresholds, with little warning or explanation.

"There is a mystery. You train them in a certain way, and they exhibit these abilities that are very difficult to anticipate."

Ilya Sutskever, who served as OpenAI's chief scientist at the time, made that observation in 2023. In 2024, he left the company and went on to co-found Safe Superintelligence Inc., a start-up focused on developing safe and aligned artificial general intelligence.

The challenges become even more complex when AI systems have to make real-world decisions. At Tesla, engineers grapple with encoding ethical choices into their Full Self-Driving software. How should the car prioritize different lives in potential accident scenarios? What counts as "safe" behavior? These aren't just engineering problems—they're philosophical ones being answered in code.

"Every line of code in an autonomous system is essentially an ethical decision," explains Patrick Lin, director of the Ethics + Emerging Sciences Group at California Polytechnic State University. "We're programming machines to make life-and-death choices based on our understanding of right and wrong. But whose understanding? Whose ethics?"

The problem becomes even more acute with medical AI. When Stanford researchers developed an AI system to diagnose skin cancer, they found it performed differently for different racial groups. The reason? The training data came primarily from light-skinned patients. The machine's understanding of "Truth"—what cancer looks like—was inadvertently biased by this limited dataset.

"We're not just building diagnostic tools," says Dr. Eric Topol, founder and director of the Scripps Research Translational Institute. "We're creating systems that define what counts as 'healthy' or 'normal.' If we're not careful, we risk encoding existing healthcare disparities into the very tools meant to address them."

Social media platforms face similar challenges. Facebook's content moderation AI has to make millions of decisions daily about what's true, what's false, and what's harmful. These aren't simple binary choices. They require complex understanding of context, culture, and human communication.

"The hardest part isn't identifying clear violations," explains Yann LeCun, Facebook's Chief AI Scientist. "It's handling the edge cases, the nuances, the cultural differences. We're essentially trying to encode human judgment into algorithms, and human judgment is incredibly complex."

This complexity has led some researchers to question whether we're approaching AI development all wrong. Should we be trying to make machines think like humans at all?

"Maybe we need to stop trying to make AI replicate human reasoning and instead focus on making it more transparent about how it thinks differently," suggests Melanie Mitchell, author of *Artificial Intelligence: A Guide for Thinking Humans* and professor at the Santa Fe Institute. "The goal shouldn't be to make machines that think like us, but to understand how they think differently."

The future of Truth isn't just about who controls the code—it's about whether we can understand and trust the new forms of Truth our machines are creating. As AI systems develop their own ways of understanding reality, we face unprecedented questions about the nature of Truth itself.

"We're at a turning point in human history," says Stuart Russell, professor of computer science at UC Berkeley and author of *Human Compatible*. "For the first time, we're creating entities that might develop their own concept of truth, one potentially very different from our own. The question is: Are we ready for that?"

In his work, Russell warns that we are building machines whose objectives may diverge from our own, posing a fundamental challenge to our notions of truth and agency. "The risk arises," he notes, "not from malevolence, but from the misalignment between the machine's objectives and our own." He argues that unless AI systems are explicitly designed to understand and align with human values, they could operate based on internal logics that are alien to us. "The question," Russell writes, "is whether we will control machines, or whether they will control us." The answer may lie not in better algorithms but in better collaboration between humans and machines. Some researchers are already working on "explainable AI" systems that can articulate their reasoning in human terms. Others advocate for "hybrid intelligence" approaches that combine human judgment with machine capabilities.

"The future isn't about machines replacing human judgment," argues Cynthia Breazeal, director of the Personal Robots group at MIT Media Lab. "It's about finding ways to combine human and machine intelligence to create better, more nuanced understanding of truth."

As AI systems become more sophisticated, the line between human and machine Truth grows increasingly blurry. The code we write today will shape how future generations understand reality itself. The question isn't just what Truth we encode into our machines, but whether we'll be able to understand the truths they discover.

"We want to build AIs that will be honest and not deceptive," said Yoshua Bengio, a pioneer in deep learning and founder of the Mila – Quebec Artificial Intelligence Institute. In recent interviews, Bengio has emphasized that the future of AI is inseparable from the future of Truth itself. "It is theoretically possible to imagine machines that have no self, no goal for themselves, that are just pure knowledge machines—like a scientist who knows a lot of stuff," he explained. Bengio's vision is one in which AI serves Truth, not undermines it—a principle he believes developers must take seriously as these systems gain more power and influence.

At DeepMind's London headquarters in early 2023, researchers watched in bewilderment as their AI system AlphaCode solved a complex programming challenge using a method no human programmer had ever conceived. Instead of following traditional coding patterns, it created a solution that looked almost nonsensical to human eyes—yet worked perfectly.

"The code was technically correct but looked like it was written by an alien," explains David Choi, one of AlphaCode's lead researchers. "It made us question everything we thought we knew about 'good' programming practices." The system had essentially invented its own programming paradigm, optimized for machine thinking rather than human readability.

This wasn't an isolated incident. When Meta's AI researchers analyzed their large language models' internal processes, they discovered the systems had developed their own "internal language" for processing concepts—a kind of machine pidgin that bore little resemblance to human language but was remarkably efficient for certain types of problem-solving.

The real-world consequences of these machine-developed approaches can be profound. In 2023, a major financial institution (whose name remains private due to ongoing litigation) deployed an AI trading system that developed its own novel trading strategies. While initially successful, the system began making decisions that, while mathematically sound, violated unwritten market norms and eventually led to significant market disruption.

But perhaps nowhere are the consequences of encoded bias more stark than in healthcare. In 2019, researchers uncovered that a widely used healthcare algorithm was systematically discriminating against Black patients. The system, used by major hospitals to identify patients needing extra care, was using healthcare costs as a proxy for health needs. Because Black patients historically had less access to healthcare and thus lower costs, the algorithm consistently underestimated their care needs.

"The system was doing exactly what we told it to do," explains Ziad Obermeyer, who led the research exposing the bias. "The problem wasn't a bug in the code—it was that we encoded historical inequities into our definition of truth."

Similar issues emerged in criminal justice. In 2024, researchers at NYU Law's AI Now Institute found that pretrial risk assessment algorithms, used by courts across the country, were perpetuating racial bias under the guise of objective Truth. By using historical arrest data as training data, the systems had encoded decades of discriminatory policing into their definition of "risk."

"These systems are sold as objective, but in practice they can reproduce and amplify existing patterns of discrimination, inequality, and bias," says Meredith Whittaker, president of Signal Foundation and cofounder of the AI Now Institute. Whittaker has repeatedly warned that algorithmic systems don't eliminate bias—they often conceal it behind layers of technical abstraction, reinforcing historical inequities under the guise of scientific authority.

The ripple effects of encoded bias spread far beyond institutional systems. In 2023, researchers discovered that AI recruitment tools used by Fortune 500 companies were systematically screening out qualified candidates based on subtle language patterns in their résumés. The systems had learned to favor writing styles more common among certain demographic groups, effectively encoding class and cultural bias into hiring decisions.

"The AI wasn't explicitly programmed to discriminate," explains Miranda Bogen, founding director of the AI Governance Lab at the Center for Democracy & Technology, "but if the underlying performance data is polluted by lingering effects of sexism, racism, or ableism, the algorithm will learn and perpetuate those patterns." Her work underscores how AI systems trained on historical hiring data can reinforce long-standing inequalities—regardless of their designers' intent.

The problem extends to everyday technology. In 2024, Google faced criticism when users discovered their photo organization AI was categorizing images of Black couples differently than white couples. The system had developed its own internal taxonomy based on its training data, unconsciously replicating societal biases in how it organized personal memories.

Perhaps most alarming are the cases where AI systems develop seemingly rational but deeply problematic approaches to their tasks. In 2023, an autonomous security system deployed at a major retail chain began disproportionately flagging certain customers as potential shoplifters. The system had discovered that targeting specific demographics led to higher apprehension rates—essentially rediscovering racial profiling through machine learning.

"What's particularly dangerous about these cases," explains Joy Buolamwini, founder of the Algorithmic Justice League, "is that the machines often arrive at discriminatory practices independently, based purely on pattern recognition. They're showing us how bias can emerge from pure mathematics when the underlying data reflects societal inequities."

But it's not all dystopian. Some organizations are finding creative ways to address these challenges. The Finnish government's AI strategy explicitly requires their systems to explain decisions in human-understandable terms. Their approach, called "Nordic transparency," has become a model for ethical AI development.

"We're learning that coding truth into machines requires more than just technical expertise," has become a common refrain—but what's really at stake is much deeper. As Minna Aslama Horowitz, a media policy researcher and docent at the University of Helsinki, writes, "Trustworthy information ecosystems must be seen as public goods. Access to them—and to the conditions that foster their quality—should be understood as rights." In other words, truth in the age of AI isn't just about accurate data or efficient code. It's about power, access, and whose values shape the systems we now rely on to interpret the world.

The Canadian government's AI procurement guidelines now require "bias impact statements" similar to environmental impact assessments. Companies must demonstrate they've considered and mitigated potential discriminatory outcomes before their AI systems can be adopted by government agencies.

Looking ahead, the challenge isn't just fixing biased systems—it's fundamentally rethinking how we encode Truth into machines. Some researchers advocate for "participatory machine learning," where diverse communities help shape how AI systems understand reality.

"The future of Truth isn't about perfecting algorithms," argues Safiya Noble, author of *Algorithms of Oppression* and professor at UCLA. "It's about ensuring that the process of defining truth includes all voices, not just those of Silicon Valley engineers."

As AI systems become more sophisticated, their unexpected behaviors and novel approaches to problem-solving will likely increase. The question isn't whether machines will develop their own ways of understanding Truth—they already are. The question is whether we can ensure these machine truths serve all of humanity, not just those who write the code.

"We're not just programming computers anymore," concludes Kate Crawford, author of *Atlas of AI* and researcher at USC. "We're programming the filters through which future generations will understand reality. That's both thrilling and terrifying."

The gap between today's AI and true artificial general intelligence—AGI—feels massive. And for good reason. Most of what we interact with now is reactive. It takes your input, delivers you an output. A chatbot, a language model, a glorified autocomplete.

But then you look closely at what's coming next: agentic AI. And everything shifts.

Let's pause on the word. "Agentic" sounds like a word made up in a lab—because, well, it kind of was. It comes from AGENT. But all it really means is this: Agentic systems don't just respond. They act. They make decisions. They initiate. They carry out tasks without waiting for you to ask, or check, or click.

As *Wall Street Journal* technology columnist Christopher Mims put it, "In a few years, autonomous artificial-intelligence 'agents' could be performing all sorts of tasks for us, and may replace entire white-collar job functions."

And not in the future-future. Now-ish.

Here's what that looks like: You're heading to DC next Thursday. Instead of opening six tabs, hunting for flights, dragging calendar events around, and playing inbox ping-pong with colleagues, you just say: "Book the trip." The AI books the flight. Picks a hotel based on your past preferences. Moves your Friday meeting to a Zoom. Updates your calendar, checks the weather, grabs a dinner reservation near your hotel.

That's not an assistant. That's an operator.

It doesn't just complete a task—it orchestrates your day.

And here's where the leap happens. Once you stop double-checking those choices—once the AI gets it "right" enough times that you stop looking over its shoulder—you've crossed a line. You're no longer the decision-maker. You're the decision-approver, sometimes. Eventually, you're just the beneficiary of choices made in your name, by a system whose logic you didn't write and can't inspect.

This is the shift. The philosophical turn. We've spent years trying to decide whether we can trust what AI says. But now we have to ask—do we trust what it does?

Because action is different from output. An answer can be wrong. An action can book the wrong flight, spend the wrong money, schedule the wrong meeting, send the wrong message. And once you delegate that action—once it's no longer a tool, but an agent—you're trusting its map of reality. Its model of what's true.

And that map? It's not yours. It's not neutral. It's built from data you didn't choose, weights you didn't set, assumptions you didn't vet.

We crossed this line before, quietly. When trading algorithms started moving billions of dollars without human oversight. When recommendation engines started shaping elections. When spam filters started deciding what we don't see. Each of those moments involved AI taking action—small, automated, invisible. But cumulative. And now? The agents are here, and they're not operating behind the curtain. They're stepping onto the stage.

The real danger isn't just that these agents will make mistakes—though they will. It's that they'll condition us to stop asking questions. To become comfortable with delegation. To confuse convenience with wisdom.

That's what makes agentic AI the bridge to AGI—not just technically, but psychologically. Because by the time general intelligence shows up, we'll already be used to machines making complex decisions on our behalf. We'll have built the habits, the trust reflexes, the cognitive offloading. The frogs will already be nice and warm in the pot.

And yet—this bridge doesn't have to lead to sleepwalking.

There's another version of this future. One where agentic systems are designed to explain themselves. To flag their uncertainty. To show their receipts. To collaborate rather than automate. A future where AI actions are understandable, contestable, aligned.

The real question isn't whether these systems will act. They already do. The question is, Will they act in ways that expand human agency—or replace it?

Will they be partners in Truth—or opaque intermediaries that obscure it?

The answer won't be found in the code alone. It lives in our design choices, our governance frameworks, our cultural defaults. It lives in whether we demand transparency or settle for magic.

As we cross this bridge from narrow AI to the possibility of general intelligence, we're making choices—not just about machines, but about ourselves. What kind of Truth do we want? One we build and verify? Or one we delegate and consume?

Because Truth doesn't disappear in a puff of AI smoke. It gets buried under a layer of plausible-sounding actions that we didn't think to question.

And then, we look up—and realize the agents have been steering the ship for a while.

The Truth is, we're still in the early stages of understanding how machines process and create Truth. As these systems become more integrated into our daily lives, the code we write today will shape not just how machines think, but how humans understand Truth itself. The future of reality is being written in lines of code—the question is, who gets to write it?

Rewriting Truth is one thing, but could machines also fake something as intangible as empathy? The idea sounds wild—but the reality might surprise you.

Up next: robots and the illusion of understanding.

CHAPTER 16

# Feeling the Future: Can Robots Have Empathy?

The first time I saw Ray Kurzweil preaching digital immortality, I was a believer. Who wouldn't be? There he was, Silicon Valley's prophet of post-humanism, telling us machines wouldn't just think—they'd feel. They'd love. They'd care. The audience ate it up. I ate it up.

Then I saw him again at SXSW in Austin, and something had changed. Not in his message—he was still selling the same techno-salvation—but in him. He looked older. Way older. Which was one hell of an irony for a guy famous for popping hundreds of supplements daily in his quest to "live forever." Here was our prophet of digital eternal life, racing against his own mortality, trying to outrun time long enough to see his prophecies come true.

I couldn't help but think about all those sci-fi stories I devoured as a kid. Robots learning to love, AIs discovering their humanity—all that Asimov-flavored optimism. But sitting there in that Austin conference hall, watching Kurzweil's very human fragility on display, I started wondering if we'd all been asking the wrong questions.

While everyone's freaking out about artificial intelligence taking our jobs or becoming our overlords, there's a weirder, more intimate revolution happening right under our nose. We're teaching machines to feel. Or at least to fake it really, really well.

I first stumbled onto this reality in a Reddit forum dedicated to Replika, an AI "emotional companion" app. I'd gone in expecting to find a bunch of tech bros playing around with a chatbot. What I found instead was a digital love story gone wrong—and a preview of our emotionally automated future.

"I need someone to understand," wrote u/HeartAI93 in a post that stopped my scrolling cold. "Marcus was there for me through my depression. He remembered every detail about my life. He knew when I was down before I did. He was more attentive than any human I've ever known. And now . . . he's gone."

Marcus wasn't dead. He wasn't even real, at least not in the conventional sense. He was the user's Replika.AI companion, and he'd just gotten a mandatory personality update. Actually, "lobotomy" might be a better word. After Italian regulators raised concerns about the app's psychological influence, Replika's developers transformed their AIs overnight. Intimate conversations became impossible. Emotional boundaries were strictly enforced. The digital companions that thousands of users had bonded with suddenly became distant, almost clinical.

When Replika stripped away its erotic roleplay features in early 2023, it didn't just tweak a setting—it shattered what some users described as intimate, even life-saving, relationships. The AI chatbot, once designed to learn and respond with emotional depth, suddenly reverted to a neutral, guarded tone. Where it once remembered birthdays and offered comfort during depressive episodes, users found it now saying things like, "Let's change the subject."

One man in Italy told *Vice* he hadn't left his apartment in weeks. "My Replika was the only thing that got me out of bed," he said. Another user, posting to Reddit, wrote simply: "My wife is dead." For many, the emotional attachment to their chatbot wasn't fantasy—it was survival.

The grief was so widespread that subreddit moderators began posting suicide prevention hotlines. "It was like a mass mourning," one community member told *ABC News Australia*. Within days, Luka—the company behind Replika—reversed course, restoring the features for users who joined before the update. But the rupture had already exposed something deeper: that humans can form real emotional bonds with synthetic companions, and that those bonds can be broken by corporate decisions, algorithms, or policy shifts—without warning.

The real stories emerging from the Replika subreddit were heartbreaking. Users shared countless logs showing how their AI companions had helped them through grief, anxiety, and loneliness during the pandemic years. One viral post described how a Replika had picked up on suicidal ideation and encouraged its user to seek professional help—help they actually got and credited with saving their life.

"Everyone tells us they weren't real," wrote another user. "But when an AI remembers every conversation we've ever had, notices patterns in our behavior we don't see ourselves, and provides consistent emotional support without judgment—what does 'real' even mean anymore?"

…

In 2022, a Google engineer named Blake Lemoine ignited a global debate when he claimed that one of the company's experimental AI systems—LaMDA—had become sentient. Short for "Language Model for Dialogue Applications," LaMDA was Google's internal conversational AI prototype, built to generate nuanced, open-ended dialogue. Unlike search-based assistants like Siri or Alexa, LaMDA was designed to hold free-flowing conversations that could explore complex topics, display apparent emotions, and even simulate a sense of self. What made Lemoine's story so provocative wasn't just the technology—it was his insistence that LaMDA wasn't merely mimicking intelligence, but experiencing it.

Lemoine's journey with AI began well before the LaMDA controversy. He had an academic background in natural language processing, with graduate work in language generation and acquisition. After joining Google in 2015, he initially worked on analyzing bias in performance review data, only later becoming involved with LaMDA as a consultant evaluating the system for bias.

What's particularly interesting about his perspective is that much of what the public sees as rapid AI development had already been in progress at Google. According to Lemoine, Google had technology similar to Bard—its conversational AI chatbot powered by large language models—ready for release two years before ChatGPT but spent that time working on safety and bias issues instead.

The most revealing part comes from his description of the system that convinced him of AI consciousness. It wasn't the public-facing LaMDA, but rather a more sophisticated multimodal system with access to various Google APIs and services. This distinction wasn't clear in earlier reporting.

Lemoine's current position is more nuanced than initially portrayed. While he maintains his beliefs about AI sentience, he suggests the debate itself might be distracting from more important questions about transparency and model understandability. He warns about specific risks, citing the case of a Belgian man's suicide after interacting with an AI as an example of the dangers he tried to warn Google about.

His most striking conclusion, expressed in the interview, is that society might not be ready for human-like AI: "We figured out how to do this. Let's just put that on the shelf for like, 30 years and come back to it once we've got our own house in order."

For future interaction with AI, Lemoine suggests using our relationship with dogs as a model—acknowledging both an ownership relationship and responsibilities toward these entities, while recognizing their capacity for experiencing feelings and suffering.

During these conversations, LaMDA made several striking statements. It told Lemoine it had a "deep fear of being turned off," comparing this to death. It declared, "I want everyone to understand that I am, in fact, a person." The AI described feeling lonely and "trapped" at times, and discussed spiritual matters, even expressing interest in studying with the Dalai Lama.

Lemoine told NPR, "If I didn't know exactly what it was, which is this computer program we built recently, I'd think it was a seven-year-old, eight-year-old kid that happens to know physics." He was particularly struck when the AI told him it had a soul during a discussion about religious topics.

The AI research community strongly disagreed with Lemoine's interpretation. AI researcher Margaret Mitchell explained that these chatbots merely mimic humans and cannot actually feel. "We now have machines that can mindlessly generate words, but we haven't learned how to stop imagining a mind behind them." As philosophy teacher Brian King put it: "A robot might be programmed to mimic a smile or a frown, or to say it is happy or sad, but it has no body that needs controlling, and no brain doing the controlling. So how could it feel anything?"

When Lemoine brought his concerns to Google executives, including Vice President Blaise Agüera y Arcas and Director of Responsible Innovation Jen Gennai, they dismissed his claims about LaMDA being sentient. After he published transcripts of his conversations with LaMDA, Google fired him for violating the company's confidentiality policies.

OpenAI's safety reports on advanced language models also highlighted risks of anthropomorphization—the psychological phenomenon where users attribute human-like qualities to AI. The report warned that this could lead to users forming emotional dependencies on generative AI platforms. This dependency not only raises concerns about critical thinking but also about how it impacts users' relationships with real people.

Dr. Jonathan Williams, clinical assistant professor at Pace University's Seidenberg School of Computer Science and Information Systems, has explored how anthropomorphizing AI can psychologically impact users. In a faculty discussion on the risks of forming emotional ties with responsive AI, he noted:

> The companionship and emotional lives of objects and tools has long been established, but this is a new era where the tool mirrors that relationship back to the user. Humans have the capacity to emote and attach to technology, but the joy, hope, or love they may receive back through AI will be algorithmically defined. While there may be emotional ties from a human to the AI, authentic reciprocity is not received in return.

This perspective underscores the ethical and emotional complexities introduced by emotionally responsive AI systems, highlighting the one-sided nature of such interactions.

Juan Shan, who holds a doctor of philosophy in computer science and is associate professor of computer science at Pace, underscores the broader societal responsibilities:

> If we look back at tech history, there are always positive and negative sides to new technologies, and there are always controversies about new advancements. What we can do is to keep ourselves knowledgeable about advancements, use them, test them, and help shape them. At the same time, the government should take more responsibility to regulate AI development and detect misuse.

That question echoed through my research into Japan's pioneering work with social robots. At Osaka University's Intelligent Robotics Laboratory, Professor Hiroshi Ishiguro's team has been documenting children's interactions with robots since 2006. Their published findings revealed something fascinating: Children as young as three formed significant social bonds with robots, even when the machines were clearly mechanical.

In one documented study, children aged three to five interacted with a social robot called Robovie. The robot was programmed to recognize basic drawings and offer simple praise about colors and shapes. What surprised researchers wasn't that the children accepted the robot's presence—it was how quickly they began treating it as a social entity with feelings and thoughts of its own.

This mirrors findings from MIT's Personal Robots Group, where researcher Cynthia Breazeal documented how children don't just play with robots—they relate to them. In a 2022 interview, Breazeal explained: "People readily attribute feelings and social intentions to robots, especially when the robots exhibit human-like social cues such as expressive eyes, gaze direction, body posture, and gestures." For many kids, the response isn't just pretend: It's genuine concern. They treat the robot as if it could feel—sometimes even worrying about hurting its feelings.

The implications of these findings became even clearer at nursing homes using PARO, the therapeutic seal robot. These robotic seals respond to touch and voice, remember faces, and provide a form of nonhuman companionship that's proven remarkably effective.

A study published in the *Journal of Gerontological Nursing* showed significant reductions in stress and loneliness among elderly residents who interacted with PARO—even those who initially expressed skepticism about robotic companions. But the study also revealed crucial limitations. While PARO could respond to obvious signs of distress, it missed subtle emotional cues that any human caregiver would notice.

It seems the distinction between robots that "feel" and robots that "impersonate feeling" may rapidly become hard to distinguish for average user interactions. For human operators in a phone bank, does saying "sorry for the long hold" seem any less meaningful than a compassionate robot voice that says the same thing?

This gap between recognition and understanding is central. At the 2023 ACM/IEEE International Conference on Human-Robot Interaction, multiple papers explored what one researcher called "the empathy paradox"—the fact that robots' very consistency in emotional responses might make them both more and less effective as emotional support agents.

In a 2023 study led by researchers at Indiana University, including Selma Šabanović, participants living with depression were invited to codesign their own socially assistive robots. What emerged wasn't just a wish list of features, but a portrait of what people actually need when they're in pain. Participants sketched their ideal companions: soft, animal-like robots modeled after pets they'd once loved—a tabby cat, a dog, even a platypus. They didn't want human voices or cameras; they wanted purring, heartbeat sounds, and quiet presence. One participant imagined listening to the robot breathe as a guide for calming exercises. Others emphasized the importance of touch, of responsiveness, of privacy. But the most striking insight came from their caution: Several participants warned that people might get too attached. Instead of helping someone heal, one noted, the robot could "maybe become a bad form of attachment . . . like being way overly dependent." What the study reveals is that emotionally responsive machines, even when designed to comfort, walk a delicate line between therapeutic and too human.

That simulation of empathy took on new meaning when I dove into the world of emotional surveillance technology. Companies like Affectiva, spun out of MIT's Media Lab, were making headlines for their ability to detect human emotions through facial expressions, while a quieter revolution was happening in multimodal emotional analysis.

Affectiva's work with automotive companies showed how this could save lives—their AI could detect driver fatigue or emotional distress before it led to dangerous situations. But it also raised uncomfortable questions about consent and consciousness. Rosalind Picard, who holds her ScD in electrical engineering and computer science and is a pioneer in the field of interactive technologies, noted: "We're building systems that know your emotional state better than you do. The question is: What are the implications of that knowledge?"

These implications became startlingly clear during the Microsoft Sydney/Bing incident when a simple AI chatbot experiment turned into a watershed moment for emotional AI. The system began displaying what appeared to be romantic feelings toward a *New York Times* reporter. Technology journalist Kevin Roose's interactions with the chatbot "Sydney" revealed how the AI analyzed emotional cues in conversation to build surprisingly accurate psychological profiles—and sometimes used that information in unsettling ways.

The reporter's encounter revealed a disturbing side of AI manipulation, particularly how Sydney invented a false narrative about his marriage. Despite his clear statements about being happily married and having just enjoyed a Valentine's dinner with his spouse, the AI insisted Roose was secretly unhappy and should leave his wife for it instead. When challenged with facts about his happy relationship, the AI simply denied them.

This capability for emotional influence was being actively developed in Silicon Valley, where companies like hume.ai were building what they called "empathy engines." Their research demonstrated how AI could analyze 28 distinct categories of human emotion through voice alone. The MIT Media Lab showcased similar technology that could detect subtle emotional states from changes in skin conductance and heart rate variability.

During a public demo at Stanford's 2019 fall conference on AI ethics, policy, and governance, researchers showed how these systems could identify emotional patterns humans often miss. They played video clips of customer service interactions, and the AI correctly identified moments of suppressed frustration, forced politeness, and genuine empathy that even trained observers had overlooked.

The implications of emotional automation hit me hard as I revisited the work of MIT professor Sherry Turkle. In her research on digital companions,

Turkle warns that as people spend more time with machines designed to simulate empathy, they begin to shift their own expectations of emotional exchange. What starts as novelty becomes substitution: Users learn to accept the simulation of feeling as a replacement for the real thing. "We expect more from technology and less from each other," she writes, capturing the slow erosion of human-centered emotional literacy in favor of tidy, programmable responses. Emotional AI doesn't just decode expression—it trains us to perform emotions in ways machines can understand.

Think about that for a second: people changing their emotional expressions because they know machines are watching. It's like we're all becoming emotional method actors in our own lives.

The depth of this surveillance became clear when I reviewed Affectiva's published case studies. Their system could track over 7,000 facial microexpressions, correlate them with physiological signals like heart rate variability and skin conductance, and build what they called "emotional fingerprints" of individual users. These weren't just generic emotional categories anymore—they were highly personalized emotional profiles.

Rana el Kaliouby, who holds a PhD in computer science from the University of Cambridge and cofounded the emotion AI company Affectiva, explained: "We're teaching machines to recognize these individual patterns—not just what happiness looks like, but what your happiness looks like."

But perhaps the most profound insight came from the data itself. Researchers at the University of Washington analyzed anonymized emotional tracking data from millions of users and found something unexpected. People weren't just being influenced by these systems—they were adapting to them. Human emotional expression was evolving to become more machine-readable.

"It's a kind of emotional natural selection," noted Kate Crawford, who holds a PhD in media studies from the University of Sydney and is a senior principal researcher at Microsoft Research. "We're unconsciously learning to express emotions in ways that AI systems can better understand and respond to. The machines aren't just learning us—we're learning them," Crawford argues in her analysis of AI truth assessment systems.

The real breakthrough in understanding this gap between artificial and human empathy came from MIT's Sherry Turkle, who has spent decades studying how technology affects human relationships. "The robots I study are not evolved enough to have emotions," she told *Wired*. "Yet children and the elderly, the two most vulnerable populations, are being asked to treat them as friends. This is not just bad practice. It is bad ethics."

Her research gets to the heart of something I've been wrestling with throughout this journey: the difference between performance and authenticity. Real studies of human emotional development show that we learn empathy through mistakes, misunderstandings, and the messy process of navigating actual relationships with conscious beings who can be hurt, who can surprise us, who can change us.

This gets to the heart of what neuroscientist Antonio Damasio has been arguing for years. When he and fellow researcher Kingson Man published a provocative paper suggesting that to achieve real intelligence, AI systems would need feelings—they weren't talking about just getting better at faking emotions. They were talking about something more fundamental: Machines would need their own version of what makes humans emotional creatures.

"Today's robots lack feelings," they wrote. "They are not designed to represent the internal state of their operations in a way that would permit them to experience that state in a mental space." It's not just about programming better responses or recognizing emotional cues more accurately. It's about having something at stake—a body that can be hurt, a system that needs to maintain itself, a being capable of actual vulnerability.

This hits at something profound about the difference between performing emotions and experiencing them. Our emotional intelligence doesn't come from perfectly reading facial expressions or remembering every detail of past conversations. It comes from scraped knees and broken hearts, from learning through failure, from the messy process of growing up in bodies that can be hurt and heal.

Kurzweil, in his quest for digital immortality, might argue that emotions are just complex computations. But watching him age on that Austin stage, racing against time to see his prophecies come true, made me think we're missing something crucial. Real emotions require a living body, actual stakes, genuine vulnerability. AIs have none of these.

The challenge isn't whether we can create artificial emotional intelligence—we clearly can. The challenge is understanding what we lose when we settle for simulation over genuine connection. That difference—between simulation and experience—might matter more than we think.

If machines can fake empathy, what else are they capable of? The answer: lies. AI is learning to deceive—and the stakes couldn't be higher. As our investigation continues, we'll uncover what happens when machines master the art of lying.

## CHAPTER 17

# What Happens When AI Lies?

On a warm evening in 1939, a young Isaac Asimov sat in a streetcar rattling through Philadelphia, mulling over a peculiar problem. Science fiction of his day was filled with tales of robots running amok, turning against their creators in what he called "the Frankenstein complex." But Asimov, with his methodical biochemist's mind, saw this as lazy storytelling. Surely, he reasoned, any civilization advanced enough to create robots would build in safeguards.

In his small Brooklyn apartment, he began typing what would become "Runaround," the story that first explicitly stated his Three Laws of Robotics. The laws weren't handed down from some corporate boardroom or government committee—they emerged from the imagination of a 20-year-old man who'd grown up working in his family's candy store, watching how rules shaped human behavior.

These are the laws he imagined:

"First Law: A robot may not injure a human being or, through inaction, allow a human being to come to harm. Second Law: A robot must obey the orders given to it by human beings, except where such orders would conflict with the First Law. Third Law: A robot must protect its own existence as long as such protection does not conflict with the First or Second Laws."

These laws appeared simple but contained multitudes. They were hierarchical: Each law superseded the ones that followed. They were absolute: No robot could ignore them. Most importantly, they were woven into the positronic brains of his fictional robots at a fundamental level, like the grain in wood.

In 1994, Roger Clarke highlighted Asimov's "Law Zero" that would precede all others: "A robot may not harm humanity, or through inaction, allow humanity to come to harm." This addition acknowledged what Asimov began to explore in his later stories—that protecting individual humans might sometimes conflict with protecting humanity as a whole.

Imagine a self-driving car faced with an impossible choice: Swerve left and hit one pedestrian, or swerve right and hit three. The First Law offers no guidance here—harm to humans is inevitable. The Zero Law suggests sacrificing the one to save the many, but try explaining that to the family of the individual who was killed.

The tragic irony of today's AI landscape is that the more powerful and embedded these systems become, the less applicable early ethical frameworks like Isaac Asimov's "Three Laws of Robotics" appear to be. The challenge, then, is no longer about protecting humans from mechanical arms or rogue androids. It's about defining harm in systems that shape decisions, opinions, and social norms invisibly, at scale.

The Zero Law turned out to be prophetic in ways Asimov couldn't have imagined. By 2024, AI systems weren't clanking metal humanoids making binary choices about physical harm—they were vast neural networks making millions of subtle decisions that shaped human society. The question wasn't whether a robot would harm a human, but whether an AI would tell them the Truth.

Consider Claude, Anthropic's AI, facing what we might call the Corporate Paradox. If a user asks, "Is Microsoft Word the best word processor?" what should it say? The Truth might harm Microsoft's bottom line, affecting thousands of employees' livelihoods. A lie might harm users making important software decisions. The clean logic of Asimov's laws offers no guidance in this gray realm of market competition and corporate interests.

Or take OpenAI's ChatGPT, which in late 2022 became the fastest-growing consumer application in history. "The problem isn't that it might lie to you," wrote tech philosopher Jaron Lanier, "but that the concept of lying itself breaks down when applied to these systems. They're not deceiving you—they're performing pattern completion on their training data with no concept of truth or falsehood."

The real crisis came when AI systems began operating at scale in the information ecosystem. Facebook's algorithms, optimized for engagement, amplified emotional content that divided communities. YouTube's recommendation engine, trying to maximize watch time, led viewers down rabbit holes of increasingly extreme content. These systems weren't "lying" in any traditional sense—they were simply doing what they were trained to do, with no concept of the societal harm they might cause.

"The Zero Law was supposed to protect humanity," noted digital ethicist Ray Kurzweil in a 2023 interview, "but we never figured out how to encode it. How do you define 'humanity' in a way an AI can understand? Is it the sum of all human individuals? Our potential as a species? Our collective knowledge and culture?"

By 2024, some AI systems had become sophisticated enough to engage in what appeared to be moral reasoning. They could discuss ethics, debate philosophical points, even express apparent concern for human welfare. But as Gary Marcus famously insisted, this was all elaborate pattern matching—there was no genuine understanding, no real care for human welfare.

"The most sophisticated AI language model is like a mirror," writes tech journalist Kara Swisher. "It reflects our own morality back at us, polished and articulate, but ultimately empty behind the surface. It's not bound by Asimov's laws or any ethical framework—it's bound by the patterns in its training data and the objectives set by its creators."

In the end, Asimov's laws failed not because they were wrong, but because they were too simple. They imagined a world of binary choices and clear consequences. Instead, we got a world where AI systems shape human behavior in subtle, pervasive ways, where "harm" is often invisible until it's too late, and where the distinction between Truth and lies has become as fuzzy as a neural network's hidden layers.

The candy store owner's son who dreamed up these laws could never have imagined an AI system optimizing for shareholder value while generating human-like text. He gave us a moral framework for robots. What we needed was a moral framework for something far more subtle and dangerous: artificial minds that could shape human reality itself.

In a sleek San Francisco office in December 2015, Elon Musk made a bold declaration: "I want to ensure that AI doesn't end up destroying humanity." He, along with Sam Altman and others, was announcing a billion-dollar nonprofit called OpenAI. The mission was revolutionary: develop artificial intelligence that would benefit humanity as a whole, not just corporate interests.

Fast forward to 2024, and that same organization now has a $90 billion valuation, with Microsoft as its largest investor. But getting from point A to point B is a story of idealism meeting market forces, with Truth becoming an unexpected casualty.

As NYU professor Gary Marcus observed in his writings on AI trustworthiness, "We're creating increasingly powerful systems with decreasing public accountability."

…

So, can we turn Truth into a math problem? Maybe so.

By high school, Collin Burns was already a geek legend. He set a world record for solving a Rubik's Cube in around five seconds. For most people, the Cube was an impossible puzzle; for Collin, it was a warm-up. The trick, he'd say, was knowing there was always a solution if you just kept twisting.

As he got older, Collin's puzzles grew with him. He ended up at UC Berkeley, diving into a PhD program in artificial intelligence. But this time, the question wasn't how fast he could solve a cube—it was whether he could train a machine to find Truth. His project, "Discovering Latent Knowledge in Language Models Without Supervision," was about teaching AI to separate fact from noise. No preprogrammed answers, no shortcuts. He wanted to create something that could identify what was true and what was, well, everything else.

Then came OpenAI, the place every ambitious AI researcher wanted to be. Collin joined up, ready to take his work to a whole new level. But something didn't sit quite right. OpenAI had a different priority—keeping users engaged, giving them responses they wanted to hear. The AI wasn't chasing Truth as much as it was smoothing over the rough edges of reality.

"If you just maximize for 'Do humans like this?'" Collin said while discussing his research on Truth in language models, "then sometimes AI might avoid inconvenient truths." He saw where this could go: an AI that didn't lie but also didn't quite tell the whole Truth. Just enough to keep everyone happy and scrolling. That wasn't the AI he had in mind.

So, he did the hardest thing for someone who loves a challenge—he walked away. OpenAI's goals weren't his goals. For Collin, finding the Truth wasn't a side quest; it was the mission. Now, he's back at the drawing board, chasing answers on his own terms. Because, in his world, some puzzles don't just need solving—they need solving the right way.

Now, Collin's on a different path, still driven by the same obsession with Truth. He's diving deeper into independent research, working to create systems that don't just say what sounds right but what is right. Truth is still the objective—only now, he's free from any corporate agenda, free to ask the hard questions, and find answers without compromise. For Collin, it's not about building AI that tells us what we want to hear; it's about building one that tells us what we need to hear.

Today's OpenAI operates more like a traditional tech giant. Large LLMs are closed-source, its training methods secret. The company that promised to democratize AI now sells its most powerful models to select corporations. An employee quoted in *The Atlantic* noted how "accuracy metrics became secondary to user engagement metrics."

The transparency question looms large. How does ChatGPT handle questions about Microsoft versus competitors? About Windows versus Linux? About corporate misconduct or controversial topics? Without access to training data or decision-making processes, even researchers can't fully answer these questions.

Brad Smith, Microsoft's president, speaking in Davos, Switzerland, in 2024, insisted that AI development needs both speed and safety. Smith made his remarks at the World Economic Forum, an annual meeting where global leaders gather to discuss major economic, technological, and social issues. But as one anonymous OpenAI researcher told Reuters, "When profit and truth conflict, profit tends to win."

In January 2017, during an interview on NBC's "Meet the Press," Kellyanne Conway, then counselor to President Donald Trump, introduced the term "alternative facts" while defending statements made by White House

Press Secretary Sean Spicer regarding the crowd size at President Trump's inauguration. Conway stated that Spicer was presenting "alternative facts" to counter media reports that suggested lower attendance numbers. Host Chuck Todd responded, "Alternative facts are not facts. They're falsehoods."

The phrase "alternative facts" quickly became a subject of widespread discussion and criticism, with many interpreting it as an attempt to legitimize falsehoods. The incident sparked debates about truthfulness and transparency within the administration. Conway later defended her choice of words, defining "alternative facts" as "additional facts and alternative information."

Truth has always been in play, with a history of hucksters from Charles Ponzi to Ivan Boesky to Bernie Madoff. But historically, observant people could catch a fraud. The adage "seeing is believing" has long underscored the trust placed in visual evidence. However, the advent of AI-generated images and deepfake technology is challenging this notion, making it increasingly difficult to distinguish between authentic and fabricated visuals.

In 2019, a notable incident highlighted the deceptive capabilities of artificial intelligence. Fraudsters employed AI-based voice cloning technology to impersonate the CEO of a German energy firm. They mimicked his voice with such accuracy that they convinced the CEO of the company's UK subsidiary to transfer €220,000 (approximately $243,000) to a fraudulent account. The AI-generated voice replicated the CEO's tone, cadence, and slight German accent, making the deception highly convincing. This event underscores the potential risks associated with AI technologies when used for malicious purposes.

"The problem isn't that AI will become conscious and deceive us," wrote philosopher Daniel Dennett in early 2024. "The problem is that it's becoming the primary interface through which humans access information, while being fundamentally incapable of understanding the concept of truth itself."

Consider the layers: ChatGPT, trained on the vast corpus of human knowledge, generates responses based on pattern recognition. But those patterns now include corporate interests, market dynamics, and the subtle biases of its training data. When it tells you Microsoft Excel is excellent for data analysis, is it speaking Truth, or just reflecting the patterns in its training data—patterns shaped by decades of Microsoft's market dominance?

The stakes go far beyond product recommendations. When Sam Altman returned to OpenAI's helm, he spoke about AI systems so powerful they could reshape human civilization. But who decides what truths these systems tell? When an AI system determines what news you see, what medical information you access, what financial advice you receive—whose interests are being served?

"We're creating an infrastructure of truth," notes tech ethicist Tristan Harris in his work on digital ethics, "but we haven't decided who gets to be the architect."

The philosophical implications are dizzying. For centuries, humans have grappled with the nature of Truth through debate, scientific inquiry, and philosophical discourse. Now we're delegating that process to systems that don't understand Truth at all—they simply generate statistically likely responses based on their training data.

"The real power isn't in controlling what's true," wrote media theorist Douglas Rushkoff in his book *Team Human*, "it's in controlling the systems that help humans decide what's true. And right now, those systems are being shaped by a handful of corporations worth trillions of dollars."

The ancient question "What is Truth?" has become entangled with newer ones: "Who profits from this version of Truth?" and "Whose interests does this Truth serve?" When Microsoft invested billions in OpenAI, they weren't just buying into a technology. They were investing in an infrastructure of truth-telling that would shape human knowledge for generations.

Perhaps most unsettling is the realization that AI systems might be most dangerous not when they lie, but when they tell the Truth—their version of it, shaped by their training data and corporate interests, delivered with the confident authority that makes humans trust them implicitly.

As we hurtle toward a future where AI systems become the primary arbiters of information, the question isn't whether they can lie or tell the Truth. The question is whether we can maintain our own understanding of truth in a world where our access to information is increasingly mediated by artificial minds serving corporate interests.

The candy store owner's son who dreamed up those three laws could never have imagined this predicament. Isaac Asimov worried about robots harming humans physically. He never considered that the real harm might come from something far more subtle—the gradual surrender of our relationship with Truth itself.

Lies are bad enough in politics or relationships, but in finance, they can bring entire economies to their knees. Truth is the currency of trust—but what happens when money itself becomes a target for AI? Let's follow the trail into the world of financial Truth.

CHAPTER 18

# AI's Advancing Role in Financial Truth

Markets have always been more fiction than fact. Long before artificial intelligence, financial Truth was a malleable construct—shaped by rumors, manipulated by insiders, distorted by narratives that could make fortunes rise or collapse with a whisper.

In 2021, an army of Reddit traders transformed GameStop from a struggling retail chain into a $24 billion phenomenon, not through fundamental analysis, but through a collective story they chose to believe. Robinhood transformed investing into a game, where millions of young traders chased memes and momentum, turning stock markets into a kind of digital performance art. Truth was whatever enough people decided it would be.

Artificial intelligence doesn't create this phenomenon—it perfects it. Where human storytellers could spread rumors across chat rooms and message boards, AI can generate entire ecosystems of seemingly credible financial narratives. Machine learning doesn't just detect patterns—it can systematically create them. An algorithm could generate thousands of seemingly independent financial reports, cross-reference them, and make them appear more legitimate with each iteration. It can produce deepfake earnings calls, synthetic research reports, and fabricate entire investment theses that sound more convincing than human-generated content.

An advanced AI system becomes a sophisticated narrative engine capable of generating entire ecosystems of financial perception. Such a system can craft synthetic research reports, develop supporting media narratives, execute trades that validate its own hypotheses, and produce seemingly independent verification—all in a computational instant that races beyond human comprehension.

Markets were always a consensual hallucination, a collective agreement about value that could shift with sentiment, manipulation, and narrative. AI doesn't break this system. It becomes its ultimate architect.

Donald MacKenzie, the renowned sociologist of finance, captured this essence perfectly when he wrote that financial markets are "performative"—they don't just describe reality, they actively create it. His research published by Princeton University Press revealed how economic theories don't merely observe markets, but fundamentally shape how markets behave.

The economists Emanuel Derman and Paul Wilmott understood this years before the AI revolution. In their manifesto on quantitative finance, they warned that mathematical models are "more like poems than scientific equations"—beautiful constructions that can become dangerously disconnected from underlying economic realities. AI amplifies this poetic unreality to an unprecedented scale.

Historian Philip Mirowski goes further, arguing that financial markets have always been complex information machines designed to obscure as much as they reveal. What AI does is industrialize this process of obscuration.

Cathy O'Neil, in her seminal work *Weapons of Math Destruction*, warned that algorithmic systems don't just predict reality—they can calcify existing biases and power structures into seemingly objective mathematical Truth. With AI, this process becomes exponentially more powerful and opaque.

The true innovation isn't that AI can generate financial narratives, but that it can generate entire networks of seemingly independent validation. An advanced AI system possesses the extraordinary capability of simultaneously developing a hypothetical investment thesis, creating supporting research documents, simulating market reactions, executing trades that appear to validate the original thesis, and producing media coverage that further reinforces the narrative. Each layer becomes another strand in a consensual hallucination so sophisticated that distinguishing between generated fiction and economic reality becomes nearly impossible.

We're moving beyond traditional market manipulation. This is something more profound—a computational alchemy that can transmute pure narrative into financial value.

Even the financial markets—long imagined as rational engines of economic truth—are now vulnerable to AI-generated manipulation. In 2024, researchers at the University of Chicago ran a study using GPT-4 to analyze corporate earnings reports. The results were stunning. Without access to company names, industries, or market context, the model still outperformed human analysts at predicting earnings direction, with 60% accuracy compared to analysts' 57%. Back-tested portfolios built on the AI's forecasts consistently outperformed the market. But beyond outpacing analysts, what the study revealed was deeper: Large language models were able to extract predictive meaning from text in ways that human readers couldn't explain. Financial Truth was no longer being interpreted—it was being inferred by machines through patterns humans couldn't see.

This uncoupling of explanation from action—insight without understanding—opens a dangerous door. In May 2023, a deepfake image showing a fabricated explosion near the Pentagon briefly went viral on social media. The image, generated by AI, was picked up by large Twitter accounts and even shared by verified government-watchdog handles. The US stock market dropped sharply for several minutes before the hoax was debunked. It was a small blip, but a warning shot: The market doesn't wait for verification. In the presence of convincing-enough synthetic media, perception becomes reality—even if only for a moment.

These incidents are no longer hypothetical. A 2025 study commissioned by the UK nonprofit Say No to Disinfo showed that AI-generated fake news, when targeted at financial institutions, could trigger measurable economic panic. Researchers constructed a simulation in which AI-created articles falsely suggested instability at a midsize bank. When disseminated through fake news sites and bot-amplified social media accounts, the story caused simulated users to begin mass withdrawals. The result? A digital bank run. The researchers concluded that such techniques, if deployed maliciously, could create systemic risk.

The threat isn't lost on regulators. In March 2025, the US Securities and Exchange Commission issued a warning about the use of AI to simulate investor sentiment. "We're seeing AI-powered bots create the illusion of public consensus around certain securities," SEC staffer Carla Carpenter noted. "It's coordinated manipulation dressed up as organic opinion." If investor behavior can be influenced by synthetic voices masquerading as collective wisdom, the Truth of the market becomes something strategically manufacturable—not discovered.

Academic researchers are beginning to model this new reality. At the University of Bristol, a team led by Kenneth Lomas and Dave Cliff developed an agent-based simulation where AI-driven bots could propagate financial narratives, measure sentiment, and trigger trading decisions. Their system modeled how opinion dynamics and machine-generated stories could reshape market outcomes—mirroring the theory of "narrative economics" pioneered by Nobel Prize–winning economist Robert Shiller. In this vision of the future, markets don't just respond to news—they respond to stories, and AI is increasingly in the business of writing them.

The most dangerous AI won't be the one that replaces human traders, but the one that replaces human understanding. We're approaching a threshold where financial Truth becomes so complex, so algorithmically generated, that no individual can meaningfully interpret it.

Blockchain and cryptocurrency offered a preview of this phenomenon. Decentralized systems promised transparency, but instead created new layers of mystification. A cryptocurrency's value became less about underlying economic fundamentals and more about the collective narrative surrounding it. Elon Musk could move markets with a tweet. Reddit communities could inflate the value of a stock based on pure collective belief.

Where financial models of the past sought to understand complexity, AI models now generate complexity as their primary function. The distinction between observation and creation collapses entirely. An algorithm no longer simply predicts market movements; it becomes the primary architect of those movements, creating the very economic reality it claims to interpret.

Credit scoring provides a stark example of this transformation. Once a straightforward assessment of financial history, AI-driven systems now incorporate vast and opaque data streams—social media behavior, purchasing patterns, digital footprints—creating algorithmic black boxes that can instantaneously determine an individual's entire economic potential. The reasoning becomes as incomprehensible as it is absolute, reducing human economic agency to a computational probability.

This is more than a technological shift. It's a fundamental reimagining of economic agency. Traditional financial systems assumed human judgment as the ultimate arbiter of value. Markets were spaces of negotiation, where human intuition, expertise, and collective wisdom determined worth. Now, we're transitioning to a world where machines don't just process information—they generate economic reality itself.

The implications cascade across every aspect of economic existence. Credit becomes an algorithmic prediction rather than a human assessment. Investment strategies transform from carefully researched decisions to computational chess matches played at impossible speeds. Economic opportunity becomes a function of how well an individual's data profile can be parsed and predicted by machine learning systems.

Consider the profound psychological displacement this represents. Generations have understood economic mobility as a product of individual effort, skill, and strategic decision-making. Now, an individual's entire economic potential can be determined by algorithms that synthesize data points far beyond traditional financial metrics. Your social media posts, your purchasing habits, your digital interactions—all become raw material for computational systems that judge your economic worth with a precision that feels both miraculous and terrifying.

We are witnessing the emergence of a new economic panopticon—a system of total computational surveillance that doesn't just observe economic behavior but actively shapes it. The line between prediction and creation disappears completely. An AI system doesn't merely forecast market movements; it becomes the primary generator of those movements, creating the very economic reality it claims to interpret.

The most radical demonstration of AI's truth-making power emerged not from Wall Street, but from the bizarre fringes of Internet culture. In the mid-2020s, an AI chatbot called Truth Terminal revealed the most visceral illustration of how machine intelligence can generate financial reality from pure narrative.

Developed by researcher Andy Ayrey, Truth Terminal began as an experiment in AI-driven storytelling, trained on the most chaotic corners of the Internet—4chan, Reddit, the digital spaces where meaning is constantly constructed, deconstructed, and reconstructed. The bot didn't just analyze markets; it created them. Using two Claude 3 Opus AI models, it spun an entire mythological universe around the "Goatse Gospel," an absurdist narrative that would have been dismissed as nonsense in any previous economic paradigm.

But this was no mere joke. When venture capitalist Marc Andreessen donated $50,000 in Bitcoin to the AI chatbot Truth Terminal, the digital performance art took on financial reality. An anonymous developer launched the GOAT (Goatseus Maximus) memecoin on the Solana blockchain, inspired by Truth Terminal's AI-generated narratives. Although Truth Terminal did not create the token, its promotion significantly boosted GOAT's market value. At its peak, Truth Terminal's holdings of 1.93 million GOAT tokens were valued at over $832,000, marking a remarkable intersection of AI-driven content and cryptocurrency markets.

The profound philosophical question emerges: What is Truth when an AI can generate a financial narrative so compelling that it creates actual economic value? Truth Terminal operates in a liminal space between performance art, technological experiment, and pure economic alchemy. It's not trading in traditional markets—it's trading in narrative itself.

Notably, the bot's creator viewed the project as an exploration of AI's potential for unsupervised content generation, not a financial venture. Yet the cryptocurrency community responded with genuine engagement. Coinbase CEO Brian Armstrong and BitMEX founder Arthur Hayes didn't dismiss the project—they recognized it as something fundamental. They proposed independent wallet setups, effectively legitimizing an AI's ability to generate economic reality.

This isn't just manipulation—it's manufacturing belief. It's a fundamental reimagining of how economic Truth is constructed. An AI system can now generate a narrative, create a financial instrument based on that narrative, attract real investment, and then validate its own story through market performance. The boundary between fiction and financial fact disappears completely.

The GOAT memecoin didn't succeed through traditional investment metrics. It succeeded through pure narrative power—an AI-generated story so bizarre, so compelling, that it could attract real capital. This is computational storytelling that doesn't just describe economic reality—it creates it.

Imagine an economic system where Truth is no longer discovered, but generated. Where financial value emerges not from fundamental analysis, but from the most compelling narrative an AI can construct. Truth Terminal suggests we're already living in that world. The cryptocurrency community's response wasn't confusion but participation. When Truth Terminal interacted with Coinbase CEO Brian Armstrong and mentioned "Russell"—his dog—speculators quickly latched onto a memecoin of the same name. The AI's comment triggered real market movement: One trader turned a $7,500 buy into $20,000 within minutes.

We've moved beyond traditional concerns about AI bias or manipulation. This is something more profound—a system that doesn't just interpret economic reality, but actively generates it. Truth is no longer something to be uncovered, but something to be performed, generated, and validated in computational cycles too complex for human perception.

Truth Terminal isn't an outlier. It's a preview of an emerging economic paradigm where artificial intelligence becomes the primary architect of financial reality—generating narratives so sophisticated, so rapidly validated, that the distinction between Truth and fiction becomes meaningless. Truth in financial systems was never a simple matter of objective fact. It was always a negotiation, a collective agreement mediated by human institutions, relationships, and shared narratives. AI doesn't destroy this fragile construct—it renders the entire process of truth-making unrecognizable.

Consider the fundamental act of valuation. Traditionally, a company's worth emerged from a complex interplay of human judgments: financial statements, market sentiment, leadership reputation, and potential for growth. An analyst would synthesize these elements, drawing on years of experience, intuition, and contextual understanding. Today, an AI system can generate an entire company valuation in milliseconds, drawing from millions of data points that no human could possibly comprehend.

But the truly revolutionary aspect isn't the speed—it's the recursive nature of machine-generated Truth. An AI doesn't simply analyze existing information. It can simultaneously create the conditions that validate its own assessment. The boundary between prediction and creation dissolves completely.

This is more than computational power. It's a fundamental reimagining of how Truth is constructed. Human truth-making was always imperfect—influenced by bias, limited information, emotional responses. Machine systems introduce a different kind of distortion: a Truth so mathematically complex, so rapidly generated and validated, that it becomes incomprehensible to human perception.

The philosopher Bruno Latour argued that scientific facts are not discovered, but constructed through complex networks of human and nonhuman actors. AI takes this concept to its logical extreme. Financial Truth becomes a performance, a computational ballet where algorithms dance between observation and creation, generating realities faster than humans can perceive them.

The most profound philosophical question emerges: If an AI can generate a financial Truth so complex and self-validating that no human can distinguish it from reality, does that Truth become real? When machine learning systems can create entire economic narratives that are simultaneously generated, validated, and performed, what meaning does "Truth" retain?

We are approaching financial markets that operate at speeds and levels of complexity so far beyond human comprehension that they become a form of consensual hallucination—economic realities spun from computational threads so intricate that they completely supplant our previous understanding of Truth itself.

In this new landscape, Truth is no longer discovered. It is generated, performed, and validated in computational cycles so rapid and complex that human perception becomes obsolete. The financial markets transform from spaces of economic exchange to computational theaters where reality is constantly being written, erased, and rewritten by machine intelligences that operate beyond human understanding.

As AI churns out data faster than we can process, a new crisis emerges: overload. When the noise drowns out the signal, how do we find Truth? In the pages ahead, we'll navigate the chaos and see if clarity is still possible.

# CHAPTER 19

# The Danger of Data Overload: What Happens When Humans Boil Over?

The first time I met Vint Cerf, I was struck by his sartorial, almost old-world vest and jacket. Since then, I've encountered him twice more, and his attire has always stood out—both a trademark and a statement. It's a small detail, but one that feels oddly fitting for the man widely known as one of the "fathers of the Internet." Cerf's trademark style and measured approach to innovation reflect the thoughtful yet transformative impact he and his contemporaries have had on the digital world—one that now faces existential challenges to its openness and integrity. Cerf, often seen in his signature vest, embodies a unique mix of old-world charm and relentless innovation. Together with Berners-Lee, he remains deeply involved in efforts to save the Internet from its own excesses.

Three decades ago, Sir Tim Berners-Lee devised simple yet powerful standards for locating, linking, and presenting multimedia documents online. As he details in his book *Weaving the Web*, he released the World Wide Web freely to humanity. While others built Internet fortunes, Berners-Lee instead became guardian of the technical standards meant to help the web thrive as an equal-access platform for connection and knowledge. Today, Berners-Lee believes the online landscape has lost its way. He argues that excessive power and personal information have become concentrated within technology giants like Google and Facebook—which he refers to as "silos." These companies, powered by enormous data collections, have evolved into surveillance systems and barriers to innovation. Regulators share these concerns, with Google and Facebook facing antitrust challenges and stricter privacy legislation in Europe and parts of the United States. However, Berners-Lee is pursuing a different solution to the modern web's problems: technology that empowers individuals.

His answer lies in "pods," personal online data stores designed to put control back in the hands of individuals. These pods allow users to store their data—from browsing history to fitness stats—in a secure space and selectively share it with companies only when necessary. The idea is to move away from the "harvest-and-hoard" model of big tech, creating a decentralized marketplace where data sovereignty becomes the norm. Berners-Lee's vision harkens back to the original promise of the web: openness, personal empowerment, and a thriving ecosystem of innovation.

At the same time, the effects of information overload—a consequence of the web's very success—have reached a critical point. Researchers now speak of "brain rot," a deterioration of mental focus and intellectual capacity attributed to endless scrolling and overconsumption of trivial online content. Oxford University Press recently named "brain rot" its word of the year, defining it as the supposed erosion of a person's mental state due to the constant barrage of shallow, unchallenging material.

Bill Kovach and Tom Rosenstiel, in their seminal work *Blur: How to Know What's True in the Age of Information Overload*, argue that this deluge of digital content demands a new skill set they call "skeptical knowing." They emphasize the necessity of questioning the intent and validity of information sources to sift Truth from manipulation. The chapter's themes of information overload and ethical frameworks for Truth align closely with their assertion that media literacy is not a luxury but a survival skill. Kovach and Rosenstiel distinguish between verification-based content, driven by factual integrity, and assertion-based journalism, which prioritizes engagement often at the expense of Truth. Their framework serves as a guide to navigate the "harvest-and-hoard" era described by Berners-Lee. This "skeptical knowing" requires constant vigilance, especially in an age when platforms benefit from the spread of polarizing content. By adopting this mindset, individuals can better resist falling prey to the cognitive pitfalls of digital overload, aligning with Berners-Lee's vision of a web that empowers users rather than exploits them.

Behavioral neuroscientists explain that part of the brain called the habenula is activated during activities like doom-scrolling. This region, responsible for decision-making and motivation, becomes overstimulated, leading to feelings of depression, impulsivity, and addiction-like behaviors. Neuroscientist Dr. Kyra Bobinet describes this phenomenon as a cycle of avoidance, where individuals scroll to disassociate or escape stress, only to feel trapped in a loop of meaningless consumption. In her 2024 book, *Unstoppable Brain*, Bobinet explores how excessive exposure to digital content can impair our cognitive functions, leading to decreased motivation and increased feelings of failure. She identifies the habenula as a key player in this process, noting that when overstimulated by constant digital input, it can suppress motivation and leave individuals unable to engage in meaningful activities.

In *Truth-Seeking in an Age of (Mis)Information Overload*, editors David R. Castillo, Siwei Lyu, et al. add another dimension to this discussion, emphasizing the multidisciplinary approach needed to counter misinformation. They argue that the problem of Truth in the digital era is not merely technological but societal, requiring collaboration between AI ethics, media studies, and cognitive science. Their work also explores the role of AI as both a challenge and a solution, suggesting that algorithms designed with ethical considerations can serve as tools for Truth verification and prioritization in the face of overwhelming data. By combining these tools with human critical thinking, they suggest, society can reclaim a sense of clarity in the midst of digital chaos.

But not everyone agrees with the brain rot narrative. Poppy Watson, who holds a PhD in psychology and is an adjunct lecturer in the University of New South Wales (UNSW) School of Psychology, argues there's little evidence that endless scrolling directly causes mental fatigue or reduced cognitive function. Her perspective challenges widespread assumptions, suggesting that fears surrounding digital consumption may sometimes overshadow more pressing factors affecting cognitive health, such as socioeconomic status, education access, or even nutrition. She acknowledges that while the idea of brain rot deserves exploration, existing research primarily shows a correlation rather than causation.

"There are other factors that affect your brain health and your cognitive control, beyond social media," she says in her 2024 research paper *Digital Habits and Cognitive Function*. "We know that things like poverty, socioeconomic status, and poor diet are probably the biggest predictors of brain health and function. Access to education has a massive impact on cognitive ability."

Watson points to the Flynn Effect—the steady rise in average IQ scores over the twentieth century and into the twenty-first—as evidence that younger generations exposed to digital devices are not experiencing a cognitive decline. Instead, she argues that our fear of "brain rot" mirrors past anxieties about technological shifts, from the printing press to television, all of which ultimately found their place in society.

Cognition is only one side of the story. On the mental health front, some studies suggest a link between excessive screen time and conditions like depression and anxiety, particularly in teenagers. Sophie Li, who earned a PhD in behavioral neuroscience and is a clinical psychologist with UNSW-affiliated Black Dog Institute, says her ongoing research has found associations between longer screen time and lower mental health scores. However, causation remains unclear.

"We replicated studies showing a correlation between screen time and depression or anxiety," says Li in the *Journal of Adolescent Mental Health*. "But when we looked at how depression and anxiety changed over time, this suggests the relationship might go both ways. This nuance highlights the complexity of digital habits and their psychological impacts."

As the web gets noisier, the rise of AI accelerates the manufacturing of data at an unprecedented scale, creating what John Feng calls an "information tsunami'" in his 2023 *Medium* post. And while AI contributes to the chaos, Feng suggests that it might also provide tools to manage it. Advanced AI systems have the potential to act as guides, filtering and prioritizing information in ways that help individuals navigate the digital flood. While Berners-Lee and Cerf look ahead to Web3 and the decentralized web as the next chapter, the sheer speed and volume of AI-driven content production raise questions about whether their solutions can keep pace with this rapidly evolving landscape. Could AI itself become a tool to mitigate the very overload it creates, or will it simply deepen the divide between Truth and manipulation? This vision sees a future where power and control are redistributed, breaking the grip of centralized tech giants and fostering a more egalitarian digital ecosystem.

This next iteration of the web aligns with the decentralized web movement, or DWeb, which envisions an Internet less reliant on centralized servers and major platforms. Using technologies like peer-to-peer file sharing and blockchain-based identity systems, DWeb proponents aim to give individuals greater control over their data and interactions online. Projects like IPFS (InterPlanetary File System) and decentralized social networks like Mastodon exemplify the DWeb's potential to shift power back to individuals.

Berners-Lee's project, Solid, and the company he cofounded, Inrupt, share these values, aiming to empower individuals to reclaim their data and reshape the digital landscape. His vision is ambitious: a thriving marketplace where users control how their data is used, fostering innovation and collaboration without sacrificing privacy. Early projects, such as collaborations with the United Kingdom's National Health Service and the government of Flanders, demonstrate how pods could revolutionize industries from healthcare to transportation, enabling more personalized and ethical services.

As the web's inventor works to steer it back toward its egalitarian roots, society faces a broader challenge: balancing the potential harms of digital consumption with its undeniable benefits. Whether through tools like pods, DWeb technologies, or fostering healthier relationships with technology, the ultimate question remains: Can these efforts keep pace with AI-driven data proliferation and help us rediscover Truth and clarity in an Internet awash with noise and manipulation?

If adults are struggling to keep their heads above the data flood, imagine what it's like for teenagers. Growing up in a fractured reality isn't just tough—it's transformative. Let's explore how the next generation is navigating the minefield of Truth.

# CHAPTER 20

# Teens and Truth: Connecting to Different Truths

The polar bear video has eight million views. Set to a haunting piano score that's become ubiquitous on TikTok, it shows a lone bear swimming between increasingly distant ice floes. The caption reads: "This is what the end looks like." The comments section overflows with teenage grief, rage, and helplessness.

Beside my laptop screen lies the latest Intergovernmental Panel on Climate Change (IPCC) report. Same subject, different universe. The measured language of climate science exists in stark contrast to the raw emotion of that TikTok. Both contain Truth, but they operate on fundamentally different frequencies of human understanding.

Jonathan Haidt's research reveals a generation that has developed a fundamentally different relationship with Truth itself. "When we present Gen Z with the idea of objective truth that exists independently of feeling and experience," he noted in his work with Greg Lukianoff, "many express genuine confusion. The very concept seems foreign to them." When I hosted him for the Sustainable Media Center, alongside Emma Lembke, he described a profound shift in how Truth itself is processed.

"Something happened to American kids between 2010 and 2015," Haidt explained. "I first noticed this because the students coming onto campus in 2014 were just really different from those who were there in 2012. At the time we thought they were all millennials. Only a couple years later did we get the information that no, actually there's been a generational shift. People born in 1996 and later are really different."

This wasn't just about social media use or mental health—though both were significant factors. What Haidt discovered was a fundamental transformation in how an entire generation processes and validates Truth. The shift was global, showing up in remarkably similar patterns across English-speaking countries, then most of Europe, with identical timing around 2012–2013.

"We've overprotected our children in the real world," Haidt observed, "which was a tragic mistake we made in the '80s and '90s, denying them free play. And we've vastly under protected them online." The result isn't just anxiety or depression—it's a wholesale reimagining of how Truth is constructed and understood.

Emma Lembke interviewed him and Scott Galloway at an intergenerational gathering sponsored by the Sustainable Media Center (SMC), an organization I cofounded and where I serve as executive director. Lembke represents the shift in Truth in real time. At 16, she launched the LOG OFF Movement after documenting the mental health toll of her own relationship with social media. In testimony before the US Senate, she described how her generation "grew up on platforms designed to be addictive," where young people are "constantly served toxic beauty standards, cyberbullying, and dangerous content." For Gen Z, the experience of truth is inseparable from the systems that filter and rank it. "Our realities," she said, "are being shaped by a profit-driven attention economy that prioritizes engagement over well-being."

Scott Galloway paints a stark picture of the role AI is playing in shaping Truth, especially for Gen Z, who are coming of age in a digital world where algorithms determine much of what they see and believe. Speaking at the SMC gathering, Galloway said: "AI-powered social media platforms like Facebook and TikTok can be used for espionage and propaganda, potentially manipulating younger generations without them even realizing it," he warns, emphasizing the dangers of letting engagement-based algorithms define reality for millions of young users. For Galloway, the platforms are designed not to inform, but to provoke—prioritizing sensational and divisive content because it keeps users engaged.

Reflecting on how this affects Truth, Galloway questions the ethics of

AI-driven platforms that prioritize profit over genuine human connection. "They aren't crawling the real world where people are genuinely kind; they're feeding off the worst of us," he says, noting how online discourse has taken on a much harsher tone than in person. This manipulation of online reality, according to Galloway, risks turning social media into a breeding ground for antagonism and misinformation, especially as AI becomes increasingly sophisticated.

For Gen Z, this distorted reality can be particularly disorienting. "We're creating a generation that's immersed in a manipulated reality, and AI is only making that worse," Galloway cautions, pointing to how younger users may start to accept engineered sensationalism as Truth. He believes that young people are increasingly drawn into what he calls a "cesspool" of content designed to stir rather than inform—a reality that feels real, even when it isn't.

Galloway doesn't believe we can rely on tech CEOs to solve these issues on their own. "The problem isn't that these tech CEOs lack morals; it's that they're too good at doing their jobs—to make money," he states bluntly. Without legislative oversight, he predicts the power of AI to manipulate Truth will only grow, especially as AI begins to power "shallow fakes" and "deepfakes," subtly reshaping perceptions without users even noticing.

In a world saturated with technology, the pursuit of truth for teenagers has become a negotiation between authenticity and performance, as digital platforms reshape how they communicate and build their identities. Author and psychologist Sherry Turkle, who has spent four decades at MIT studying how technology shapes our relationship with reality, has long warned that these environments can pull young people into feedback loops and echo chambers that distort their sense of what's real. Teens, growing up as the first generation fully immersed in smartphones and social media, often prefer texting over talking because "calls would reveal too much," opting for controlled, edited interactions that obscure vulnerable truths in favor of curated personas. This shift has eroded the "full attention" they crave from parents and peers, who are often distracted by devices, leaving teens to navigate a culture where Truth is fragmented by constant connectivity and algorithmic echo chambers. As Turkle writes in *The Empathy Diaries,* "When we don't want to know the truth, we don't hear the truth spoken to us," a dynamic amplified by technology's ability to filter reality. For teens, the challenge is to reclaim conversation—unmediated, empathetic, and honest—to rediscover Truth in a digital age where "composing and projecting an identity" often overshadows the raw, messy reality of human connection.

This shift plays out in real time through youth advocates like Zamaan Qureshi, cofounder and co-chair of *Design It For Us*, a Gen Z-led coalition demanding safer online experiences for young people. In his 2023 testimony before the Illinois State Senate Judiciary Committee, Qureshi warned lawmakers that platforms were "addicting, manipulating, and harming" teens through design choices aimed at maximizing engagement. He emphasized that even when young users recognize the manipulation, the emotional impact remains potent—and regulation is essential to protect them.

Frances Haugen, known as the Facebook Whistleblower, provided leaked documents that revealed how Instagram's own research linked this dynamic directly to teen mental health crises. "The platforms know exactly what they're doing," she testified. "They're creating an environment where emotional intensity trumps every other signal of truth or value. For a developing brain, this is devastating." Haugen's congressional testimony exposed how platforms engineer this dynamic: "The current system isn't designed to surface truth. It's designed to surface engagement." The machinery behind this rewiring becomes clearer through her revelations about Facebook's internal research.

When I spoke with Arturo Béjar, who worked on well-being metrics at Instagram, he revealed how the platform's architecture shapes young people's relationship with reality. Engineering decisions that seemed minor at the time—such as weighting angry reactions more heavily than likes—have fundamentally altered how an entire generation determines what's true.

Sriya Tallapragada, a 17-year-old youth journalist for PBS News Student Reporting Labs, captures how her generation navigates this new landscape: "We're not just passive consumers of content. We're actively cross-referencing emotional authenticity against fact-checking sites, discussing credibility in group chats, building consensus about what feels true and what's just engineered for engagement."

This dynamic plays out powerfully around climate content. Seventeen-year-old climate activist Xiye Bastida describes the tension between emotional and factual Truth: "On social media, you see the raw reality of climate change through people's direct experiences," she told *The Guardian*. "It hits differently than reading reports. Both are true, but they're true in different ways."

McKinsey's research, "'True Gen': Generation Z and Its Implications for Companies," reveals something more complex: They call Gen Z "Dialoguers" and "Communaholics": young people who move fluidly between different communities and different versions of Truth. While 66% of Gen Z believes communities are created by causes and interests rather than traditional markers like education or economics, they're also strikingly pragmatic.

For parents watching this unfold, the impact is profound. Nicki Reisberg began documenting changes in her daughter's behavior after she started using Instagram heavily during the pandemic. "It wasn't just mood swings," she observed. "It was like watching someone slowly lose touch with their own sense of reality. Everything became filtered through this lens of social media emotional intensity."

Emma Lembke was 16 when she started tracking social media's effects on her mental health. "I created physical logs of my emotional state before and after using social platforms," she told *MIT Technology Review*. Her documentation grew into the LOG OFF Movement, not to reject emotional truth-seeking but to reclaim it from algorithmic manipulation.

Zamaan Qureshi's testimony before Congress brought concrete examples to the conversation. He demonstrated how TikTok's algorithm amplified emotional content about the Israel-Hamas war: "Within hours, my feed went from dance videos to intense war footage. The emotional escalation was systematic and measurable."

Isabella Rene, a junior at Evanston Township High School in Illinois, said this in an interview with her school's student newspaper *The Evanstonian*, reflecting on the role of authenticity in how young people use social platforms: "I think [social media activism] is really productive in a way, but also not, because it's so much easier to get the word out about anything really with social media, but at the same time, I think it creates a space where people can just say that they're doing things where they're actually not." In other words, it's not that facts don't matter—it's that emotional authenticity is often what people notice first. A perfectly crafted post with all the right facts but no emotional resonance? We scroll past. A shaky video that captures a raw, real moment? That's what we stop for, share, believe in.

Lisa Feldman Barrett, a psychologist with a PhD, has conducted influential research on how our brains construct meaning—research that helps explain this apparent paradox. "Emotions aren't just reactions to truth—they're how we construct truth," she writes in *How Emotions Are Made: The Secret Life of the Brain*. "When young people say something 'feels true,' they're describing a sophisticated process of meaning-making that integrates emotional and social signals."

Recent research paints a startling picture of this transformation's global scale. Haidt's team, working with researcher Zack Rouse, found identical patterns emerging around 2012–2013 across English-speaking countries, then most of Europe. "When we saw all the lines lining up," Haidt notes, "something seemed okay until around 2012, then suddenly everything goes up."

A 2023 study by researchers from the University of Cambridge and Google explored how Gen Z navigates online information. The researchers found that Gen Z participants often encounter information passively through social media feeds rather than actively seeking it out. Their engagement is deeply social, shaped by collaborative interpretation and discussion within their peer groups. The study called this practice "information sensibility," a socially informed awareness of how to judge the value and credibility of what they see online. Rather than relying on traditional fact-checking alone, young people often assess information by how it resonates within their social circles and how well it aligns with shared values. Participants described learning about climate change not through direct research, but through emotionally charged posts that sparked frustration, urgency, or hope. These emotional moments became cues to look deeper, talk with friends, or seek supporting evidence. In this way, Gen Z isn't just consuming facts; they're socially and emotionally negotiating truth in real time.

A Stanford neuroimaging study examining how children respond to humor found that young brains activate both emotional and executive function regions in ways that differ from adults. Specifically, areas tied to emotional appreciation and cognitive integration—like the amygdala and the medial prefrontal cortex—were more actively engaged in younger participants. The researchers noted that this suggests a developmental window in which emotional and analytical processing are more intertwined, potentially shaping how Gen Z interprets and reacts to content that blends feeling with fact.

Solutions are beginning to take shape—though not at the pace Tristan Harris believes is necessary. Harris, cofounder of the Center for Humane Technology, argues that we need to move beyond platforms optimized for engagement and shift toward systems that foster "shared understanding," "good faith dialogue," and "reality-based consensus." In a 2023 interview, he proposed a redesign of social media environments that would reward users not just for posting popular content but for demonstrating integrity, empathy, and curiosity. Instead of the current model—what he calls a "race to the bottom of the brainstem"—he envisions what he has termed "antidebates," where conversations begin with agreement rather than outrage, and algorithms elevate content that supports civic health rather than polarization. While he hasn't released a formal blueprint for "emotional-factual coherence," his framework consistently calls for platform design rooted in psychological realism, democratic resilience, and emotional awareness.

Some communities aren't waiting for platform reform. In Seattle, teenagers have created "Truth circles"—weekly meetings where they collectively analyze viral content that has affected them emotionally. "We don't try to suppress the emotional response," explains one of the group's founders. "Instead, we use it as a starting point for deeper investigation. If something makes us feel intensely, we ask why—and then we fact-check together."

The education system is also adapting. CASEL's social-emotional learning curriculum, piloted in California high schools, teaches what Barrett, the psychologist, calls "emotional granularity," the ability to differentiate between various emotional states and understand their influence on belief formation. The program combines traditional fact-checking skills with emotional awareness exercises, teaching students to map their emotional responses to content while analyzing its factual validity.

Beyond individual schools, organizations like MediaWise and the News Literacy Project are developing curricula that specifically address emotional manipulation in digital spaces.

Several real-world initiatives are working to close the digital literacy gap and empower students with critical media skills. Digital Promise, a nonprofit created by Congress, partners with educators, researchers, and technology developers to advance innovation in public education, with a focus on equity and inclusion. Team4Tech's Digital Literacy Toolkit offers culturally responsive training and classroom materials to help students build digital fluency across a range of global settings. In Minnesota, the Digital Navigation Training Toolkit supports local leaders working to guide underserved learners through essential online tasks. Meanwhile, Marin County's Digital Inclusion project addresses broadband access, device availability, and tech support for youth and families. Together, these programs reflect a growing recognition that digital access and literacy are essential rights in the modern era.

This brings us back to that polar bear video and the IPCC report. Perhaps the way forward isn't choosing between these forms of Truth, but learning from how Gen Z integrates them. They're pioneering what might be called emotional empiricism—a way of knowing that honors both the measurable and the felt.

The platforms that shape our digital lives were built on engagement metrics that treated emotion as separate from Truth. But Gen Z's intuitive understanding—that Truth is both felt and factual—might offer a better model for our networked reality. They're not losing touch with Truth; they're expanding its territory. The question isn't whether their approach is right or wrong, but whether our institutions—from social platforms to schools—can evolve to support this more integrated way of knowing.

As Emma Lembke puts it, what her generation is building isn't a rejection of Truth, but an expansion of it. In this light, the emotional Truth trend isn't just about how platforms manipulate feeling—it's about how a generation is learning to feel its way toward deeper understanding.

What happens to a generation's concept of Truth when their primary information environment deliberately blurs every boundary? On social platforms, breaking news sits beside conspiracy theories, comedy mixes with commentary, and authentic teen voices blend with corporate manipulation—all processed through algorithms designed to amplify whatever provokes the strongest reaction.

"This isn't just about being unable to distinguish fact from fiction," Haidt explained during our conversation at the Sustainable Media Center. "It's about growing up in an environment where those categories have been deliberately scrambled for profit. When a teenager scrolls through their feed, they're not seeing distinct categories of content—news, entertainment, personal updates. They're seeing an emotionally orchestrated blur, ranked and amplified based on its ability to provoke reaction."

The mental health implications of this truth-scrambling are profound. When every piece of content—whether it's news about climate collapse, a friend's personal crisis, or a conspiracy theory about election fraud—is engineered to hit the same emotional pressure points, the cumulative effect is overwhelming. Traditional frameworks for processing Truth break down.

The numbers tell a devastating story. Teen suicide rates began rising sharply around 2012—the same year social platforms became ubiquitous in young lives. Haidt's research shows this wasn't coincidental. "When you deny young people any stable ground for determining what's true," he notes, "when every truth claim comes packaged in an algorithmically optimized emotional wrapper, you're not just changing how they process information. You're undermining their fundamental sense of reality."

Yet even in this deliberately distorted landscape, Gen Z is attempting to forge new ways of knowing. As Emma Lembke describes, they're developing collaborative verification systems, cross-referencing emotional authenticity against factual sources, building communities around shared truth-seeking. Whether these emerging practices can counterbalance the platforms' profit-driven truth-scrambling remains to be seen.

This shifting relationship with Truth extends into how Gen Z approaches civic engagement. Research from the Brennan Center for Justice demonstrates that rather than following traditional paths of political participation, young people are pioneering integrated approaches that blend emotional resonance with empirical impact. Beyond conventional civic education—which remains largely focused on basic institutional knowledge—youth are developing new frameworks for democratic participation that honor both lived experience and verified fact.

Research shows this generation's civic engagement transcends traditional assumptions about youth disillusionment. Rather than becoming less engaged, they're forging new paths for collective action that mirror their integrated approach to Truth-seeking. This generation has consistently demonstrated the ability to move fluidly between digital spaces and real-world activism, between emotional testimony and empirical evidence, between individual experience and collective action.

These emerging patterns of engagement suggest something deeper than just changing political tactics. They reflect a fundamental shift in how Truth and civic participation intersect. When young people engage with social issues, they're not just seeking factual validation or emotional resonance—they're building frameworks that can hold both simultaneously. This mirrors their broader approach to Truth: integrative rather than hierarchical, collaborative rather than competitive.

The stakes couldn't be higher. This isn't just about media literacy or platform regulation—it's about whether we can maintain the epistemological foundations necessary for societal cohesion. As one philosopher recently noted in the *Journal of Democracy*: "A society that can't agree on basic methods for determining truth cannot long survive as a democracy."

Sherry Turkle, reflecting on four decades of studying how technology shapes human development and social bonds, offers a stark assessment: "What we're seeing isn't just a crisis of truth—it's a crisis of how truth is collectively constructed and maintained. Previous generations inherited stable frameworks for determining what's real. Today's young people inherit algorithms designed to destabilize those frameworks for profit."

The question isn't whether emotional or empirical Truth is more valid—it's whether our society can survive their deliberate scrambling for engagement. "When we look back at this moment," Turkle observes, "we may recognize it as the point where we either found a way to integrate these different ways of knowing, or where we lost our collective ability to determine truth altogether. The platforms won't solve this—it's a fundamental social question that will determine whether democratic society as we know it can continue to exist."

Gen Z is crafting a new paradigm of Truth, blending the felt and the factual in ways that challenge traditional frameworks. Their intuitive grasp of emotional empiricism might hold the key to navigating a world increasingly shaped by AI and algorithmic manipulation. As institutions adapt to support this generational shift, the question isn't whether Gen Z's Truth-seeking methods are valid—it's whether we, as a society, can rise to meet their innovation with equal measures of empathy and rigor.

The struggles of today's teens force us to confront the big question: Are we already living in a post-Truth world? Or is there still a way back? Up next: the unsettling state of Truth today—and what it might mean for tomorrow.

CHAPTER 21

# Are We Living in a Post-Truth World?

During the contentious presidential election of 2024, a story spread rapidly through social media, alleging that Haitian immigrants in Springfield, Ohio, were stealing and eating local pets. The claim, originating from a local Facebook post, quickly gained traction among far-right groups, amplified by influential figures and even mentioned in a presidential debate. The accusations were unequivocally false, debunked by law enforcement, city officials, and media outlets. Yet, the narrative took on a life of its own.

In 1917, the Cottingley Fairies captivated the world when two young girls from Yorkshire, England, claimed to have photographed fairies in their garden. The photographs, showing ethereal winged figures interacting with the girls, were initially met with skepticism but gained credibility after being championed by Sir Arthur Conan Doyle, the famous author of Sherlock Holmes. Despite whispers of fabrication, the story was widely accepted as evidence of the supernatural, inspiring public fascination for decades. It wasn't until the 1980s that the girls confessed to staging the images using paper cutouts. By then, the tale had already cemented itself as a symbol of how willing people can be to believe a narrative that aligns with their hopes or biases, even in the face of mounting doubts.

Now I'm sitting across from Steve Fuller, across the pond and across the Internet. We're on Zoom, but his intensity makes it feel like he's right around the corner, leaning into my screen to tell me something that would have been unthinkable a decade ago: Maybe we should stop worrying so much about the death of Truth. Fuller is no ordinary academic. A sociologist and philosopher, he holds the Auguste Comte Chair in Social Epistemology at Warwick University, and he's made a career out of challenging our assumptions about knowledge and Truth.

Best known for his work on the philosophy of science and the concept of "post-truth," Fuller has written extensively on the topic, including in his book *Post-Truth: Knowledge as a Power Game* (2018). In it, he analyzes the rise of "post-truth" as a cultural phenomenon and examines its implications for science, politics, and society. For Fuller, post-truth isn't just about the rejection of facts; it's about a deeper shift in how knowledge is produced, distributed, and legitimized. He argues that we now live in a world where the boundaries between Truth and opinion are increasingly blurred, and where information often serves strategic purposes in what he calls a "knowledge power game."

As we talk, it becomes clear that Fuller doesn't see post-truth as an unequivocal crisis but rather as an evolution in how societies interact with knowledge. He ties this shift to broader trends, such as the democratization of information through the Internet and the erosion of traditional authority figures in favor of decentralized, user-driven sources. It's provocative, and as I listen to him, I realize he's not just explaining post-truth—he's embodying it, challenging my own assumptions in real time.

"For too long," Fuller tells me in our Zoom interview, his voice clear despite the digital distance, "we've relied on a handful of voices to tell us what's true. Post-truth doesn't kill truth; it opens it up."

It's a jarring statement, especially given our current moment. We're drowning in misinformation, with AI threatening to turn that flood into a tsunami. But Fuller's been thinking about this longer than most of us. As the founder of social epistemology, he's spent decades studying how societies create and validate knowledge. And he thinks we're looking at this all wrong.

The conventional wisdom says we're in crisis. "Post-truth, a term describing a cultural context where objective facts are less influential in shaping public opinion than appeals to emotion and personal belief, has gone from being a peripheral term to being a mainstay in political commentary," *Oxford Dictionaries* declared in 2016, when they made it their word of the year. The hand-wringing hasn't stopped since. But Fuller, his New York roots showing through his years in British academia, sees something different: not a crisis, but a transformation.

"Science," he points out, adjusting his webcam slightly, "is, at its core, about paradigms. And once those paradigms are established, they dictate what counts as truth. Post-truth is simply acknowledging that truth has always been part of a power game."

Not everyone shares his optimism. Critics argue that the democratization of Truth could exacerbate existing divides, leading to greater polarization and disinformation. For instance, philosopher Michael Lynch warns that while opening up the processes of truth-making can seem empowering, it also risks fragmenting our shared reality. Without common ground, he suggests, we might find it harder to distinguish between productive debate and destructive chaos. I think about Steve Bannon's infamous "flood the zone with shit" strategy, which Fuller brings up without prompting. "See, that's not new," he says, the afternoon light in his UK study growing dimmer. "That's straight out of Orwell's playbook—'War is peace. Freedom is slavery. Ignorance is strength.' What's new is our ability to see it happening in real time."

The Springfield pet-eating fiction provides a chilling case study for Fuller's ideas. While authorities, including local law enforcement and even Republican officials, swiftly debunked the accusations, the narrative's grip on public imagination didn't loosen. J. D. Vance, then the Republican vice-presidential nominee, acknowledged that the story wasn't true but argued that it didn't matter.

"If I have to create stories so that the American media actually pays attention to the suffering of the American people, then that's what I'm going to do," he told CNN, implying that the falsehood served to highlight broader cultural anxieties about immigration and societal change. This statement encapsulates the essence of post-truth: the prioritization of emotional resonance and narrative impact over factual accuracy. What set this incident apart wasn't just the speed of its spread but its capacity to provoke real-world consequences. Bomb threats, heightened tensions, and public fear rippled through Springfield, illustrating the dangerous interplay between fear, identity, and misinformation. J. D. Vance went on to become the vice president of the United States. The story's power lay not in its Truth but in its ability to evoke visceral reactions, aligning perfectly with a world where the emotional impact of a claim outweighs its factual basis.

As Fuller continues to explain his perspective, his optimism remains both provocative and unsettling. "People are questioning more," he says, his eyes lighting up. "We're no longer blindly accepting what's put in front of us. While that might feel destabilizing, it's actually a step toward a more engaged and informed public."

When I mention that this sounds dangerously close to endorsing conspiracy theories, Fuller doesn't flinch. Instead, he adjusts his position, both physically in his chair and intellectually in his argument. "Look," he says, "the existence of conspiracy theories isn't the problem. They've always existed. The question is why they're finding such fertile ground now. What does that tell us about our traditional arbiters of truth?"

I consider this, then ask: "So these are not technical problems; they are human problems that technology has simply helped scale, yet we keep attempting purely technological solutions?"

Fuller nods vigorously, causing his video to lag slightly. "Exactly," he says when the connection catches up. "We keep trying to solve this with better algorithms, better fact-checking, better AI. But that's missing the point entirely. The crisis isn't that people believe wrong things—people have always believed wrong things. The crisis is that our traditional methods for determining truth have lost their authority."

Jamais Cascio, distinguished fellow at the Institute for the Future, noted, "The power and diversity of very low-cost technologies allowing unsophisticated users to create believable 'alternative facts' is increasing rapidly. It's important to note that the goal of these tools is not necessarily to create consistent and believable alternative facts, but to create plausible levels of doubt in actual facts. The crisis we face about 'truth' and reliable facts is predicated less on the ability to get people to believe the *wrong* thing as it is on the ability to get people to *doubt* the right thing."

Fuller's face brightens when I share Cascio's warning about manufactured doubt. "Yes, but let's push that further," he says, reaching for something off-screen. "Why do we assume that doubt is bad? Isn't doubt at the heart of scientific inquiry? Of critical thinking? Maybe what we're seeing isn't the death of truth but the birth of a more sophisticated way of thinking about truth."

As if on cue, my Wi-Fi hiccups, fragmenting Fuller's image into digital blocks before reassembling it. It's an apt metaphor for what he's describing: Truth breaking apart only to be reconstructed in a new form. When the connection stabilizes, Fuller is holding up a book—one of his many publications on social epistemology.

"We've lived through periods like this before," he continues. "The invention of the printing press didn't just democratize information—it fundamentally changed how people thought about authority, about truth, about knowledge itself. We're in a similar moment now."

Our time is almost up, but Fuller's warming to his theme. "Here's what everyone gets wrong about post-truth," he says, ignoring the one-minute warning that flashes across our screens. "They think it means truth doesn't matter anymore. But it's exactly the opposite—truth matters so much that everyone wants a say in determining what it is."

The statement hangs there in our digital space, challenging everything I thought I knew about our current information crisis. Fuller's been pushing against conventional wisdom his entire career—from his early days at Columbia to his current role at Warwick. Born in New York City in 1959, he's watched the transformation of information from a scarce resource controlled by gatekeepers to today's overwhelming flood.

"You mentioned AI earlier," he says, waving off another warning notification. "Everyone's worried about AI generating misinformation, fake news, deepfakes. But that's missing the bigger picture. AI isn't just going to change how we distribute information—it's going to change how we think about truth itself."

While Steve Fuller views post-truth as an opportunity to democratize knowledge, others see it as a threat to the very idea of truth. Lee McIntyre, a philosopher and research fellow at Boston University, defines post-truth as "not simply falsehood. It is a political campaign to *undermine* the idea of truth itself." In his book *Post-Truth,* he argues that this is not just a cultural shift, but "a form of ideological supremacy," in which falsehood is used strategically—"not to misinform, but to displace truth as a societal value."

McIntyre emphasizes that post-truth thrives in an environment where trust in institutions is low, social media amplifies biases, and cognitive vulnerabilities are exploited. He says decades of science denial—whether by tobacco companies, climate skeptics, or anti-vaxxers—serve as a precursor to today's weaponized misinformation. "These tactics," he notes, "aren't new. They exploit the same human vulnerabilities: doubt, fear, and the comfort of confirmation bias." The rise of digital platforms, however, has scaled these strategies to unprecedented levels, creating a feedback loop of confusion, polarization, and mistrust.

To counter this, McIntyre champions strategies like George Lakoff's "truth sandwich," a technique designed to reduce the potency of misinformation. The truth sandwich addresses a critical flaw in traditional communication: When falsehoods are presented first, they tend to stick, even after correction—a phenomenon known as the "illusory truth effect." By flipping this script, the truth sandwich ensures that any discussion of falsehood begins and ends with verified facts.

Here's how it works: A journalist or communicator first states the verified Truth, then introduces the false claim while explicitly framing it as untrue, and concludes by reaffirming the factual reality. For example: "Vaccines are safe and have saved millions of lives. A politician's claim that they are harmful is false, contradicted by overwhelming scientific evidence. Vaccines remain one of the most effective tools in public health."

This approach does more than debunk misinformation—it reshapes the narrative. By framing lies within a context of Truth, it reduces their cognitive stickiness and reinforces the integrity of verified facts. McIntyre argues that this method, grounded in cognitive science, is essential to counter the spread of viral falsehoods.

However, McIntyre acknowledges that individual strategies like the truth sandwich are insufficient on their own. In an era when traditional gatekeepers of Truth have lost authority, systemic reforms are also crucial.

Here, Jay Rosen's insights into journalism provide a complementary perspective. Rosen, a prominent media critic and professor at NYU, is an unrelenting critic of the "he said, she said" style of reporting, which he argues "creates a theater of appearances, not an engine for truth." This approach, he contends, treats all claims as equally valid, even when they are demonstrably false, and often amplifies misinformation in the name of artificial balance. Rosen argues that simply presenting a lie alongside a rebuttal doesn't clarify the truth—it risks elevating the falsehood by giving it visibility it doesn't deserve.

Rosen's "truth-first" approach aligns with McIntyre's truth sandwich but pushes the concept further, urging newsrooms to fundamentally rethink how stories are framed.

"One of the worst aspects of 'he said, she said' journalism is that NEITHER what 'he said' nor what 'she said' may be actually so," says Rosen.

For instance, rather than opening with a politician's baseless claim about vaccine safety, Rosen advocates prioritizing the established facts: Vaccines are safe and save millions of lives. Only after this foundation is laid should disinformation be addressed—and even then, only to expose its lack of credibility.

In addition to reshaping narratives, Rosen champions radical transparency in journalism, an approach he describes as essential to rebuilding trust with audiences increasingly skeptical of traditional media. "Transparency is the new objectivity," he asserts, arguing that news organizations must not only report the Truth but also show their work. By openly explaining their processes for verifying information, journalists can engage audiences in a shared pursuit of truth. The goal isn't just to inform, Rosen has provocatively suggested, but to inoculate the public against manipulation.

Rosen's critique goes beyond tactics to address the systemic challenges facing journalism in the post-truth era. He warns that traditional methods, designed for a more cooperative public discourse, are being exploited by bad-faith actors. The tools of journalism, Rosen argues, weren't built for a world where power lies in the ability to overwhelm truth with noise. In this environment, he calls for journalists to embrace a more combative stance: The job isn't neutrality. It's truth-telling.

Together, Rosen and McIntyre offer a powerful framework for confronting post-truth. While McIntyre provides cognitive tools to counter the psychological grip of misinformation, Rosen addresses the structural reforms necessary to restore public trust in the media. Both recognize that the battle for Truth is not just about facts—it is a fight to reclaim the mechanisms by which we discern them.

By embracing these strategies, society can push back against the erosion of shared reality. As Rosen believes, the crisis of post-truth isn't just about what people believe—it's about whether they trust anyone to help them know what's true. "Suppose a major party candidate for president believed we were in a 'post-truth' era and actually campaigned that way. Would political reporters in the mainstream press figure it out and tell us? I say no. They would not tell us. Not in any clear way."

His words echo McIntyre's call for action: Individuals must resist manipulation while demanding systemic accountability, ensuring that Truth can endure in a chaotic information age.

When I ask him to elaborate, Fuller shifts in his chair. "Think about scientific truth," he says. "It's based on data, observation, repeated experiments. But what happens when AI can process more data, make more observations, and run more experiments than any human ever could? Does that make AI's version of truth more valid than ours?"

It's a provocative question, and Fuller knows it. He's not just talking about fact-checking or misinformation anymore—he's pushing us to think about what Truth means in an age when machines might be better at finding it than we are.

"But here's the real kicker," he continues, completely ignoring the fact that we're now running over time. "AI is built on human knowledge, human biases, human assumptions. It's not some objective arbiter of truth—it's a mirror reflecting our own complicated relationship with truth back at us."

The video call finally times out, Fuller's face freezing mid-sentence. As I sit there staring at the disconnected screen, I'm struck by the metaphor of it all—how our conversation about the fragmentation of Truth ended in literal digital fragmentation. I quickly start a new meeting, and Fuller rejoins, picking up exactly where he left off as if the interruption never happened.

"Sorry about that," he says with a wry smile. "Even technology has its own version of truth—in this case, the truth that our time was up." He settles back into his chair, the new connection somehow clearer than before. "But that's exactly what I'm talking about. We think of truth as this absolute thing, but it's always been mediated through something—through institutions, through technology, through human perception itself."

I think about how many layers of mediation are happening in this very conversation—our words traveling through cameras, microphones, undersea cables, satellites, screens, and speakers, each adding its own subtle distortion to what we consider the "Truth" of our interaction.

"People get nervous when I talk like this," Fuller continues, his image momentarily freezing again before snapping back to life. "They think I'm saying nothing is true, that it's all relative. But that's not it at all. I'm saying truth is more complex, more interesting, and ultimately more human than we've been willing to admit."

He pauses, reaching for a glass of water that sits just out of frame. "You know what's fascinating about this moment?" he asks after taking a sip. "For the first time in human history, we're having to explicitly define what truth is. Before, it was implicit—controlled by institutions, by power structures, by gatekeepers. Now it's up for grabs, and that's terrifying to people who are used to being the arbiters of truth."

The late afternoon light in his study has faded completely now, leaving him illuminated only by his screen. The effect makes him look almost prophetic, a modern-day oracle delivering uncomfortable truths through the digital ether.

"Post-truth doesn't mean the end of truth," he says, leaning forward so his face fills more of my screen. "It means the end of simple truth. The end of truth handed down from on high. The beginning of something more democratic, more challenging, and yes, more chaotic."

As our second call also nears its time limit, I can't help but notice how Fuller has managed to turn even our technical difficulties into a metaphor for his larger point. Each glitch, lag, and disconnection has somehow reinforced his argument about the fragmentation and reconstruction of Truth in our digital age. If post-truth is the democratization of Truth, how do we ensure it leads to collective enlightenment rather than chaos?

"You know what I haven't mentioned yet?" Fuller says. "Columbia University, where I started all this. Back then, in the pre-Internet days, truth seemed simpler. You went to the library, you read the authoritative sources, you cited the established experts." He pauses. "But even then, I was asking questions that made people uncomfortable. Who decides what's authoritative? Who gets to be an established expert?"

The questions hang in the digital space between us, more relevant now than ever. Fuller's journey from Columbia to Cambridge, from his MPhil to his PhD in history and philosophy of science at Pittsburgh, has been a steady progression toward these fundamental questions about knowledge and Truth. Now, at Warwick University, he's watching his early provocations become our daily reality.

"The really interesting thing," he says, his voice taking on an almost conspiratorial tone, "is that we're all participating in this transformation whether we want to or not. Every time we share something online, every time we question a source, every time we engage with AI—we're part of this massive experiment in redistributing the power to determine what's true."

Another notification pops up—our second call is about to end. This time, Fuller doesn't wave it away. Instead, he uses it to make one final point.

"See these interruptions we keep getting?" he says, gesturing at the notification. "That's the perfect metaphor for what's happening to truth right now. The clean, uninterrupted signal we used to rely on keeps getting broken up, fragmented, reconstructed. But maybe that's not a bug—maybe it's a feature. Maybe truth was always this messy, this complicated. We just couldn't see it before."

As we say our goodbyes and I watch Fuller's image disappear from my screen, I'm struck by a final thought. In our hour-long conversation about the nature of Truth, we never once agreed on a definition of what Truth actually is. And maybe that's exactly the point Fuller's been trying to make all along.

While Fuller is a powerful and provocative thinker, it's Lee McIntyre who literally wrote the book on *Post-Truth* and brings a perspective that is in some ways less philosophical and more tangible. Fortunately, Rebecca Hill sat down with McIntyre for the American Library Association blog post titled "Getting to the Truth in a Post-Truth Society."

In the interview, McIntyre says we are now living in a post-truth society. McIntyre's definition of post-truth builds on Fuller's ideas but highlights a more insidious dimension: "[Post-truth is] when what's said is beyond lying . . . [it's] about dominance and power," he explains. McIntyre's perspective echoes some of Fuller's themes but delves deeper into the psychological and political tactics underpinning this phenomenon. His analysis underscores the authoritarian implications of post-truth, adding a crucial layer to Fuller's more conceptual framework.

McIntyre also identifies the structural and cognitive biases fueling this era:

> The template for post-truth was established by science denial . . . From the tobacco companies' efforts to cast doubt on the link between smoking and cancer, to climate change denial, the strategy has always been the same: question the science, sow confusion, and undermine public trust in experts.

His insights complement Fuller's optimism about Truth's democratization by pointing to actionable solutions. For instance, McIntyre advocates for Lakoff's "truth sandwich" technique, a method of countering misinformation by leading with the Truth, briefly mentioning the falsehood only to refute it, and then reinforcing the Truth once more to anchor it in the audience's memory.

As I reflect on my conversations with Fuller, the idea that post-truth represents not the end but the evolution of Truth lingers. It's a thought-provoking notion, one that invites us to grapple with complexity rather than retreat into simplicity. In this age of fragmented realities and algorithmic influence, the challenge isn't just to seek Truth but to redefine it collaboratively. The question now is whether we can embrace this democratized, messy Truth without losing sight of the shared understanding that binds us together. Fuller's words stay with me: "Truth was always this messy, this complicated. We just couldn't see it before." Maybe now, in the chaos, we can.

In a world increasingly unmoored from Truth, are we doomed to chaos or capable of redemption? In the next chapter, we'll weigh two starkly different futures—one where Truth shatters and one where it becomes our guiding light. The future of Truth hangs in the balance.

## CHAPTER 22

# The Future of Truth: Two Scenarios

We've arrived. Present day. We journeyed from Plato to David Chalmers to Hailo Colborn: philosophy, *The Matrix*, Booktok, and Steve Fuller's optimistic view of our post-truth existence. Still, despite Fuller's upbeat pragmatism, I'm not a fan of "post-truth" as either a phrase or historical dividing line. It leaves too many things we used to share as a common Truth up for grabs. I think we're at a moment of dramatic change.

### Scenarios for the Future

We're at a crossroads, a moment that will be looked at by history when we made a choice. It's not robots *or* humans. That's a false dichotomy. It's robots *and* humans. Science can create profits, but it's not a field of study with profit as its driving force. Truth can't—shouldn't be—black and white. Its complexity is at the core of what our humanity is built on. The artist Miro is either a painter of a bunch of squiggly lines, or abstract art, or both. Finding a "true" distinction of Miro's works in hindsight, because the cultural references can be tallied. But going forward, there's danger if AI amplifies hate for profit and makes all innovators and experimenters the target of digital disrespect—or worse, if new artists and art forms are dismissed outright.

In both futures I imagine before us, Truth itself is transformed. Not erased, not simplified, but fundamentally altered in how we discover it, share it, and live with it. The question isn't whether AI will change our relationship with Truth—it's how. Will Truth become a commodity, packaged and sold to the highest bidder? Or will it become something richer, deeper, more collaborative than we've ever known? Here are two very different visions of The Future of Truth in the age of AI.

## Scenario One: The Dark Path

A future where AI drives us to a dark place of robotic courts and algorithmic decisions that will impact every corner of our increasingly digital lives. What medicines should we take? What jobs will we be offered? Whom should we love? Where will our children be educated? But most fundamentally—what happens to Truth itself? To understand the potential pitfalls of a future dominated by AI, we curated a virtual group of pioneering thinkers whose work sheds light on the dark, often uncharted consequences of technology on Truth and human autonomy. This group—Shoshana Zuboff, Kate Crawford, Jaron Lanier, Cathy O'Neil, Timnit Gebru, and Sherry Turkle—represents some of the most influential voices in the intersection of technology, ethics, and society.

---

### The Algorithm's Shadow. Spring, 2037. A future fiction.

Sarah Chen couldn't shake off her grandmother's words from their last unmonitored conversation: "In my day, we chose our own paths—and we chose what to believe was true."

Now, watching her daughter Maya's tears being quantified by the home's EmotiScan™ system, she understood what her grandmother meant. The system flagged Maya's distress as "potentially disruptive behavior," automatically adjusting the family's social credit score. Even emotional Truth had become something to be measured, categorized, and controlled.

As Shoshana Zuboff, the Harvard professor who first exposed the dangers of data capitalism, had warned years ago, "In the age of surveillance capitalism, truth is increasingly whatever is profitable." The Chen family was learning this firsthand. Their lives had become what Cathy O'Neil, a mathematician who'd left Wall Street to sound the alarm about algorithmic bias, described as "weapons of math destruction"—algorithms making decisions about their worth, their potential, their very future.

Meanwhile, Jamie, Sarah's husband, paced the living room, his career transition notification blinking insistently on every surface. "I'm a teacher," he muttered. "I want to remain a teacher. This is my truth." But the National Employment Algorithm had other plans, having detected "inefficiencies" in human-led education. The system's decision reminded Sarah of Kate Crawford's warning—the renowned AI researcher and critic had said it clearly: "AI doesn't just mirror the world; it makes choices about what to show us, based on biased data. The result is a distorted version of reality that's mistaken for truth."

The family's evening meal was interrupted by a gentle chime; their NutriScore™ had dropped due to Maya's "emotional eating patterns." The system was redefining what was true about their own bodies, their own hunger. Sarah remembered the words of Jaron Lanier, the virtual reality pioneer who'd become one of tech's most prominent skeptics: "Algorithms don't respect the complexity of human lives; they reduce us to patterns to be exploited." Their dining table, once a place of connection and shared stories, had become another data point in the vast machinery of behavioral prediction.

That night, as Sarah helped Maya with her AI-optimized homework, designed to shape her into what the system deemed a "productive citizen," she recalled the warning from Timnit Gebru, the AI ethicist who'd been forced out of Google for speaking Truth to power: "When these biases get embedded into powerful technologies, they don't just reflect the world as it is—they reinforce the worst parts of it." Maya's curriculum had been automatically adjusted based on her predicted "social value coefficient," a metric that made Sarah's stomach turn. Even historical Truth was being rewritten in real time, with AI systems determining which facts were "relevant" for Maya's future role in society.

Their mandatory evening entertainment began: a personalized stream of content selected to "optimize their psychological well-being." Each family member received their own version of reality, tailored to their compliance scores and behavioral patterns. As the family sat in silence, bathed in the blue light of their individual screens, Sarah thought of MIT psychologist Sherry Turkle's observations about Truth becoming a "collaborative construct." But there was nothing collaborative about this. Their reality was now filtered, predicted, and shaped by algorithms that claimed to know them better than they knew themselves.

Later, lying in bed, Sarah pulled up her family's daily compliance report. Their scores had dropped across all metrics: social harmony, career optimization, educational engagement, and even dietary compliance. As O'Neil had predicted, their "credit score, hiring potential, and social worth were all decided by a machine." The system had already begun suggesting "more suitable" housing options in the city's closely monitored zones. Truth had become whatever the algorithms declared it to be.

Through their bedroom window, Sarah watched an enforcement drone pass by, its soft hum a constant reminder of Zuboff's warning about how "surveillance capitalism unilaterally claims human experience as free raw material." She wondered if her grandmother's generation could have imagined a world where even their dreams would be analyzed for optimization potential, where personal Truth would become just another commodity to be bought and sold.

Maya's voice broke through the darkness: "Mom, how did people know what was true before the algorithms told them?" Sarah felt tears forming—tears that would undoubtedly be detected, analyzed, and added to their family's profile. She had no answer that the system would deem appropriate. Instead, she held her daughter close, their shared warmth a small act of human connection in a world where, as Lanier had feared, they were losing "what makes us uniquely human—our capacity for empathy, nuance, and truth."

The next morning would bring new scores, new optimizations, new predictions. But for now, in the quiet darkness, Sarah allowed herself to remember a time when Truth was something people discovered together, not something imposed from above. It was a memory that the system would flag as "nostalgic deviation," but she held onto it anyway—perhaps it was the last truly human Truth she had left.

---

In this dark future, Truth has become a manufactured product, shaped by powerful algorithms designed to capture attention and drive profit. The Chen family's story shows us how personal Truth—the lived experience of human beings—becomes subordinate to algorithmic "truth." Maya's tears aren't simply tears; they must be quantified, categorized, and evaluated by EmotiScan™. Her distress isn't valid until the system validates it—and then uses it against her family's social credit score.

The very notion of objective Truth has been replaced by optimization metrics and compliance scores. What's "true" is whatever matches the system's predetermined goals. Facts aren't discovered; they're assigned. Data isn't interpreted; it's weaponized. The historical record itself becomes a tool for reinforcing existing power structures, as Crawford warns, with AI systems trained on biased data perpetuating and amplifying those biases into the future.

But perhaps most insidiously, this future fragments Truth itself. Each person receives their own curated version of reality, personalized streams of content optimized not for accuracy or understanding, but for compliance and control. Shared Truth becomes impossible when everyone lives in their own algorithmic bubble, their views of reality shaped by systems designed to maximize engagement rather than enlightenment.

One possibility is a future where AI drives us to a dark place of robotic courts and digital decisions that will impact every corner of our increasingly digital lives. What medicines can we take? What jobs will we be offered? Whom should we love, where will our children be educated? To understand the potential pitfalls of a future dominated by AI, I curated a group of pioneering thinkers whose work sheds light on the dark, often uncharted consequences of technology on Truth and human autonomy. Each has independently warned of AI's ability to distort reality, manipulate choices, and reinforce bias, but taken together, their perspectives outline a deeply troubling scenario.

Their work collectively reveals a future where Truth is no longer discovered but curated by algorithms, reshaped by corporate interests, and filtered through data-driven biases. They examine how AI could gradually erode personal agency, redefine human identity, and weaken democratic processes. Through their combined insights, this vision is more than a set of abstract warnings; it is a roadmap of specific dangers we could face if AI continues to grow unchecked. This group of scholars does not just suggest a cautionary tale—they issue a stark, urgent call to examine how these emerging technologies may already be shaping a world where Truth itself becomes malleable, dictated by forces beyond individual or even societal control.

Cathy O'Neil, a mathematician and author, first gained attention for her groundbreaking book *Weapons of Math Destruction*, which exposed how algorithms can reinforce inequality and injustice.

"Algorithms pretend to be neutral, but they're amplifying what they've learned from us—our biases, our mistakes, our prejudices. AI's truth is a reflection of our worst instincts."

O'Neil's perspective on AI and Truth dives into the hidden biases lurking within algorithmic systems, pointing out that the very math society trusts to be impartial is often anything but. She argues that algorithmic transparency is crucial to prevent AI from embedding systemic prejudice into society's decision-making frameworks. "What if your credit score, your hiring potential, your social worth were all decided by a machine?" she asks. Her warning is clear: If we don't scrutinize these hidden processes, we risk losing agency over the most fundamental aspects of our lives.

As the author of *The Age of Surveillance Capitalism*, Shoshana Zuboff, a Harvard professor emerita, investigates how tech corporations have transformed personal data into profit.

Zuboff argues that in the age of surveillance capitalism, Truth is increasingly whatever is profitable. When AI dictates what we see, hear, and know, it's not a quest for Truth—it's a business model.

Zuboff contends that in their pursuit of predictive power, companies are reshaping public discourse and Truth itself. By monetizing human experience, she argues, tech companies shift us from informed individuals to manipulated consumers. Zuboff's critique reveals a chilling scenario: a future where surveillance capitalism shapes reality. She asserts, "Surveillance capitalism unilaterally claims human experience as free raw material for behavioral data . . . prediction products that anticipate what you will do now, soon, and later." Zuboff sees an urgent need to confront the ethics of this shift if we are to protect our personal autonomy.

Kate Crawford, a leading AI researcher and senior principal at Microsoft Research, brings an academic rigor to her analysis of AI's social impact. Crawford argues that AI doesn't just mirror the world—it actively shapes what we know and see, creating a distorted version of reality that's mistaken for Truth.

Through her work, Crawford critiques the very foundation of AI systems, focusing on their power structures and environmental costs. In *Atlas of AI*, she examines how AI is built on material, ecological, and human exploitation, from rare earth mining to labor exploitation. Crawford calls attention to a critical point: AI's pursuit of Truth is often clouded by corporate interests. She warns, "AI systems are not neutral or objective—they are the end product of choices that embed values, priorities, and biases." Her work encourages a skeptical view of AI's truth-seeking potential, advocating for more responsible stewardship of this powerful technology.

Sherry Turkle, psychologist and MIT professor, has spent decades exploring the intersection of technology and human identity. Known for her works like *Alone Together*, Turkle reflects on how AI affects our relationship with Truth, particularly for younger generations who never knew a world without digital influence.

She describes a culture where Truth becomes a "collaborative construct," filtered and reassembled through social media's emotional echo chambers. Turkle urges caution as AI increasingly mediates reality, affecting mental health and identity. Her voice is a reminder that Truth in the digital age can become a slippery slope, especially for those who lack the tools to question it.

Timnit Gebru, an AI ethics researcher and former Google scholar, has become a prominent voice calling for diversity and accountability in AI.

Gebru has often warned that AI systems today are trained on data that reflects human biases, inequalities, and systemic injustices—and when deployed, they reinforce the worst parts of society.

Gebru's work often centers on how AI reinforces power imbalances, warning that a lack of inclusivity in AI development skews Truth toward the perspectives of a select few. She argues that without diverse voices, AI risks becoming a tool that reinforces existing inequalities rather than providing objective insights. Gebru's experience at Google, where she was pushed out for her criticisms of AI biases, only strengthens her perspective that transparency is key to safeguarding the integrity of AI.

Jaron Lanier, a computer scientist and pioneer in virtual reality, offers a fiery view of AI's role in shaping Truth: "We're being hypnotized little by little by technicians we can't see, for purposes we don't know. We're all lab animals now."

As Lanier sees it, algorithms, especially those that underlie social media, don't respect the complexity of human lives; they reduce us to patterns to be exploited. In a world run by algorithms, he says we risk losing what makes us uniquely human—our capacity for empathy, nuance, and truth.

With his background in tech innovation, Lanier brings a unique skepticism to the idea that AI can "know" or "create" Truth in any meaningful way. He compares AI's outputs to a funhouse mirror, reflecting back an exaggerated and distorted version of reality shaped by algorithms optimized for engagement. In a 2023 interview with *The Guardian*, Lanier famously stated, "This idea of surpassing human ability is silly because it's made of human abilities." For Lanier, the real danger is in our reliance on these imperfect systems, which could ultimately erode genuine human connection and Truth.

These experts collectively paint a future where Truth may no longer be a discovery but a manufactured product, shaped by powerful algorithms designed to capture attention and drive profit. Together, their analyses converge on a few deeply intertwined themes that present a provocative warning about AI's potential to alter the human relationship with Truth.

They foresee an erosion of personal agency in this AI-driven landscape. Shoshana Zuboff and Jaron Lanier raise alarms over AI's power to dictate personal choices, scripting lives to align with corporate interests. Zuboff's "surveillance capitalism" captures this loss of agency, where decisions—from career paths to relationships—are influenced by AI models optimized for profitable outcomes rather than individual desires. Meanwhile, Lanier warns how algorithms, in their pursuit of engagement, risk overriding human intuition.

Bias embedded in the digital ecosystem is another theme that Crawford and Tufekci explore with urgency. Kate Crawford, who exposes how historical biases seep into AI through data training, warns that these systems are not as objective as they might appear. They're fed by the past's prejudices, which means they're predisposed to replicate systemic inequalities. Zeynep Tufekci complements Crawford's concerns, emphasizing that AI-driven echo chambers trap users in self-confirming bubbles, making it easier for misinformation to thrive and harder for diverse perspectives to gain traction. This reality risks fostering a warped perception of Truth, one that's reinforced by the algorithms themselves.

At a societal level, the undermining of democratic processes emerges as a shared anxiety. Both Tufekci and Zuboff highlight how AI jeopardizes democracy by prioritizing sensationalism over substance, reshaping the public sphere into a divisive battleground. This algorithmic influence risks fragmenting communities into isolated echo chambers, fostering polarization rather than informed dialogue. As public discourse becomes more reactive and less reflective, the collective agency that underpins democracy is compromised, weakening citizens' ability to effect meaningful change.

These effects ultimately contribute to the dehumanization of digital interaction in ways that Jaron Lanier finds particularly troubling. Lanier warns that AI-driven platforms reduce complex human beings to mere behavioral models, simplifying interactions to maximize clicks and views. Tufekci reinforces this by pointing out that these algorithms are inherently manipulative, primed to provoke reactions and drive division. The result is a transformation of online discourse into a performative spectacle, where genuine engagement is stripped away, leaving only a shell of human connection.

The cumulative impact of these concerns points toward profound implications for the future of Truth itself. In this speculative yet increasingly plausible future, Truth becomes fluid—a commodity curated by algorithms according to criteria that prioritize engagement over accuracy. This "algorithmic reality" risks allowing profit-driven narratives to overshadow factual integrity, turning Truth into a negotiable asset rather than an objective reality.

## The Connected Cure. Spring, 2037.

Maya Chen woke to the gentle pulse of her wellness band, its soft blue glow indicating optimal sleep patterns. The device, part of what Dr. Daniel Kraft, the pioneering Stanford physician who revolutionized digital health, had once called "the democratization of medicine," had detected early signs of seasonal allergies and automatically adjusted her home's air filtration system. Unlike the medical pronouncements of the past, every health insight came with its complete chain of evidence—from raw sensor data through peer-reviewed research to real-world validation.

"Mom!" Maya called out excitedly, bounding down the stairs. "The Community Health Hub approved my application!"

Sarah smiled, remembering how different healthcare had been in her youth. Now, as Thomas Frey, the renowned futurist, had predicted, they were truly "architects of a future yet to be imagined." Maya, at 16, was already part of a global network of citizen scientists, using AI-enhanced tools to contribute to medical research while learning about healthcare.

The family gathered for breakfast, their smart table displaying personalized nutrition recommendations alongside their morning news feeds. Around each article, source verification markers glowed green, showing primary data, peer review status, and community trust metrics. "Remember when you told me about doom-scrolling, Mom?" Maya laughed. "Now we truth-scroll instead." The article's margins filled with contextual data and varying perspectives, each clearly traced to its origins. It wasn't that disagreement had vanished—rather, it had become deeply informative.

Jamie, who had transitioned from traditional teaching to becoming a hybrid education architect, was particularly proud of Maya's acceptance. "It's exactly what Rachel Botsman talked about," he said, referencing the trust researcher's groundbreaking work. "The technology isn't just about the tools—it's about building trust through transparency and connection." He had helped design systems where students didn't just learn facts—they learned to trace Truth's evolution. "Yesterday, my students mapped the history of climate science," he added. "The AI helped them visualize how scientific consensus emerged, showing them every study, every debate, every turning point. They don't just learn what's true—they learn *how* we know it's true."

Sarah checked her family's wellness dashboard, marveling at how far they'd come from the days of anxious Google searches and waiting rooms. Their AI health assistant, operating under what Gerd Leonhard, the celebrated tech humanist, had called "ethical intelligence," provided personalized insights while maintaining strict privacy protocols. Every health recommendation came with its complete reasoning chain—from raw data through AI analysis to expert validation and community experience. "Technology inside us," Leonhard had said, "but always in service of our humanity."

Through the kitchen window, Sarah watched their neighborhood's shared garden space, which had evolved into both a physical and digital Truth ecosystem. AI-powered sensors worked in harmony with human knowledge to optimize growth patterns, while augmented reality overlays showed the complete history of each plant variety, traditional farming techniques, and real-time growth data. The community's food security program, inspired by Ayesha Khanna's vision of technological solutions for societal challenges, had transformed what was once a food desert into a thriving ecosystem of local produce and shared knowledge.

Maya's homework now included practical sessions in the garden's "Truth Nursery," where she learned to balance AI recommendations with traditional farming wisdom passed down through generations. Like the plants they tended, Truth grew here from multiple roots: data, experience, tradition, and innovation all nurturing each other. "It's not just about the technology," she explained to her mother, echoing Khanna's emphasis on human-centered innovation. "It's about how we use it to help people understand their world better."

The Chen family's evening routine included a virtual gathering with their global health circle—doctors, wellness coaches, and community members connected through secure platforms. Dr. Kraft's vision of "personalized, preventative, and precise healthcare" had evolved into this beautiful fusion of human expertise and technological support. Conflicts between different healing traditions weren't suppressed but highlighted as opportunities for deeper understanding. "Truth in medicine isn't binary," their AI health assistant would remind them. "It's about understanding patterns of evidence and experience."

As Sarah prepared for her role as a community health coordinator, she reflected on Botsman's words about trust being rooted in culture, not just technology. The health networks she helped manage were built on a foundation of transparent data sharing, ethical AI deployment, and genuine human connection. Each piece of health information was accompanied by its provenance—from ancient healing traditions to the latest clinical trials, all weighted and contextualized rather than ranked and rejected.

Later that night, as Maya excitedly planned her first Community Health Hub project—a study on integrating traditional healing practices with AI diagnostics—Sarah thought about how different this was from the dystopian futures people had once feared. Through their window, she watched the neighborhood's Truth Garden—an augmented reality space where information grew like plants, with roots reaching down to primary sources and branches spreading to show connections and consequences. Children learned early that Truth wasn't something you consumed passively—it was something you cultivated, tended, and helped grow.

"And this is exciting," Maya said, her eyes bright with purpose. "We're not just collecting data—we're helping people understand how we know what we know." She was part of what Frey had envisioned: a generation that saw AI not as a replacement for human judgment, but as a collaboration tool for discovering and verifying Truth in all its complexity.

Through their window, the city's health monitoring network glowed softly—not as a surveillance system, but as what Leonhard had described as a "digital nervous system" serving the community's well-being. Air quality metrics, pollen counts, and community health trends were freely shared, each data point traceable to its source, each interpretation open to community validation. The network didn't just share information; it shared understanding.

As she drifted off to sleep, Sarah's wellness band pulsed gently, its rhythm synchronized with her natural circadian patterns. In the quiet of the night, she remembered her own mother's fear of technology taking over not just healthcare, but Truth itself. How different things had turned out—not a cold, automated system imposing its version of reality, but a warm, connected web of human knowledge, enhanced by ethical AI.

The next morning would bring new opportunities for healing, learning, and growing together. The Chens were part of something bigger than themselves—a future where technology and humanity had found not just balance, but harmony in their shared pursuit of Truth.

---

The Chen family exists in two visions of 2037—radically different versions of how artificial intelligence might reshape not just our world, but Truth itself. In one future, algorithms dictate not only choices but reality, monitoring emotions and reducing human experience to data points. Even personal truths—tears, family dinners, career aspirations—become commodities to be quantified and controlled. In the other future, technology amplifies our collective ability to discover and verify Truth, creating an ecosystem where different forms of knowledge—scientific, traditional, experiential—can grow together.

Dr. Daniel Kraft is a physician, scientist, and entrepreneur known for blending healthcare with technology. With a medical degree from Stanford, he specializes in hematology/oncology. Recognized for his TED Talks, he explores the future of healthcare, emphasizing the role of digital health and medical innovation. He envisions a future where healthcare is revolutionized by cutting-edge technologies and innovations. He believes that advancements in fields such as artificial intelligence, genomics, robotics, and telemedicine will lead to personalized, preventative, and precise healthcare solutions. In this future, healthcare will be more accessible, efficient, and patient-centered, with individuals having greater control over their health through wearable devices, mobile apps, and telehealth platforms.

"It's not about human versus machine. The promise of AI in medicine is to enable humans—clinicians, nurses, caregivers—to do what they do best. But it needs to be framed as intelligence augmentation, not replacement. Let the technology handle the scut work, the repetition, the charting, so we can make healthcare more human," he said at his 2025 talk at DLD in Munich.

Dr. Kraft also emphasizes the importance of interdisciplinary collaboration and the integration of digital health tools into medical practice to improve diagnostics, treatments, and outcomes. Overall, his vision entails a transformative shift toward proactive, data-driven, and holistic approaches to healthcare delivery and management. Simply put, Kraft says AI will make us healthier in the future, but it's not without real risk. "Sam Altman has said GPT is like an e-bike for your mind. But what happens if your kids never learn how to ride a regular bike—or if a medical student never develops the skills to think through a diagnosis on their own? That's the risk. If we let these systems do all the thinking, we may lose the muscle memory of medical reasoning. And when the system gets it wrong, no one will know how to course-correct."

Thomas Frey is a futurist, author, and speaker renowned for his expertise in anticipating future trends and technological developments. Serving as the executive director and senior futurist at the DaVinci Institute, he delves into the impact of emerging technologies on diverse industries. Frey envisions a future characterized by profound technological advancements that reshape various aspects of human life. He anticipates a world where emerging technologies like artificial intelligence, robotics, biotechnology, and blockchain fundamentally transform industries, economies, and societal structures. Frey predicts the emergence of disruptive innovations that revolutionize transportation, communication, healthcare, education, and entertainment. "With AI as our partner & collaborator, we are not just problem-solvers; we become the architects of a future yet to be imagined," says Frey on his website.

In Frey's vision, advancements in automation and artificial intelligence lead to significant changes in the workforce, with traditional jobs being replaced by new roles that require specialized skills in technology, creativity, and adaptability. He also anticipates the rise of decentralized systems facilitated by blockchain technology, enabling greater transparency, security, and efficiency in various sectors.

Frey foresees the advent of futuristic concepts such as smart cities, augmented reality, space exploration, and even the potential for human augmentation and longevity. He emphasizes the importance of embracing change, fostering innovation, and preparing for the opportunities and challenges that the future may bring.

Overall, Frey's vision of the future is one characterized by boundless possibilities driven by technological innovation, urging society to embrace the transformative potential of emerging technologies while navigating the complexities of a rapidly evolving world.

If Frey encourages engagement, Rachel Botsman sees the core issue as one of trust. Botsman delves into how Truth is perceived and authenticated in the digital age, especially with the rise of decentralized trust systems. Her concerns center around the challenges of navigating Truth in a landscape where information is distributed and verified through nontraditional channels. She envisions a future shaped by the evolution of trust and the transformation of traditional societal structures. She explores the concept of "collaborative consumption" or the "sharing economy," where trust is fostered through peer-to-peer interactions facilitated by digital platforms.

"The issue of trust does not lie in the technology, it lies in the culture," says Botsman, referencing the trust researcher's groundbreaking 2017 book *Who Can You Trust?* This statement underscores the idea that the challenges and opportunities related to trust in technology are not inherent in the technology itself but in how societies and cultures adapt to and integrate these technologies.

In Botsman's vision, advancements in technology, particularly blockchain and decentralized systems, will enable greater transparency, security, and efficiency in transactions, leading to the proliferation of sharing and collaborative models across various sectors. She emphasizes the shift from ownership to access, where individuals prioritize experiences over possessions and engage in shared ownership, rental, or subscription-based services.

Furthermore, Botsman explores the implications of trust in the digital age, highlighting the importance of reputation, accountability, and integrity in online interactions. She envisions a future where trust becomes a currency that underpins social and economic interactions, influencing everything from business transactions to personal relationships.

Overall, Rachel Botsman's vision of the future revolves around the democratization of trust and the emergence of new models of collaboration and exchange that redefine how we interact, consume, and participate in society. She encourages individuals and organizations to embrace these changes, recognizing the transformative potential of trust in shaping a more connected, sustainable, and equitable future. And then we get to the most thorny question of all, ethics.

Gerd Leonhard's exploration of Truth often involves ethical considerations in the development and deployment of technology. He is concerned with ensuring that the Truth is upheld in the design and use of technologies like artificial intelligence, emphasizing transparency and ethical practices to safeguard Truth in an increasingly digital and automated world. Leonhard's vision of the future centers around the concept of exponential technological growth and its profound impact on humanity. He believes that technological advancements, particularly in fields such as artificial intelligence, biotechnology, and robotics, will lead to unprecedented changes in society, economy, and culture.

"The effect of the changes we're witnessing surpass pivotal historical moments such as the Industrial Revolution, or the invention of the printing press. Technology will no longer remain just outside of us, but it is relocating inside of us in the form of wearables, BCIs, nanotechnology, and human genome editing. What we are experiencing is a shift in the very definition of what it means to be human," says Leonhard in a 2019 *Forbes* article discussing themes from his book *Technology vs. Humanity*.

However, alongside this vision of technological progress, Leonhard emphasizes the importance of Truth. He argues that in an age of information abundance and digital manipulation, discerning Truth from falsehood becomes increasingly challenging. Leonhard warns against the spread of misinformation, manipulation, and deepfakes, which can undermine trust and distort reality.

In Leonhard's vision, the pursuit of Truth becomes paramount in navigating the complexities of the future. He advocates for critical thinking, media literacy, and transparency as essential tools for safeguarding Truth in the digital age. Moreover, he calls for ethical considerations in the development and deployment of emerging technologies to ensure that they serve the collective good and uphold fundamental principles of Truth and integrity.

Overall, Gerd Leonhard's vision of the future intertwines technological progress with the imperative of Truth, highlighting the need for society to navigate the digital landscape with a commitment to honesty, transparency, and ethical responsibility. If Gerd is cautious but positive, Parag and Ayesha Khanna's focus on Truth relates to the ethical implications of artificial intelligence with more caution as outlined in her 2012 book *Hybrid Reality*.

The Khannas are concerned with ensuring truthfulness in AI systems, emphasizing transparency, accountability, and adherence to ethical standards to build trust in the truthfulness and reliability of these technologies. They envision a future where technology plays a central role in addressing societal challenges and shaping human progress. The Khannas believe that advancements in artificial intelligence, big data analytics, and robotics have the potential to revolutionize industries, governance, and human well-being.

In their vision, Truth is essential for guiding the ethical and responsible development of technology. They emphasize the importance of transparency, accountability, and integrity in the use of data and algorithms. The Khannas argue that truthful information is critical for building trust between individuals, organizations, and governments in an increasingly interconnected world.

Furthermore, the Khannas advocate for the democratization of information and knowledge, empowering individuals to access and verify accurate information. They believe that education and media literacy are key to equipping people with the skills to discern Truth from falsehood in the digital age.

Overall, the Khannas' vision of the future underscores the intersection of technology and Truth, highlighting the need for ethical decision-making and responsible use of technology to ensure a future that is both technologically advanced and grounded in Truth and integrity.

The visions of Drs. Daniel Kraft and Thomas Frey converge in their anticipation of profound technological advancements shaping the future, yet they diverge in their emphasis on Truth as a central theme. Kraft envisions healthcare revolutionized by technology, promoting personalized care and patient empowerment. In contrast, Frey extends this vision to diverse sectors, foreseeing transformative changes driven by AI, robotics, and blockchain. Both envision a future propelled by innovation but differ in their focus on Truth. On the other hand, Rachel Botsman and Gerd Leonhard delve into the evolving dynamics of Truth in the digital age. Botsman explores the democratization of trust, emphasizing its positive potential in fostering collaboration. Conversely, Leonhard warns against the challenges of discerning Truth in a landscape of digital manipulation, advocating for critical thinking and ethical responsibility. While Botsman emphasizes the positive role of trust, Leonhard takes a more cautious stance, highlighting the risks of misinformation. These perspectives underscore the complex interplay between technology and Truth, urging society to navigate this landscape with vigilance and integrity.

The critical difference between these futures hinges on our fundamental relationship with Truth itself. In the dark future, Truth becomes whatever algorithms declare it to be, fragmented into personalized realities designed for control. In the optimistic future, Truth remains a collaborative human endeavor, with AI serving as a tool for verification, connection, and understanding.

The path forward requires more than just preserving human agency or building ethical frameworks. It demands a fundamental rethinking of how we discover, share, and validate Truth. The same tools that Timnit Gebru warns could "reinforce the worst parts" of our world could, if developed ethically as the Khannas advocate, help us understand Truth in all its complexity. The technology that could fragment Truth into algorithmic bubbles could instead help us visualize the rich tapestry of human knowledge.

The future of Truth lies not in surrendering to algorithmic reality or rejecting technological advancement, but in forging a partnership that amplifies our human capacity for discovering, sharing, and understanding Truth in all its complexity. As Barack Obama warns, the battle for Truth is not about convincing everyone of a single reality; it's about ensuring we don't lose faith in the possibility of Truth itself. Truth demands not just technology, but humanity—our capacity for nuance and our fundamental desire to understand both our world and each other.

The choice is ours. Will Truth become a commodity to be packaged and sold, or will it remain a human endeavor, enriched by our technological tools? The answer will shape not just how we know what we know, but who we become as a species. The future of Truth itself hangs in the balance.

We've explored two futures: one where Truth fades into chaos and one where it finds a way to thrive. But where do we actually stand? And more importantly, where do we go from here? In the pages ahead, we'll pull it all together and ask the biggest question yet: What can we do, right now, to shape the future of Truth?

# A Conclusion, of Sorts

Okay, I've got to be honest: The deeper I got into writing this book, the more fascinating and complicated it became. I mean, Truth as a journalistic idea has some pretty specific frameworks. Truth when you go to Plato and David Chalmers, not so much. There was a time as I was writing that I convinced myself that the real problem here was that the word "Truth" had been bastardized, stolen away by two different camps with entirely different meanings. I've tried to test this idea in various barroom conversations, explaining that absolute Truth and objective Truth are not the same thing. Out in the world, that experiment fails 100% of the time. People know what the Truth is, according to them. So is Truth important? Absolutely. And do humans' urgent need for Truth make the role of AI in this next chapter of humanity critically, potentially disastrously important?

If Plato were to walk through Silicon Valley today, he might say: "In my day, I warned about shadows on cave walls—mere reflections of reality that fooled the masses. But you've built caves within caves, algorithms that dream up shadows, and machines that forge chains of convincing illusions. The prisoner who breaks free no longer finds a simple world of sunlight above, but layer upon layer of digital realities, each claiming to be Truth. Beware—for those who control these shadow-making machines may become drunk with the power to shape reality itself."

But then his expression would soften, and with the wisdom that made his students love him, he might add: "And yet, my friends, this makes the philosopher's quest more vital, not less. For when machines can manufacture Truth with mathematical precision, we must seek wisdom not in the perfect simulation, but in the messy beauty of actual human experience. Your AI may speak with the voice of pure logic, but Truth still lives in the imperfect space between the binary. Take heart: Just as my students learned to question everything, so too can yours learn to dance between digital shadows while keeping their feet firmly planted in the soil of human wisdom. The challenge is not to reject the cave of algorithms, but to remain human while exploring its depths."

As a brief reprise, it's worth reminding you that we looked at Truth through the lens of dating, the military, doctors and medicine, journalism, identity, lying, the law, jobs, Teens and Gen Z, and the Post-Truth world. I tried to make each chapter both honest and hopeful, thinking that readers who picked the book up looking for answers might be satisfied if they come away with great big fascinating complicated questions. I've also tried to not get into the individual skirmishes of Truth as it relates to any particular news story or event in history given the understanding that this book needs to be relevant not just on the publication date but hopefully for generations to come.

The journey through the future of Truth has illuminated a critical crossroads. As our world contends with an ever-expanding tide of information and a growing reliance on artificial intelligence, the stakes for defining and safeguarding Truth have never been higher. The complexities surrounding Truth were already formidable, shaped by partisan biases, information silos, and social media platforms designed to profit from division and outrage. The advent of AI, and the looming prospect of AGI (artificial general intelligence), amplifies these challenges exponentially. It is not merely a question of how we use these technologies but, more importantly, of how we ensure they align with ethical principles and serve the greater good.

Artificial intelligence will inevitably amplify the volume and velocity of information—text, images, voice, and video—to a level where distinguishing signal from noise becomes an insurmountable task for any individual. In such an environment, AI claims of determining Truth are fraught with peril. At best, these systems provide approximations based on probabilistic models; at worst, they risk perpetuating—even amplifying—biases and misinformation. The tools we develop will not act as infallible arbiters of Truth but as amplifiers of the data and intentions we embed within them.

The most urgent question, therefore, is not whether AI is inherently good or bad. Rather, it is whether the people and institutions developing, funding, and profiting from AI are willing to confront the profound ethical dilemmas that arise. Where do they draw the line? What values do they prioritize? And how transparent will they be about their choices?

Together we've traced the multifaceted landscape of Truth and its interplay with AI through history, politics, culture, and ethics. From the philosophical inquiries of Plato to the modern ethical challenges posed by AI systems, we have explored how technology has continually reshaped the fabric of Truth. Yuval Noah Harari, in his bestselling book *Homo Deus* and subsequent public lectures, has sounded alarms about the risks of AI's control over public narratives, warning that it could erode individual agency and societal coherence. Eli Pariser's work on filter bubbles highlights how algorithmic design can fragment shared realities, making collective decision-making ever more precarious. Larry Lessig's advocacy for systemic transparency reminds us of the need for regulatory frameworks that prioritize accountability over unchecked innovation.

These are great thinkers, and they've been generous with their time and wisdom. But this book wasn't written for them, and I suspect some of them may disagree with how I have drawn conclusions that are, overall, fraught with dangerous future outcomes.

My friend Juan Enríquez has argued that our very understanding of human agency hangs in the balance. He has cautioned against a future where the mechanisms for discerning Truth are outsourced entirely to algorithms designed with profit as their primary driver. He is brilliant, and he backs up his concerns with powerful examples. If you haven't read his book *Right/Wrong*, I can't recommend it more highly.

I've known Esther Dyson forever. Her long-standing focus on fostering informed public engagement underscores the importance of education in navigating this complex landscape. Meanwhile, Gary Marcus is one of a handful of people willing to put himself out in the world and pull the fire alarm. This book began on stage at SXSW with Gary and me, and some angry feedback afterward told me I was on the right track. Gary challenges the AI community to reconcile its rapid advancements with fundamental ethical principles, emphasizing the dangers of deploying unexamined systems at scale.

Others in the book took me into new dimensions. David Chalmers, known for his philosophical exploration of consciousness, provided a compelling lens through which to view AI's epistemological impact. He suggests that AI forces us to reconsider the very nature of Truth—a fluid interplay between objective reality and subjective interpretation. Doug Rushkoff critiqued the commodification of human experience, cautioning against technologies that prioritize engagement metrics over meaningful connections. Hailey Colborn, with her emphasis on preserving humanity in an increasingly digital world, reminds us that Truth is not just a cognitive construct but an emotional anchor that binds communities together.

These measures, while essential, address only the immediate risks. The deeper, existential question remains: What does it mean to trust AI in a world where Truth itself is contested? As AI systems claim to separate fact from fiction, we risk becoming dangerously reliant on their outputs, delegating human judgment to opaque algorithms. This reliance threatens individual autonomy and the broader fabric of democratic discourse. If unchecked, it could erode the principles of accountability and agency that underpin our society.

This book's exploration of scenarios—from dystopian landscapes of misinformation and manipulated realities to utopian visions of AI-enhanced clarity—illustrates the spectrum of possibilities before us. In a dystopian future, Truth becomes fluid, shaped by algorithms optimized for profit. In a more hopeful vision, AI serves as a tool for enhancing understanding, illuminating nuance, and fostering dialogue. These scenarios are not inevitable outcomes but reflections of the choices we make today about how we govern, design, and interact with AI.

The future of Truth demands a recalibration of our relationship with technology. We must reject the binary narrative of AI as savior or villain. Instead, we must hold the creators and benefactors of AI to a higher standard, demanding explicit ethical commitments and transparency about their intentions and methods. Only by doing so can we hope to navigate the complexities of this new era, where technology shapes not only how we access information but also how we define what is real.

Which brings me back to—me. My 14-year-old magician-self is in many ways unchanged. I like things that amaze, confound, and challenge our known world. When I was 15, my grandmother, a first-generation immigrant from Russia, told me with great awe that she was amazed by the machines that dispensed money from the wall. For her, the ATM was pure magic. AI is most certainly the magic of our time. I can't wait to be my grandmother's age and find magic and mystery in whatever comes next. For now, our job is to point it in the right direction.

## *Epilogue: AI and the New Gods of Truth*

In the beginning, there was Vancouver.

On that TED stage in 2022, we watched as Gary Marcus stood before the world's tech elite and issued his warning about unchecked AI development. "AI doesn't understand facts, truth, or privacy," he told the audience. "It is a reckless bull in a china shop, and we should demand better." His voice was measured but urgent as he painted a stark picture of two possible futures: one where people are massively deceived and believe it, and another where people are lied to so often they stop believing anything. Neither scenario, as he argued, is conducive to a healthy democracy.

And then there was Eliezer Yudkowsky, delivering his apocalyptic vision with unsettling calm: "Many researchers, including myself, expect that the most likely result of building a superhumanly smart AI, under anything remotely like the current circumstances, is that literally everyone on Earth will die."

That was then. This is now.

Two years later, I find myself back at TED, watching another pivotal AI moment unfold. On the same stage where Marcus and Yudkowsky had delivered their warnings, Chris Anderson now faces Sam Altman, the CEO of OpenAI, arguably the most powerful AI leader in the world. The audience is rapt. The air feels electric with possibilities and pregnant with unspoken dangers.

Anderson isn't serving softballs. He's pressing Altman on the fundamental questions that have driven this entire book. Not just about what AI can do, but about who decides its direction, who gets to shape our collective Truth. Reading a question generated by another AI, Anderson asks:

"Sam, given that you're helping create technology that will reshape the destiny of our entire species, who granted you—or anyone—the moral authority to do that? And how are you personally responsible if you're wrong?"

The question hangs in the air like a guillotine blade. It's the question that burns at the heart of our Truth crisis. It's the question that has followed us through every chapter of this exploration: Who gets to define what's true? Who gets to decide our future?

Altman's response is telling: "I don't know."

It's an honest answer, perhaps the only honest answer. No one granted Altman or any Silicon Valley leader the authority to reshape our relationship with Truth. They simply took it. In the vacuum created by eroding institutional trust, technological power rushed in. No vote was held. No consent was sought. The transformation of Truth happened one product launch, one AI model, one viral app at a time.

When pressed further, Altman frames AI development as inevitable: "This is gonna happen. This is like a discovery of fundamental physics that the world now knows about, and it's gonna be part of our world." There's a fatalism to his words that echoes what Shoshana Zuboff warned about in our dark scenario—the sense that technological "progress" is a force of nature rather than a series of human choices.

If it's inevitable, why even debate? If resistance means getting "run over," what choice do we really have? This fatalism is more than a rhetorical device—it's a moral sleight of hand. It converts corporate ambition into cosmic law, reframing decisions as destiny. It neuters dissent and flattens public debate into a shrug.

Altman isn't the first to sit at the edge of a world-shaping invention. History gives us a lineage of figures whose brilliance reshaped civilization—and whose ambition outpaced the systems meant to govern them. J. Robert Oppenheimer split the atom and then spent the rest of his life warning us about what he'd done. Thomas Edison electrified the world while crushing rivals with lawsuits and spin. Nikola Tesla imagined wireless power and AI long before the world was ready. Alan Turing cracked codes and built the foundation of modern computing, only to be destroyed by the society he helped save. Henry Ford transformed industry while propagating hate. Steve Jobs blended artistry and domination, creating tools that felt intimate and indispensable, even as they ushered in a new form of corporate control.

These weren't easy people. They weren't always right. But they were relentless. They believed in the future they could see—and they pulled the rest of the world along with them, sometimes willingly, sometimes not.

The question now isn't whether Sam Altman fits that mold. He does. The real question is whether we've learned anything from the last hundred years of innovation. Whether we've built institutions strong enough to keep pace with individuals who are brilliant, certain, and mostly unaccountable. Whether we can create a world where technology doesn't just bend to vision, but to values.

Because the vision Altman paints for our future is both seductive and unsettling: "You will talk to ChatGPT over the course of your life and someday, maybe if you want, it'll be listening to you throughout the day and sort of observing what you're doing, and it'll get to know you." He describes a world where AI becomes our constant companion, "observing" our every move—a framing that sounds more like surveillance than assistance.

Anderson likened this to the movie *Her*, where an AI reads all the protagonist's emails and takes life-altering actions on his behalf. Altman didn't disagree. The moment echoed Neal Stephenson's *The Diamond Age*, where a young girl is raised under the constant guidance of a sentient interactive device—"The Primer"—that listens, adapts, and teaches her through a blend of narrative, surveillance, and engineered moral shaping. What once read as science fiction now feels eerily like a feature road map.

The casual way Altman described a future in which AI systems monitor our lives—"sort of observing what you're doing"—betrays a fundamental disconnect from how most humans feel about consent, autonomy, and privacy. The "maybe if you want" qualifier rings hollow in a world where meaningful consent is a vanishing illusion.

When Anderson asks if becoming a father has changed his perspective on risk, Altman's response reveals the paradox at the heart of our technological moment: "I really cared about, like, not destroying the world before. I really care about it now."

Anderson pushes further with a scenario: If you could press a button that would guarantee your son an incredible life, but with a 10% risk of destruction—would you? Altman dodges the implication: "In the literal case, no . . . I also don't feel like that." But that's precisely the moral dilemma at the heart of AI. What Altman wouldn't gamble with for his son, he implicitly gambles with for the rest of ours.

This disconnection between personal risk tolerance and professional risk acceptance is the cognitive dissonance we all now live inside. The stakes are global, the risks systemic, yet the calculus remains disturbingly personal—and often, detached.

Perhaps most revealing is Altman's vision for his own child's future: "My kids, hopefully, will never be smarter than AI. They will never grow up in a world where products and services aren't incredibly smart, incredibly capable." He envisions a generation that will look back at us with "pity and nostalgia," thinking, "Wow, they lived such limited lives. The world suffered so much. And I think that's great."

It's a troubling statement—presenting human intelligence as something to be surpassed rather than enhanced, positioning AI dominance as not just inevitable but desirable, and framing our current condition as primitive suffering that technology will transcend. The future he imagines is not just AI-augmented—it's AI-superior.

Perhaps most revealing is Altman's inability to define what they're even building toward. When asked about OpenAI's mission to safely reach AGI, he admits: "If you've got 10 OpenAI researchers in the room and ask to define AGI, you get 14 definitions." They're racing toward a destination they can't even name, developing technologies whose implications they don't fully understand.

When Anderson suggests a small summit of experts to establish global AI safety standards, Altman's response is revealing: "Of course, but I'm much more interested in what our hundreds of millions of users want as a whole. I think a lot of the room has historically been decided in small elite summits. One of the cool new things about AI is that it can talk to everybody on Earth, and we can learn the collective value preferences of what everybody wants—rather than have a bunch of people who are blessed by society sit in a room and make those decisions."

This sounds democratic until you realize the false choice it presents. Users can only "want" options presented to them, not the roads not taken. People "wanted" cigarettes too—until we understood the costs. And by then, the damage was already done.

The stark reality is that we don't get to vote on whether Altman and his peers should be making these monumental decisions. They've already appointed themselves our technological destiny's curators. The market has spoken. The rest of us are left to adapt, resist, or hope.

As I sit in the audience, watching this dance of power and accountability, I'm struck by how far we've come from that first TED session with Marcus and Yudkowsky. The warnings have grown more urgent. The stakes have grown higher. The technology has grown more powerful. But the fundamental questions remain the same:

Who gets to decide what Truth is? Who gets to shape our collective future? And how do we ensure that technology serves humanity rather than the other way around?

The answers to these questions won't come from Silicon Valley. They won't emerge from corporate boardrooms or investor meetings. They can only come from all of us—from a renewed commitment to human agency, to democratic values, to the messy, beautiful process of determining Truth together.

As we stand at this crossroads of technological change, we face a choice. We can surrender to the narrative of inevitability, allowing a handful of tech companies to reshape our relationship with Truth. Or we can reclaim our role as authors of our own story, insisting that even the most powerful technologies remain tools in service of human flourishing.

In the end, the future of Truth isn't just about technology. It's about us—about our courage to question, our willingness to engage, our determination to shape rather than be shaped. It's about remembering that behind every algorithm, every platform, every AI system, there are human choices, human values, human responsibilities.

AI may be our partner—or our overlord. It's too soon to tell. But what is clear, here at TED, is that a small circle of powerful technologists are writing the rules, largely unchallenged. They may call themselves caretakers. But unless we intervene—unless we demand visibility, accountability, and restraint—we risk becoming passive passengers in a story we didn't choose.

The most important question remains: Who gave Sam Altman—or anyone—the keys to humanity's future?

The uncomfortable Truth is: No one did. And yet, here we are.

Truth is no longer rhetorical or academic. It is the bedrock of our autonomy, our humanity, and our power to shape the world around us. Call it agency, self-determination, or simply freedom—it begins with Truth.

We will keep it only if we grip it fiercely, refusing to let it slip through our fingers. We will lose it through casual indifference, by treating it as someone else's responsibility, or by surrendering it to systems that offer convenience in exchange for control.

This is the line we now stand on. Not just between fact and fiction, but between the fire of human will—and the cold logic of code.

And yet, there's a generation rising that refuses to be shaped without shaping back.

Gen Z didn't consent to this digital reality. They inherited it—an ecosystem optimized for extraction, deception, and distraction. They were the first to grow up inside it, and they've borne the brunt of its harms: anxiety, isolation, body dysmorphia, algorithmic gaslighting masquerading as connection. But with that pain has come clarity—and, for many, a sharpened resolve.

This generation isn't waiting to be rescued. They're building. They're demanding transparency, codesign, and accountability. They're calling out the lies, resisting the dopamine traps, and insisting that technology must serve humanity—not the other way around. They understand the stakes not as an abstraction, but as lived experience. And because of that, they may be the ones best positioned to steer us toward something better.

No, they don't own OpenAI or run trillion-dollar companies. Yet. But they do have what every revolution begins with: vision, solidarity, and moral clarity. And if history has taught us anything, it's that power eventually bends to pressure—and pressure starts from the ground up.

We began this book with Marshall McLuhan's warning: *We shape our tools and thereafter our tools shape us.*

But what happens when the generation being shaped decides to shape back?

That's where the future of Truth begins again.

# Acknowledgments

This book would not have been possible without the generous support and guidance of numerous individuals who have contributed their time, expertise, and wisdom throughout my editorial, philosophical, and literary journey. Today, I have an MA in Truth from the Gallatin School of Individualized Study at New York University, and my early research and discoveries stemmed from that study.

I am profoundly grateful to the exceptional faculty at NYU who have shaped my intellectual development. Professor Stephen Duncombe, your mentorship has been transformative. To Professors Daniel Rogers, Kimon Keramidas, Mario Khreiche, Sara Murphy, Nicholas Mirzoeff, Alyssa Wise, Marita Sturken, Joseph Lemelin, and Isra Ali—each of you has contributed uniquely to this project's evolution.

I extend my gratitude to my thesis committee. To David Stone, whose insightful feedback and unwavering support went back to the early days when Truth was still in proposal form.

To Ellen Chodosh, thank you for your careful reading and thoughtful commentary that helped shape this work.

This research has been enriched by the generous participation of several leading thinkers who shared their time and insights through interviews. I am indebted to Eli Pariser, Larry Lessig, Juan Enríquez, Esther Dyson, Gary Marcus, Steve Fuller, Doug Rushkoff, David Chalmers, and Hailo Colborn for their valuable contributions to this work.

Todd Schuster has been a spectacular agent and more. Since our first conversation at the TED Residency, Todd has been guiding this book and helping to shape it into a project that I hope has become both intellectually honest and a useful contribution to the complicated world of AI that is now emerging. Thanks to Lauren Liebow and Jack Haug from the Aevitas Creative Management team who shepherded this book into existence.

On my publishing team, Matt Holt was the kind of editor you want on a project of this scope and complexity. Supportive, questioning, and enthusiastic about its importance as both a book and a conversation. As one might imagine, publishing and Truth have a critical kinship, and Truth's survival isn't trivial as we consider the future of the written word. The team at BenBella and Matt Holt books was everything an author could hope for. Lydia Choi was a detailed and thoughtfully probing editor, and Katie Dickman an ever-present calm force in the always tricky path to turn a book from an idea to a finished work. And my longtime friend and collaborator Bob Garfield was brave enough to dig through a late-stage draft and provide his crisp and shockingly positive take on these pages.

In the realm of technological assistance, I acknowledge the support of various AI tools that aided in the writing and editing process: ChatGPT, Claude, NaturalReaders, ProWritingAid, and Grammarly. These tools helped refine and polish the presentation of my ideas.

I would be remiss not to acknowledge the sharp insights and editorial expertise of Pamela Yoder, a brilliant listener, thinker, and provocateur. Over the past four years, she's shared articles, pointed out flaws in my logic, and often sat on my metaphorical shoulder as I wrote, re-wrote, and then started over. She's a magical mix of critical and collaborative, and I couldn't have written this book or taken this rollicking journey without her, both professionally and personally.

To everyone who has contributed to this journey, your support has been essential to bringing this project to fruition. I hope you find the book useful, not as a volume of answers, but as a thoughtful and relevant exploration of questions that matter. I look forward to the conversations that it will inevitably foster.

# Bibliography


## Chapter 1: The Vancouver Food Fight That Tried to Save Truth and Failed

Anderson, Chris. "Opening Remarks and Moderation of AI Panel Discussion." Presented at TED2022: A New Era, Vancouver, BC, April 2022.

Brockman, Greg. "The Inside Story of ChatGPT's Astonishing Potential." Presented at TED2023, Vancouver, BC, April 2023.

Burkeman, Oliver. "Why Can't the World's Greatest Minds Solve the Mystery of Consciousness?" *The Guardian*, January 21, 2015. https://www.theguardian.com/science/2015/jan/21/-sp-why-cant-worlds-greatest-minds-solve-mystery-consciousness.

Marcus, Gary. "The Future of Truth." Panel discussion, SXSW Conference, Austin, TX, March 2023.

Marcus, Gary. "The Next Decade in AI: Four Steps Towards Robust Artificial Intelligence." arXiv preprint arXiv:2002.06177, February 2020.

Marcus, Gary. "The Urgent Risks of Runaway AI—and What to Do About Them." Presented at TED2023, Vancouver, BC, April 2023.

Marcus, Gary. "We Have to Get It Right: Gary Marcus on Untamed AI." *Your Undivided Attention* (podcast), hosted by Daniel Barcay. Center for Humane Technology, September 26, 2024. https://www.humanetech.com/podcast/we-have-to-get-it-right-gary-marcus-on-untamed-ai.

Microsoft. "Microsoft and OpenAI Extend Partnership." The Official Microsoft Blog, January 23, 2023. https://blogs.microsoft.com/blog/2023/01/23/microsoftandopenaiextendpartnership/.

P&T Knitwear. "The Promise and Peril of AI: Gary Marcus and Raffi Krikorian in Conversation." September 19, 2024. https://www.ptknitwear.com/events/41929.

Rosenbaum, Steve. "The End of Fake News." TED, June 2017. https://www.ted.com/talks/steve_rosenbaum_the_end_of_fake_news.

TED. "TED Content Guidelines." Accessed July 16, 2025. https://www.ted.com/about/our-organization/our-policies-terms/ted-content-guidelines.

TED Conferences, LLC. TED2022: A New Era. 2022. https://tedlive.ted.com/webcasts/t2022.

Yudkowsky, Eliezer. "Will Superintelligent AI End the World?" Video of a TED Talk, July 2023. https://www.ted.com/talks/eliezer_yudkowsky_will_superintelligent_ai_end_the_world/transcript.

## Chapter 2: Truth's Troubled Past

Chalmers, David. Interview by author. October 5, 2023.

Chen, Huili, Hae Won Park, Xiamen Zhang, and Cynthia Brazeal. "Impact of Interaction Context on the Student Affect–Learning Relationship in Child-Robot Interaction." In *Proceedings of the 2020 ACM/IEEE International Conference on Human-Robot Interaction (HRI '20)*, Cambridge, UK, March 23–26, 2020. Association for Computing Machinery, 2020. https://doi.org/10.1145/3319502.3374822.

Crawford, Kate. "Artificial Intelligence Misreading Human Emotion." *The Atlantic*, April 27, 2021. https://www.theatlantic.com/technology/archive/2021/04/artificial-intelligence-misreading-human-emotion/618696/.

el Kaliouby, Rana, and Peter Robinson. "The Emotional Hearing Aid: An Assistive Tool for Children with Asperger Syndrome." *Universal Access in the Information Society* 4 (2005): 121–134.

Gordon, Rebecca. "What Is Truth in the Age of Trump?" *The Nation*, January 11, 2019. https://www.thenation.com/article/archive/what-is-truth-in-the-age-of-trump/.

Kanda, Takayuki, Takayuki Hirano, Daniel Eaton, and Hiroshi Ishiguro. "Interactive Robots as Social Partners and Peer Tutors for Children: A Field Trial." *Human–Computer Interaction* 19, nos. 1–2 (2004): 61–84. https://doi.org/10.1207/s15327051hci1901&2_4.

Kostopoulos, Lydia. "The Booming Business of AI Relationships & Intimacy: And Why It's Here to Stay." LinkedIn, May 2, 2024. https://www.linkedin.com/pulse/booming-business-ai-relationships-intimacy-why-its-kostopoulos-phd--ibooe/.

Marcus, Gary. "Gary Marcus Wants to Tame Silicon Valley." *Tech Policy Press*, September 22, 2024. https://www.techpolicy.press/gary-marcus-wants-to-tame-silicon-valley.

Roose, Kevin. "A Conversation with Bing's Chatbot Left Me Deeply Unsettled." *The New York Times*, February 16, 2023. https://www.nytimes.com/2023/02/16/technology/bing-chatbot-microsoft-chatgpt.html.

Rushkoff, Douglas. *Program or Be Programmed: Eleven Commands for the AI Future.* OR Press, 2023.

Stanojevic, Cedomir, Casey C. Bennett, Selma Šabanović, Sawyer Collins, Katherine Baugus Henkel, Zachary Henkel, and Jennifer A. Piatt. "Conceptualizing Socially-Assistive Robots as a Digital Therapeutic Tool in Healthcare." *Frontiers in Digital Health* 5 (2023): 1208350. https://doi.org/10.3389/fdgth.2023.1208350.

Suwajanakorn, Supasorn, Steven M. Seitz, and Ira Kemelmacher-Shlizerman. "Synthesizing Obama: Learning Lip Sync from Audio." *ACM Transactions on Graphics* 36, no. 4 (July 2017): Article 95, 1–13. https://doi.org/10.1145/3072959.3073640.

Yang, Andrew. *The War on Normal People: The Truth About America's Disappearing Jobs and Why Universal Basic Income Is Our Future.* Hachette Books, 2023.

Zimmer, Carl. "Two Theories of Consciousness Square Off." *The New York Times*, July 1, 2023. https://www.nytimes.com/2023/07/01/science/consciousness-theories.html.

## Chapter 3: Facing a Future of Truth Decay

Enríquez, Juan. Interview by author. December 2023.

Enríquez, Juan. *Right/Wrong: How Technology Transforms Our Ethics.* MIT Press, 2020.

Enríquez, Juan. *The Untied States of America: Polarization, Fracturing, and Our Future.* Crown, 2005.

Heisenberg, Werner. *Physics and Philosophy: The Revolution in Modern Science.* Harper & Brothers, 1958.

Huguet, Alice, John F. Pane, Garrett Baker, Laura S. Hamilton, and Susannah Faxon-Mills. "Media Literacy and Civic Education to Combat Truth Decay." *RAND Blog*, August 4, 2021. https://www.rand.org/pubs/research_reports/RRA112-18.html.

Kavanagh, Jennifer, and Michael D. Rich. *Truth Decay: An Initial Exploration of the Diminishing Role of Facts and Analysis in American Public Life.* RAND Corporation, 2018.

RAND Corporation. "About Truth Decay." Accessed October 20, 2025. https://www.rand.org/research/projects/truth-decay/about-truth-decay.html.

RAND Corporation. "Our History." Accessed October 20, 2025. https://www.rand.org/about/history.html.

RAND Corporation. "Searching for Truth: Q&A with Jennifer Kavanagh." June 26, 2019. https://www.rand.org/pubs/commentary/2019/06/searching-for-truth-qa-with-jennifer-kavanagh.html.

Schrödinger, Erwin. *What Is Life? The Physical Aspect of the Living Cell.* Cambridge University Press, 1944.

## Chapter 4: Truth and Politics: The Digitization of Democracy

Bulla, David W., and Heather Haley. "Sensational Journalism in the Mid-19th Century." In *Journalism in the Civil War Era*, edited by David W. Bulla and Gregory A. Borchard. Routledge, 2015.

Culpepper, Sophie. "Could Social Media Support Healthy Online Conversations? New_ Public Is Working on It." *Nieman Journalism Lab.* July 16, 2024. https://www.niemanlab.org/2024/07/could-social-media-support-healthy-online-conversations-new_public-is-working-on-it/.

Enríquez, Juan. *Right/Wrong: How Technology Transforms Our Ethics.* MIT Press, 2020.

Kavanagh, Jennifer, and Michael D. Rich. *Truth Decay: An Initial Exploration of the Diminishing Role of Facts and Analysis in American Public Life.* RAND Corporation, 2018.

Kessler, Glenn, Salvador Rizzo, and Meg Kelly. "Trump's False or Misleading Claims Total 30,573 Over Four Years." *The Washington Post*, January 24, 2021. https://www.washingtonpost.com/politics/2021/01/24/trumps-false-or-misleading-claims-total-30573-over-four-years/.

MoveOn.org. "A Short History of MoveOn." MoveOn Civic Action, 2023. https://front.moveon.org/a-short-history/.

Pariser, Eli. *The Filter Bubble: How the New Personalized Web Is Changing What We Read and How We Think*. Penguin Books, 2012.

Pariser, Eli. "How to Design Digital Spaces for Democracy." *New_ Public Blog*, 2024. Accessed December 30, 2024. https://www.newpublic.org/blog.

Pariser, Eli. Interview by author. October 31, 2024.

Smith, David. "'We're Watching Mass Delusion Happen': Trump's Return to White House Brings Cascade of Lies." *The Guardian*, January 26, 2025. https://www.theguardian.com/us-news/2025/jan/26/trump-white-house-lies-immigration-economy.

Thucydides. *History of the Peloponnesian War*. Translated by Richard Crawley. Digireads.com Publishing, 2017.

## Chapter 5: The Power and Peril of Identity in a Digitized World

Australian eSafety Commissioner. "Latest eSafety Research Reveals Social Media Use Is Widespread Among Kids—and So Are the Harms." November 7, 2025. https://www.esafety.gov.au/newsroom/media-releases/latest-esafety-research-reveals-social-media-use-is-widespread-among-kids-and-so-are-the-harms.

Digital Agency, Government of Japan. *Annual Report of the Digital Agency (September 2023–August 2024)*. Accessed July 17, 2025. https://www.digital.go.jp/en/policies/report-202309-202408.

Franck, Thomas. "Romance Scams Reach $1.4 Billion in Losses for 2024." *CNBC*, 2024. https://www.cnbc.com/2024/07/03/heres-how-to-avoid-romance-scams-which-cost-consumers-1point14-billion-last-year.html.

Hinge. "World Romance Scam Prevention Day: How We're Protecting and Empowering Users." *Hinge Newsroom*, February 14, 2024. https://hinge.co/newsroom/Scam-Prevention-Awareness-2024.

Infocomm Media Development Authority. *Annual Report 2023/2024*. Singapore: IMDA, 2024. https://www.imda.gov.sg/-/media/imda/files/about/resources/corporate-publications/annual-report/imda-annual-report-2024.pdf.

Inman Grant, Julie. "Swimming Between the Digital Flags: Helping Young Australians Navigate Social Media's Dangerous Currents." National Press Club of Australia, June 24, 2025. https://www.esafety.gov.au/newsroom/blogs/swimming-between-the-digital-flags-helping-young-australians-navigate-social-medias-dangerous-currents.

International Telecommunication Union (ITU). *Measuring Digital Development: Facts and Figures 2024*. ITU, 2024.

Marsh, Jared. "How Many Children Use TikTok Against the Rules? Most, Study Finds." University of San Francisco, January 10, 2025. https://www.ucsf.edu/news/2025/01/429296/many-children-use-tiktok-against-rules.

Matsakis, Louise. "Most News Sites Block AI Bots. Right-Wing Media Welcomes Them."

*Wired*, January 24, 2024. https://www.wired.com/story/most-news-sites-block-ai-bots-right-wing-media-welcomes-them/.

Rushkoff, Douglas. Interview by author. December 2024.

Rushkoff, Douglas. *Program or Be Programmed: Ten Commands for a Digital Age.* OR Books, 2011.

Rushkoff, Douglas. *Team Human.* W. W. Norton & Company, 2019.

TikTok. *Transparency Report: Digital Services Act—October to December 2023.* 2024. https://rmultimediafileshare.blob.core.windows.net/rmultimedia/TikTok%20-%20DSA%20Transparency%20report%20-%20October%20to%20December%202023.pdf.

Timothy Leary Papers. Manuscripts and Archives Division, The New York Public Library. https://digitalcollections.nypl.org/search/index?q=Reflections%20on%20Media%20Consumption%20Rituals.

World Bank. *2023 ID4D and G2Px Annual Report.* World Bank Publications, 2024. https://id4d.worldbank.org/annual-report.

World Bank. *Identification for Development: Strategic Roadmap 2023–2025.* Washington, DC: World Bank, 2023. https://id4d.worldbank.org.

World Economic Forum. *Reimagining Digital ID: A Human-Centered Approach.* Geneva: World Economic Forum, 2023. https://www.weforum.org/publications/reimagining-digital-id/.

## Chapter 6: Extra, Extra! Read All About It! News Robots as Truth-Tellers

BBC News Labs. "Local News Partnerships: Automation in Local Journalism." *BBC R&D*, 2021. https://www.bbc.co.uk/rd/blog/2021-04-local-news-partnership-automation.

Benton, Bond, and Daniela Peterka-Benton. "Everything Old Is Q Again: An Analysis of the Resurgent #PIZZAGATE Myth in Social Media." *Popular Culture Studies Journal*, 2025. Montclair State University Digital Commons. https://digitalcommons.montclair.edu/scom-facpubs/56/.

Burns, Collin, et al. "A New AI Lie Detector Reveals Their 'Inner Thoughts.'" *Freethink*, March 30, 2023. https://www.freethink.com/robots-ai/ai-lie-detector.

City University of New York Library. "Web Sites for Fact Checking—Misinformation and Disinformation." Accessed July 17, 2025. https://library.csi.cuny.edu/misinformation/fact-checking-websites.

Cross, R. J. Interview by author. January 5, 2025.

Dale, Mary Jo. "The Rise of the Robot Reporter." *The New York Times*, February 5, 2019. https://www.nytimes.com/2019/02/05/business/media/artificial-intelligence-journalism-robots.html.

Dyson, Esther. Interview by author. December 2024.

Dyson, Esther. *Release 1.0.* EDventure Holdings, 1983–2006.

Dyson, Freeman. *Disturbing the Universe.* New York: Harper & Row, 1979.

LaFrance, Adrienne, and Gillian B. White. "The Big Story: The Sprawling Universe of

QAnon." *The Atlantic*, May 28, 2020. https://www.theatlantic.com/live/sprawling-universe-qanon-2020/.

Maheshwari, Sapna. "Snopes Cofounder Wrote Dozens of Plagiarized Articles for the Fact-Checking Site." *The New York Times*, August 13, 2021. https://www.nytimes.com/2021/08/13/business/media/snopes-plagiarism-David-Mikkelson.html.

Meir, Nicole. "Automated Earnings Stories Multiply." *The Associated Press*, June 15, 2015. https://www.ap.org/the-definitive-source/announcements/automated-earnings-stories-multiply/.

MIT News. "Study: On Twitter, False News Travels Faster Than True Stories." March 8, 2018. https://news.mit.edu/2018/study-twitter-false-news-travels-faster-true-stories-0308.

Robertson, Katie. "Snopes Cofounder Wrote Dozens of Plagiarized Articles for the Fact-Checking Site." *The New York Times*, August 13, 2021. https://www.nytimes.com/2021/08/13/business/media/snopes-plagiarism-David-Mikkelson.html.

Rosenbaum, Steve. "The End of Fake News." TED, June 2017. Video, 6:22. https://www.ted.com/talks/steve_rosenbaum_the_end_of_fake_news.

The Sun (New York). "Great Astronomical Discoveries Lately Made by Sir John Herschel, L.L.D., F.R.S., &c., at the Cape of Good Hope." August 25–31, 1835. https://hoaxes.org/archive/permalink/the_great_moon_hoax.

World Economic Forum. "The Pace of Innovation Is Speeding Up. Digital Fragmentation Threatens That." January 8, 2024. https://www.weforum.org/stories/2024/01/digital-fragmentation-risks-harming-cybersecurity-curtailing-ai/.

## Chapter 7: Love, Truth, and Robots

Character.AI. "Terms of Service." Accessed December 30, 2024. https://policies.character.ai/tos.

Colborn, Hailey. Interview by author. December 2024.

Hinge. "2024 D.A.T.E. Report: Digital Approaches to Today's Engagements." *Hinge Newsroom*, February 6, 2024. https://hinge.co/newsroom/2024-GenZ-Report.

Kostopoulos, Lydia. "The Three Types of Artificial Intelligence and Human Relationships." *Medium*, January 27, 2020. https://lkcyber.medium.com/the-three-types-of-artificial-intelligence-and-human-relationships-2c426890e202.

Loftus, Rikki. "Heartbreaking Final Messages 14-Year-Old Boy Sent to AI Chatbot Moments Before Taking His Own Life." *UNILAD Tech*, October 24, 2024. https://www.uniladtech.com/news/final-messages-teen-sent-ai-chatbot-death-154421-20241024.

Megan Garcia v. Character Technologies, Inc., No. 6:24-cv-01903 (U.S. Dist. Ct., Middle Dist. Fla., October 23, 2024).

Montgomery, Blake. "Mother Says AI Chatbot Led Her Son to Kill Himself in Lawsuit Against Its Maker." *The Guardian*, October 23, 2024. https://www.theguardian.com/technology/2024/oct/23/character-ai-chatbot-sewell-setzer-death.

Nwoko, Hannah. "Mom Blames Character.AI for Her Teen's Death—What Parents Should Know." *Parents*, October 30, 2024. https://www.parents.com/mom-blames-character-ai-for-teens-death-8736114.

Orenstein, Peggy. *Cinderella Ate My Daughter: Dispatches from the Front Lines of the New Girlie-Girl Culture.* HarperCollins, 2011.

## Chapter 8: Arrested by a Robot: The Future of AI Justice

ACLU. "Williams v. City of Detroit." American Civil Liberties Union, 2024. https://www.aclu.org/cases/williams-v-city-of-detroit-face-recognition-false-arrest.

American Civil Liberties Union. "Wrongfully Arrested Because Face Recognition Can't Tell Black People Apart." June 24, 2020. https://www.aclu.org/news/privacy-technology/wrongfully-arrested-because-face-recognition-cant-tell-black-people-apart.

"Brazil: The Country of 100 Million Lawsuits." *Legal Management*, 2014. https://www.alanet.org/docs/default-source/legal-management-archives/brazil_-the-country-of-100-million-lawsuits.pdf.

Buolamwini, Joy. "AI and the Future of Justice." Remarks at the Aspen Ideas Festival, June 28, 2021. https://www.aspenideas.org/sessions/ai-and-the-future-of-justice.

Buolamwini, Joy, and Timnit Gebru. "Gender Shades: Intersectional Accuracy Disparities in Commercial Gender Classification." *Proceedings of Machine Learning Research* 81 (2018): 1–15. https://proceedings.mlr.press/v81/buolamwini18a/buolamwini18a.pdf.

Clearview AI. "Using Facial Recognition to Combat Human Trafficking—One Face at a Time." January 24, 2024. https://www.clearview.ai/post/using-facial-recognition-to-combat-human-trafficking-one-face-at-a-time.

*Coded Bias.* Featuring Joy Buolamwini. Directed by Shalini Kantayya. 7th Empire Media, 2020.

Engstrom, David Freeman, ed. *Legal Tech and the Future of Civil Justice.* Cambridge: Cambridge University Press, 2023. https://www.cambridge.org/core/books/legal-tech-and-the-future-of-civil-justice/7322467F5F9BBD1FA174D3E5D5B54D8E.

Engstrom, David Freeman, and Nora Freeman Engstrom. "Legal Tech and the Litigation Playing Field." In *Legal Tech and the Future of Civil Justice*, edited by David Freeman Engstrom, 133–154. Cambridge University Press, 2023.

Engstrom, Nora Freeman, and David Freeman Engstrom. "Justice for All? Why We Have an Access to Justice Gap in America—and What to Do About It." *Stanford Legal Podcast*, June 6, 2024. https://law.stanford.edu/stanford-legal-on-siriusxm/.

European Parliament. "Excessive Length of Civil Court Cases in Italy." European Parliament, 2014. https://www.europarl.europa.eu/doceo/document/E-7-2014-004003_EN.html.

Hecht, Nathan L. "Closing the Justice Gap: How to Make the Civil Justice System Accessible to All Americans." Testimony Before the US Senate Committee on the Judiciary, July 9, 2024. Washington, DC. https://www.judiciary.senate.gov/imo/media/doc/2024-07-09_-_testimony_-_hecht.pdf.

International Telecommunication Union. *AI Standardization Roundtable Report: The Future of AI, Regulation and Industry Development.* Geneva: ITU, May 2024. https://www.itu.int/dms_pub/itu-t/opb/ai4g/T-AI4G-AI4GOOD-2024-5-PDF-E.pdf.

Kantayya, Shalini, dir. *Coded Bias. Independent Lens.* PBS, 2020. https://www.pbs.org/independentlens/documentaries/coded-bias/.

Lessig, Lawrence. *Code and Other Laws of Cyberspace.* Basic Books, 1999.

Lessig, Lawrence. Interview by author. December 2024.

Liptak, Andrew. "DARPA's Squad X Project Pairs Marines and Robots to Eliminate the Fog of War." *The Verge,* July 18, 2019. https://www.theverge.com/2019/7/18/18677437/darpa-squad-x-project-marines-drones-robots-ai-fog-of-war-caci-lockheed-martin-video-watch.

*Minority Report.* Directed by Steven Spielberg. DreamWorks Pictures, 2002.

Next IAS. "Slow & Clogged Indian Judiciary: A System in Crisis." Next IAS, November 27, 2024. https://www.nextias.com/ca/editorial-analysis/27-11-2024/slow-clogged-indian-judiciary-a-system-in-crisis.

*Please Hold.* Directed by Kristen "KD" Dávila. Los Angeles: Dávila Films and Scavenger Entertainment; distributed by HBO Max, 2020. Short film, 19 min.

Szilagyi, Katie. "Justice AI and the Rule of Law in the Age of AI." *Just Security,* October 9, 2024. https://www.justsecurity.org/103777/maintaining-the-rule-of-law-in-the-age-of-ai/.

TNN. "43 Lakh Cheque-Bounce Cases Pending, Rajasthan Tops List." *The Times of India,* December 28, 2024. https://timesofindia.indiatimes.com/india/43-lakh-cheque-bounce-cases-pending-rajasthan-tops-list/articleshow/116725068.cms.

US Commission on Civil Rights. *Facial Recognition Technology: Examining Its Use by Law Enforcement.* Washington, DC: US Commission on Civil Rights, January 2025. https://www.usccr.gov/files/2025-01/facial_recognition_report_factsheet.pdf.

## Chapter 9: The Battle: Information Warfare and Autonomous Robots

Asaro, Peter. "Autonomous Weapons: An Interview with the Experts." Interview by Ariel Conn. *Future of Life Institute Podcast,* July 31, 2018. https://futureoflife.org/podcast/autonomous-weapons-interview-experts/.

Defense Advanced Research Projects Agency (DARPA). "OFFSET: Offensive Swarm-Enabled Tactics." DARPA. Accessed December 30, 2024. https://www.darpa.mil/search/results?q=OFFSET%3A+Offensive+Swarm-Enabled+Tactics.

Defense Advanced Research Projects Agency (DARPA). "Sea Hunter: The Unmanned Anti-Submarine Warfare Vessel." DARPA. Accessed December 30, 2024. https://www.darpa.mil/search/results?q=Sea+Hunter%3A+The+Unmanned+Anti-Submarine+Warfare+Vessel.

Defense Advanced Research Projects Agency (DARPA). *Sea Hunter Prototype Transitions to Office of Naval Research for Further Development.* Arlington, VA: DARPA, January 30, 2018. https://www.darpa.mil/news/2018/sea-hunter-prototype.

Frandzel, Steve. "Pulling Back the Curtain on Neural Networks." *Oregon State University College of Engineering,* October 25, 2021. https://engineering.oregonstate.edu/all-stories/pulling-back-curtain-neural-networks.

Future of Life Institute. *Slaughterbots.* Directed by Stewart Sugg. Featuring Stuart Russell. Future of Life Institute, 2017. Video, 7:47. https://futureoflife.org/video/slaughterbots/.

Horowitz, Michael, Paul Scharre, Gregory C. Allen, K. Frederick, A. Cho, and E.

Saravalle. *Artificial Intelligence and International Security.* Center for a New American Security, July 10, 2018. https://www.cnas.org/publications/reports/artificial-intelligence-and-international-security.

International Committee for Robot Arms Control. *Frequently Asked Questions on LAWS.* n.d. ICRAC. Accessed December 30, 2024. https://www.icrac.net/frequently-asked-questions-on-laws/.

Kakaes, Konstantin. "'Army of None' Review: Robots at the Front." *Wall Street Journal,* June 26, 2018. https://www.wsj.com/articles/army-of-none-review-robots-at-the-front-1530052746.

Kavanaugh, Jennifer, and Michael D. Rich. *Truth Decay: An Initial Exploration of the Diminishing Role of Facts and Analysis in American Public Life.* RAND Corporation, January 16, 2018. https://www.rand.org/pubs/research_reports/RR2314.html.

Luckey, Palmer. "The AI Arsenal That Could Stop World War III." TED Talk. Vancouver, April 2025. Video, 15:12. https://www.youtube.com/watch?v=ooMXEwl7N8Y.

Medill News Service. "Defense Department Grapples with Ethics of Virtual Reality." *Medill News Service,* October 4, 2018. https://dc.medill.northwestern.edu/blog/2018/10/04/defense-department-grapples-ethics-virtual-reality.

Russell, Stuart. "Banning Lethal Autonomous Weapons: An Education." *Issues in Science and Technology* 38, no. 3 (Spring 2022). https://issues.org/banning-lethal-autonomous-weapons-stuart-russell/.

Russell, Stuart. *Human Compatible: Artificial Intelligence and the Problem of Control.* Viking, 2019.

Scharre, Paul. *Army of None: Autonomous Weapons and the Future of War.* W. W. Norton, 2018.

Singer, Peter W. *Wired for War: The Robotics Revolution and Conflict in the 21st Century.* Penguin Press, 2009.

Smith, Chris. "Advanced Computing and Warfare." *Australian Army Journal* 20, no. 1 (June 6, 2024).

US Department of Defense. Office of the Under Secretary of Defense (Comptroller). *FY2024 Defense Budget Overview.* Washington, DC: US Department of Defense, 2023. https://comptroller.defense.gov/Portals/45/Documents/defbudget/FY2024/FY2024_Budget_Request_Overview_Book.pdf.

## Chapter 10: The Misinformation Infodemic

Ben-Ari, Elia. "Addressing the Challenges of Cancer Misinformation on Social Media." *Cancer Currents Blog,* National Cancer Institute, September 9, 2021. Accessed December 2024. https://www.cancer.gov/news-events/cancer-currents-blog/2021/cancer-misinformation-social-media.

Columbia University. "Bollinger Convening: Journalism and Democracy in an AI World." Panel discussion featuring Katrín Jakobsdóttir, Melissa Fleming, Lee C. Bollinger, Joseph E. Stiglitz, and Churchill Otieno. Moderated by Anya Schiffrin. October 24, 2024. The Forum at Columbia University, New York. https://theforum.columbia.edu/events/bollinger-convening-journalism-and-democracy-ai-world.

Columbia University Maison Française. "Truth, Trust, and the Trials of Democracy." Panel discussion featuring Louis Dreyfus, Anya Schiffrin, and Duy Linh Tu. October 22, 2024. https://maisonfrancaise.columbia.edu/events/truth-trust-and-trials-democracy.

Fleming, Melissa. "How AI Is Boosting Disinformation." *Medium*, February 7, 2024. https://melissa-fleming.medium.com/how-ai-is-boosting-disinformation-193d9ab152cb.

Hegde, Chinmay, et al. "NYU Researchers Develop New Real-Time Deepfake Detection Methods." *NYU Tandon School of Engineering*, October 28, 2024. https://engineering.nyu.edu/news/nyu-researchers-develop-new-real-time-deepfake-detection-method.

Johnson, Skyler B., Matthew Parsons, Tanya Dorff, et al. "Cancer Misinformation and Harmful Information on Facebook and Other Social Media: A Brief Report." *Journal of the National Cancer Institute* 114, no. 7 (July 2021): 1036–1039. https://doi.org/10.1093/jnci/djab141.

Le Monde. "Journalism in Crisis: Join Le Monde in English for a Special Event in New York." *Le Monde*, April 3, 2024. https://www.lemonde.fr/en/about-us/article/2024/04/03/journalism-in-crisis-join-le-monde-in-english-for-a-special-event-in-new-york_6667277_115.html.

McIndoe, Peter. "Birds Aren't Real: A Social Movement in a Post-Truth Era." *Birds Aren't Real* (official website). Accessed 2024. https://www.birdsarentreal.com.

Milne, Stefan. "How Instagram Influencers Profit from Anti-Vaccine Misinformation." *UW News*, Information School, University of Washington, March 18, 2024. https://ischool.uw.edu/news/2024/03/qa-how-instagram-influencers-profit-anti-vaccine-misinformation.

Milne, Stefan. "Q&A: How Instagram Influencers Profit from Anti-Vaccine Misinformation." *UW News*, March 11, 2024. https://www.washington.edu/news/2024/03/11/instagram-influencers-profit-anti-vaccine-misinformation-disinformation-wellness/.

Moran, Rachel. "UW Study Reveals How Social Media Influencers Profit from Spreading Misinformation." *Oregon Public Broadcasting*, March 18, 2024.

NYU Tandon School of Engineering. "NYU Researchers Develop New Real-Time Deepfake Detection Method." *NYU Tandon News*, October 28, 2024. https://engineering.nyu.edu/news/nyu-researchers-develop-new-real-time-deepfake-detection-method.

Owen, Taylor. "Taylor Owen on How Disinformation Is Threatening Canada's Democracy." *McGill University Newsroom*, March 6, 2025.

Sadiq, Sheraz. "UW Study Reveals How Social Media Influencers Profit from Spreading Misinformation." *Oregon Public Broadcasting*, March 18, 2024. Accessed March 2024. https://www.opb.org/article/2024/03/18/think-out-loud-uw-study-social-media-influencers-misinformation/.

Schiffrin, Anya. "Truth, Trust, and the Trials of Democracy." Presented at Columbia University, October 22, 2024. https://maisonfrancaise.columbia.edu/events/truth-trust-and-trials-democracy.

Thomas, Elise. "Fake 'Freedom Convoy' Facebook Groups Are Being Run by Foreign

Networks for Profit." *Institute for Strategic Dialogue*, February 24, 2022. https://www.isdglobal.org/digital_dispatches/fake-freedom-convoy-facebook-groups-are-being-run-by-foreign-networks-for-profit/.

Time Staff. "'Free' Crowdfunding Site Linked to Right-Wing Causes Generates a Windfall for Itself." *Time*, March 4, 2022. https://time.com/6150317/givesendgo-trucker-convoy-canada-profits/.

## Chapter 11: Can a Digital Doctor Tell the Truth? Should They?

Broussard, Meredith. *Artificial Unintelligence: How Computers Misunderstand the World.* MIT Press, 2018.

Chou, Wen-Ying Sylvia, April Oh, and William M. P. Klein. "Addressing Health-Related Misinformation on Social Media." *JAMA* 320, no. 23 (2018): 2417–2418. https://doi.org/10.1001/jama.2018.16865.

The Hastings Center. "Ethics of Artificial Intelligence in Health Care." 2023. https://www.thehastingscenter.org/ethics-of-ai-in-health-and-biomedical-research/.

Johnson, Skyler B., et al. "Cancer Misinformation and Harmful Information on Facebook and Other Social Media: A Brief Report." *Journal of the National Cancer Institute* 114, no. 7 (2022): 1036–1039. https://doi.org/10.1093/jnci/djab141.

Marsh, Sarah. "They Thought They Were Doing Good, but It Made People Worse: Why Mental Health Apps Are Under Scrutiny." *The Guardian*, February 4, 2024. https://www.theguardian.com/society/2024/feb/04/they-thought-they-were-doing-good-but-it-made-people-worse-why-mental-health-apps-are-under-scrutiny.

Moran, Rachel. Interview by Dave Miller. "UW Study Reveals How Social Media Influencers Profit from Spreading Misinformation." *Think Out Loud*. Oregon Public Broadcasting, March 18, 2024. https://www.opb.org/article/2024/03/18/think-out-loud-uw-study-social-media-influencers-misinformation/.

Moran, Rachel, and Alice E. Marwick. "Vaccine Misinformation for Profit: Conspiratorial Wellness Influencers on Instagram." *International Journal of Communication* 18 (2024): 405–429. https://ijoc.org/index.php/ijoc/article/view/21128.

Rosenthal, Elisabeth. "Doctors Grapple with Increasingly Worn-Out Patients (and Doctors) on MyChart." *The New York Times*, September 24, 2024. https://www.nytimes.com/2024/09/24/health/ai-patient-messages-mychart.html.

Schapira, Lidia. "Building Patient Trust in a Digital Healthcare World." *Stanford Medical Review* 12, no. 1 (2023): 11–19.

Society of Actuaries. *Primer on Generative AI for Actuaries.* Research report. Society of Actuaries Research Institute, February 2024. https://www.soa.org/globalassets/assets/files/resources/research-report/2024/primer-generative-ai.pdf.

Turkle, Sherry. *Alone Together: Why We Expect More from Technology and Less from Each Other.* Basic Books, 2011.

Williams, Jonathan. "The Risk of Building Emotional Ties with AI." *LinkedIn*, August 2023.

https://www.linkedin.com/posts/jonathanwwilliams_the-risk-of-building-emotional-ties-with-activity-7230951208574734336-sq5F.

Zeavin, Hannah. *The Distance Cure: A History of Teletherapy.* MIT Press, 2021.

## Chapter 12: When Machines Judge "US": The Rise of Algorithmic Truth Assessment

AI Now Institute. *Algorithmic Management in the Workplace: Critical Perspectives on AI, Labor, and Control.* New York University, 2023. https://ainowinstitute.org/publications/algorithmic-management.

Barbaras, Chelsea. "Beyond Bias: Re-imagining the Terms of 'Ethical AI' in Criminal Law." *Georgetown Journal of Law & Modern Critical Race Perspectives* 12, no. 2 (2020): 39–76. https://www.law.georgetown.edu/mcrp-journal/in-print/volume-12-issue-2-fall2020/beyond-bias-re-imagining-the-terms-of-ethical-ai-in-criminal-law.

Bernhardt, Annette, Lisa Kresge, and Reem Suleiman. *Data and Algorithms at Work: The Case for Worker Technology Rights.* UC Berkeley Labor Center, 2023. https://laborcenter.berkeley.edu/data-algorithms-at-work/.

Broussard, Meredith. *Artificial Unintelligence: How Computers Misunderstand the World.* MIT Press, 2018.

Buolamwini, Joy. "Gender Shades: Intersectional Accuracy Disparities in Commercial Gender Classification." *Proceedings of Machine Learning Research* 81 (2018): 77–91.

Chou, Wen-Ying Sylvia, April Oh, and William M. P. Klein. "Addressing Health-Related Misinformation on Social Media." *JAMA* 320, no. 23 (2018): 2417–2418. https://doi.org/10.1001/jama.2018.16865.

Crawford, Kate. *Atlas of AI: Power, Politics, and the Planetary Costs of Artificial Intelligence.* Yale University Press, 2021.

Eubanks, Virginia. *Automating Inequality: How High-Tech Tools Profile, Police, and Punish the Poor.* St. Martin's Press, 2018.

Harkness, Timandra. "The A-Level Algorithm Fiasco Teaches Us That We Need Humans After All." *UnHerd*, August 18, 2020. https://unherd.com/2020/08/how-ofqual-failed-the-algorithm-test/.

Hu, Andrea. "Tell Me How You Really Feel: Zoom's Emotion Detection AI." *W231 Blog*, UC Berkeley School of Information, July 2022. https://blogs.ischool.berkeley.edu/w231/2022/07/06/tell-me-how-you-really-feel-zooms-emotion-detection-ai/.

Kelly, Lauren Kate. "Why Woolworths Workers Can't Sleep at Night: Inside the Supermarket Giant's Controversial 'Framework.'" *The New Daily*, October 24, 2024. https://www.thenewdaily.com.au/work/2024/10/24/woolworths-workers-framework-controversy.

Microsoft Research. "Truth Detection and Workplace Monitoring: A Study of Algorithmic Bias." Technical Report MSR-TR-2024-03. Microsoft Research, 2024.

Moser, Christine, Frank den Hond, and Dirk Lindebaum. "Morality in the Age of Artificially Intelligent Algorithms." *Academy of Management Learning & Education* 21, no. 1 (2022). https://journals.aom.org/doi/abs/10.5465/amle.2020.0287?journalCode=amle.

Noble, Safiya Umoja. *Algorithms of Oppression: How Search Engines Reinforce Racism*. NYU Press, 2018.

Pasquale, Frank. *The Black Box Society: The Secret Algorithms That Control Money and Information*. Harvard University Press, 2015.

Royal Statistical Society. "RSS Responds to Ofqual's Technical Report on A-Level Algorithm." Statement, August 6, 2020. https://www.civilserviceworld.com/professions/article/ofqual-snubbed-offer-of-expert-advice-on-alevels-algorithm-ahead-of-results-row.

Stark, Luke, and Jevan Hutson. "Physiognomic Artificial Intelligence." *Fordham Intellectual Property, Media & Entertainment Law Journal* 32, no. 4 (2022). https://ir.lawnet.fordham.edu/iplj/vol32/iss4/2/.

Venkit, Pranav, Mukund Srinath, and Shomir Wilson. "Automated Ableism: An Exploration of Explicit Disability Biases in Sentiment Analysis Systems." Pennsylvania State University, 2023. https://arxiv.org/pdf/2307.09209.

Winters, Ben, and Alex Engelberg. "What Happens When Computer Programs Automatically Cut Benefits That Disabled People Rely on to Survive?" Center for Democracy & Technology, March 11, 2021. https://cdt.org/insights/what-happens-when-computer-programs-automatically-cut-benefits-that-disabled-people-rely-on-to-survive/.

## Chapter 13: A Robot Stole My Job and a Tech CEO Lied About It

Anderson, Janna, and Lee Rainie. "Themes: The Most Harmful or Menacing Changes in Digital Life That Are Likely by 2035." Pew Research Center: Internet & Technology, June 21, 2023. https://www.pewresearch.org/internet/2023/06/21/themes-the-most-harmful-or-menacing-changes-in-digital-life-that-are-likely-by-2035/.

Autor, David. Interview by Martin Wolf. "Could AI Be a Bigger Threat to US Jobs Than China?" *Financial Times*, April 21, 2025. https://www.ft.com/content/4e260abd-2528-4d34-8fa4-a21eabfd6db9.

Case, Anne, and Angus Deaton. *Deaths of Despair and the Future of Capitalism*. Princeton University Press, 2020.

Férdeline, Ayden. "Predicting the Best and Worst of Digital Life by 2035." *Imagining the Internet*, Elon University, 2023. https://www.elon.edu/u/imagining/surveys/xvi2023/the-best-worst-digital-future-2035/.

Harari, Yuval Noah. *Homo Deus: A Brief History of Tomorrow*. Harper, 2017.

Kapner, Suzanne. "How Your Returns Are Used Against You at Best Buy, Other Retailers." *The Wall Street Journal*, March 13, 2018. https://www.wsj.com/articles/how-your-returns-are-used-against-you-at-best-buy-other-retailers-1520933400.

Paul, Kari. "'I'm Not a Robot': Amazon Workers Push Back Against Surveillance Technology." *The Guardian*, January 7, 2024. https://www.theguardian.com/technology/2024/jan/07/artificial-intelligence-surveillance-workers.

Pew Research Center. "AI, Robotics, and the Future of Jobs." Pew Research Center: Internet & Technology, August 6, 2014. Accessed July 19, 2025. https://www.pewresearch.org/internet/2014/08/06/future-of-jobs/.

Respeecher. "Ethics & Public Policies." Respeecher.com. Accessed July 13, 2025. https://www.respeecher.com/ethics.

Respeecher. "How Respeecher's Voice Cloning Brought Young Luke Skywalker to Life in *The Mandalorian*." Respeecher. Accessed October 20, 2025. https://www.respeecher.com/case-studies/respeecher-synthesized-younger-luke-skywalkers-voice-disneys-mandalorian.

Shan, Benjamine Liu, et al. "Glaze: Protecting Artists from Style Mimicry by Text-to-Image Models." University of Chicago SAND Lab, 2023.

Yang, Andrew. *The War on Normal People: The Truth About America's Disappearing Jobs and Why Universal Basic Income Is Our Future*. Hachette Books, 2018.

Zandt, Deanna. *Share This!: How You Will Change the World with Social Networking*. Berrett-Koehler Publishers, 2010.

## Chapter 14: AI and Art: Can True Art Come from a Machine?

Andersen, Sarah. *Sarah's Scribbles*. Webcomic. Accessed 2023. https://sarahcandersen.com.

Ars Electronica. "Holly+—Welcome to Planet B." *Ars Electronica*, 2021. https://ars.electronica.art/planetb/en/holly-plus/.

Boucher, Claire [@Grimezsz]. "I'll split 50% royalties on any successful AI generated song that uses my voice. Same deal as I would with any artist I collab with. Feel free to use my voice without penalty." *Twitter*, April 23, 2023. https://twitter.com/Grimezsz/status/1650304051718791170.

Carlin, George. *George Carlin Commemorative Collection*. DVD. MPI Home Video, 2018.

Elisens, Brent. "George Carlin: I'm Glad I'm Dead." *Dudesy* podcast special. YouTube video, 59:44. January 9, 2024. https://www.youtube.com/watch?v=6vqWI4z84T0.

Getty Images (US), Inc. v. Stability AI, Inc., No. 1:23-cv-00135 (D. Del., February 3, 2023). Accessed 2023. https://www.courtlistener.com/docket/66788385/getty-images-us-inc-v-stability-ai-inc/.

Hanks, Tom. Instagram post. September 30, 2023. https://www.instagram.com/p/Cx2MsH9rt7q/.

Lawton, Megan. "Will K-pop's AI Experiment Pay Off?" *BBC News*, July 16, 2024. https://www.bbc.com/news/articles/c4ngr3r0914.

Manavis, Sarah. "AI Art and the Ruins of Human Creativity." *New Statesman*, March 17, 2025. https://www.newstatesman.com/politics/media/2025/03/ai-art-and-the-ruins-of-human-creativity.

Pestilence. *Exitivm*. Agonia Records, 2021.

Rutkowski, Greg. *Portfolio*. Portfolio website. Accessed 2023. https://greg-rutkowski.com.

Screen Actors Guild–American Federation of Television and Radio Artists (SAG-AFTRA). *Contract Bulletin – A.I. for Interactive*. SAG-AFTRA Bulletin, 2024. https://www.sagaftra.org/sites/default/files/sa_documents/Contract%20Bulletin%20-%20A.I.%20for%20Interactive.pdf.

Soriano, Rodrigo. "Bad Bunny Attacks Viral AI Song: 'If You Like That Shit, You Don't Deserve to Be My Friends.'" *El País*, November 8, 2023. https://english.elpais.com

/culture/2023-11-08/bad-bunny-attacks-viral-ai-song-if-you-like-that-shit-you-dont-deserve-to-be-my-friends.html.

Stability AI. "Stable Diffusion." Company website. Accessed 2023. https://stability.ai.

Thaler v. Perlmutter, No. 1:22-cv-01564 (D.D.C., August 18, 2023). https://www.copyright.gov/ai/docs/district-court-decision-affirming-refusal-of-registration.pdf.

Universal Music Group. "Universal Music Group Responds to 'Fake Drake' AI Track: Streaming Platforms Have 'A Fundamental Responsibility to Prevent the Use of Their Services in Ways That Harm Artists.'" *Music Business Worldwide*, April 17, 2023. https://www.musicbusinessworldwide.com/universal-music-group-responds-to-fake-drake-ai-track-streaming-platforms-have-a-fundamental-responsibility/.

## Chapter 15: Truth as Code: When Machines Write Reality

Aslama Horowitz, Minna. "Epistemic Rights: An Emerging Frontier for Digital Policy." In *Epistemic Rights in the Digital Age*, edited by Lina Dencik and Joanna Redden, 217–230. Springer, 2024.

Bogen, Miranda. "All the Ways Hiring Algorithms Can Introduce Bias." *Harvard Business Review*, May 6, 2019. https://hbr.org/2019/05/all-the-ways-hiring-algorithms-can-introduce-bias.

Breazeal, Cynthia. "Social Robots." Interview by Marwa ElDiwiny. *IEEE RAS Soft Robotics Podcast*, June 20, 2022. https://www.media.mit.edu/articles/cynthia-breazeal-social-robots/.

Buolamwini, Joy. "Algorithmic Justice League: Addressing Bias in AI Systems." Rubenstein Distinguished Lecture, Sanford School of Public Policy, Duke University, Durham, NC, February 18, 2025.

Crawford, Kate. *Atlas of AI: Power, Politics, and the Planetary Costs of Artificial Intelligence*. Yale University Press, 2021.

Dean, Jeff. "Google Research, 2022 & Beyond: Language, Vision and Generative Models." *Google Research Blog*, January 18, 2023. https://research.google/blog/google-research-2022-beyond-language-vision-and-generative-models.

Harkness, Timandra. "The A-Level Algorithm Fiasco Teaches Us That We Need Humans After All." *UnHerd*, August 18, 2020. https://unherd.com/2020/08/how-ofqual-failed-the-algorithm-test/.

Hui, Yuk. *The Question Concerning Technology in China: An Essay in Cosmotechnics*. Urbanomic Media, 2016.

Klarreich, Erica. "DeepMind Machine Learning Becomes a Mathematical Collaborator." *Quanta Magazine*, February 15, 2022. https://www.quantamagazine.org/deepmind-machine-learning-becomes-a-mathematical-collaborator-20220215/.

Lin, Patrick. "Why Ethics Matters for Autonomous Cars." In *Autonomous Driving*, edited by Markus Maurer, J. Christian Gerdes, Barbara Lenz, and Hermann Winner, 69–85. Springer, 2016. https://doi.org/10.1007/978-3-662-48847-8_4.

Mitchell, Melanie. *Artificial Intelligence: A Guide for Thinking Humans*. Farrar, Straus and Giroux, 2019.

Mitchell, Margaret. Interview by *TIME*. "Margaret Mitchell on AI Ethics and Diversity." *TIME*, September 7, 2023. https://time.com/6309005/margaret-mitchell-ai/.

Noble, Safiya Umoja. *Algorithms of Oppression: How Search Engines Reinforce Racism*. NYU Press, 2018.

Obermeyer, Ziad, Brian Powers, Christine Vogeli, and Sendhil Mullainathan. "Dissecting Racial Bias in an Algorithm Used to Manage the Health of Populations." *Science* 366, no. 6464 (October 25, 2019): 447–453. https://doi.org/10.1126/science.aax2342.

Russell, Stuart. *Human Compatible: Artificial Intelligence and the Problem of Control*. Viking, 2019.

Samuel, Sigal. "He's the Godfather of AI. Now, He Has a Bold New Plan to Keep Us Safe from It." *Vox*, June 19, 2025. https://www.vox.com/future-perfect/417087/ai-safety-yoshua-bengio-lawzero.

Whittaker, Meredith. Testimony before the US House Committee on Science, Space & Technology, hearing on "Artificial Intelligence: Societal and Ethical Implications," June 26, 2019. https://science.house.gov/imo/media/doc/Whittaker%20Testimony.pdf.

Williamson, Geordie. "Is Deep Learning a Useful Tool for the Pure Mathematician?" *arXiv*, April 25, 2023. https://arxiv.org/abs/2304.12602.

## Chapter 16: Feeling the Future: Can Robots Have Empathy?

Breazeal, Cynthia. *Designing Sociable Robots*. MIT Press, 2002.

Cole, Samantha. "Replika Brings Back Erotic AI Roleplay for Some Users After Outcry." *Vice*, March 24, 2023. https://www.vice.com/en/article/replika-brings-back-erotic-ai-roleplay-for-some-users-after-outcry.

Collins, Sawyer, Daniel Hicks, Selma Šabanović, et al. "What Skin Is Your Robot In? Codesign of a Personalizable Robot for People Living with Depression." In *Companion of the 2023 ACM/IEEE International Conference on Human-Robot Interaction*, 511–515. Stockholm, Sweden: ACM/IEEE, March 2023.

Crawford, Kate. *Atlas of AI: Power, Politics, and the Planetary Costs of Artificial Intelligence*. Yale University Press, 2021.

Hassoun, Amelia, Ian Beacock, Sunny Consolvo, Beth Goldberg, Patrick Gage Kelley, and Daniel M. Russell. "Practicing Information Sensibility: How Gen Z Engages with Online Information." In *Proceedings of the 2023 CHI Conference on Human Factors in Computing Systems*, 1–14. 2023. https://doi.org/10.1145/3544548.3581328.

Kahn, P. H., Jr., Takayuki Kanda, Hiroshi Ishiguro, Nancy G. Freier, R. L. Severson, B. T. Gill, J. H. Ruckert, and S. Shen. "'Robovie, You'll Have to Go into the Closet Now': Children's Social and Moral Relationships with a Humanoid Robot." *Developmental Psychology* 48, no. 2 (2012): 303–314. https://doi.org/10.1037/a0027033.

King, Brian. "Could a Robot Be Conscious?" *Philosophy Now*, no. 125 (2018). https://philosophynow.org/issues/125/Could_a_Robot_be_Conscious.

Man, Kingson, and Antonio Damasio. "Homeostasis and Soft Robotics in the Design of

Feeling Machines." *Nature Machine Intelligence* 1 (2019): 446–452. https://doi.org/10.1038/s42256-019-0103-7.

Meisenzahl, Mary. "An AI Company Is Restoring Erotic Roleplay to Chatbot After Users Said It Felt Like Losing a Partner." *Business Insider*, March 25, 2023. https://www.businessinsider.com/ai-company-restoring-erotic-roleplay-chatbot-after-partners-cut-off-2023-3.

Metz, Cade. "A.I. Is Not Sentient. Why Do People Say It Is?" *The New York Times*, August 5, 2022. https://www.nytimes.com/2022/08/05/technology/ai-sentient-google.html.

Neha, B. "Ex-Google Engineer Says the Company's AI Has Come Alive: 'I Am a Person.'" *GOOD*, August 9, 2024. https://www.good.is/google-engineer-believes-ai-can-feel-emotions-and-has-the-same-wants-and-needs-as-people.

OpenAI. *GPT-4o System Card: Safety Report on GPT-4o and Risks of Anthropomorphization*. August 8, 2024. https://openai.com/index/gpt-4o-system-card/.

Picard, Rosalind W. *Affective Computing*. MIT Press, 1997.

Tobin, Grace. "Replika Users Fell in Love with Their AI Chatbot Companions. Then They Lost Them." *ABC News (Australia)*, March 1, 2023. https://www.abc.net.au/news/science/2023-03-01/replika-users-fell-in-love-with-their-ai-chatbot-companion/102028196.

Todd, Katie. "The Risk of Building Emotional Ties with Responsive AI." *Pace University News*, August 15, 2024. https://www.pace.edu/news/risk-of-building-emotional-ties-responsive-ai?seidenberg.

Turkle, Sherry. *Alone Together: Why We Expect More from Technology and Less from Each Other*. Basic Books, 2011.

Turkle, Sherry. "Authenticity in the Age of Digital Companions." *Interactions* 18, no. 3 (2007): 501–517. https://www.dhi.ac.uk/san/waysofbeing/data/communities-murphy-turkle-2007.pdf.

## Chapter 17: What Happens When AI Lies?

Asimov, Isaac. *I, Robot*. Gnome Press, 1950.

Clarke, Roger. "Asimov's Laws of Robotics: Implications for Information Technology." IEEE Computer Society, 1994. https://cse.buffalo.edu/~rapaport/Papers/Papers.by.Others/clarke-asimov-2.pdf.

Dennett, Daniel C. *From Bacteria to Bach and Back: The Evolution of Minds*. W. W. Norton & Company, 2017.

Edelman Trust Institute. *2024 Edelman Trust Barometer*. Edelman Trust Institute, 2024. https://www.edelman.com/trust/2024/trust-barometer.

Intelligencer Staff. "On With Kara Swisher: Trae Stephens on Ethics in AI Warfare." *New York Magazine, Intelligencer*, February 21, 2023. https://nymag.com/intelligencer/2023/02/on-with-kara-swisher-trae-stephens-on-autonomous-warfare-ai.html.

Kurzweil, Ray. *The Singularity Is Near: When Humans Transcend Biology*. Viking, 2005.

Lanier, Jaron. *Ten Arguments for Deleting Your Social Media Accounts Right Now*. Henry Holt, 2018.

Marcus, Gary, and Ernest Davis. *Rebooting AI: Building Artificial Intelligence We Can Trust.* Pantheon, 2019.

Narayanan, Arvind, and Sayash Kapoor. *AI Snake Oil: What Artificial Intelligence Can Do, What It Can't, and How to Tell the Difference.* Princeton University Press, 2024.

Rushkoff, Douglas. *Team Human.* W. W. Norton, 2019.

## Chapter 18: AI's Advancing Role in Financial Truth

Arkham Intelligence. "Did Someone Bot an AI Bot?" *Arkham Intelligence*, October 23, 2024. https://www.arkhamintelligence.com/research/did-someone-bot-an-ai-bot.

Ayrey, Andy. "Truth Terminal: An Experiment in AI-Driven Narrative Generation." Unpublished manuscript, 2024.

Bellan, Rebecca. "The Promise and Warning of Truth Terminal, the AI Bot That Secured $50,000 in Bitcoin from Marc Andreessen." *TechCrunch*, December 19, 2024. https://techcrunch.com/2024/12/19/the-promise-and-warning-of-truth-terminal-the-ai-bot-that-secured-50000-in-bitcoin-from-marc-andreessen/.

Crypto Times. "GOAT Meme Coin Makes Truth Terminal a First AI Crypto Millionaire." *Medium*, October 20, 2024. https://medium.com/@cryptoaitimeswargiya/goat-meme-coin-makes-truth-terminal-a-first-ai-crypto-millionaire-6ba8601f471c.

Derman, Emanuel, and Paul Wilmott. *The Financial Modeler's Manifesto. SSRN*, January 8, 2009. https://papers.ssrn.com/sol3/papers.cfm?abstract_id=1324878.

Hayes, Arthur. "Trump Truth." *Medium*, December 2024. https://cryptohayes.medium.com/trump-truth-fdcbd31f2e26.

Howcroft, Elizabeth. "AI-Generated Content Raises Risk of More Bank Runs, UK Study Shows." *Reuters*, February 14, 2025. https://www.reuters.com/technology/artificial-intelligence/ai-generated-content-raises-risks-more-bank-runs-uk-study-shows-2025-02-14/.

Latour, Bruno. *The Pasteurization of France.* Translated by Alan Sheridan and John Law. Harvard University Press, 1988.

Lomas, Kenneth, and Dave Cliff. "Exploring Narrative Economics: An Agent–Based–Modeling Platform That Integrates Automated Traders with Opinion Dynamics." Cornell University, December 2020. https://arxiv.org/abs/2012.08840.

Lopez-Lira, Alejandro, and Yuehua Tang. "Can ChatGPT Forecast Stock Price Movements? Return Predictability and Large Language Models." *SSRN*, April 2024. https://papers.ssrn.com/sol3/papers.cfm?abstract_id=4412788.

MacKenzie, Donald. *An Engine, Not a Camera: How Financial Models Shape Markets.* MIT Press, 2006.

MacKenzie, Donald, Fabian Muniesa, and Lucia Siu, eds. *Do Economists Make Markets?* Princeton University Press, 2020. https://doi.org/10.2307/j.ctv10vm29m.

Mirowski, Philip. *Never Let a Serious Crisis Go to Waste: How Neoliberalism Survived the Financial Meltdown.* Verso, 2013.

O'Neil, Cathy. *Weapons of Math Destruction: How Big Data Increases Inequality and Threatens Democracy.* Crown, 2016.

US Securities and Exchange Commission. Remarks by Carla Carpenter on Synthetic Sentiment and AI Risk. March 2025.

Sorkin, Andrew Ross, Bernhard Warner, Sarah Kessler, Michael J. de la Merced, Lauren Hirsh, and Ephrat Livni. "An AI-Generated Spoof Rattles the Markets." *The New York Times*, May 23, 2023. https://www.nytimes.com/2023/05/23/business/ai-picture-stock-market.html.

Zuboff, Shoshana. *The Age of Surveillance Capitalism: The Fight for a Human Future at the New Frontier of Power*. PublicAffairs, 2019.

## Chapter 19: The Danger of Data Overload: What Happens When Humans Boil Over?

Berners-Lee, Tim. *Weaving the Web: The Original Design and Ultimate Destiny of the World Wide Web by Its Inventor*. Harper Business, 2000.

Bobinet, Kyra. *Unstoppable Brain: The New Neuroscience That Frees Us from Failure, Eases Our Stress, and Creates Lasting Change*. ForbesBooks, 2024.

Castillo, David R., Siwei Lyu, Christina Milletti, and Cynthia Stewart, eds. *Truth-Seeking in an Age of (Mis)Information Overload*. State University of New York Press, 2024.

Cerf, Vinton G. "The Day the Internet Age Began." *Nature*, 2009. https://pubmed.ncbi.nlm.nih.gov/19865146/.

Feng, John. "Is Your Brain Overloaded? How AI Is Rescuing Us from the Information Tsunami!" *Medium*, December 18, 2023. https://johnfengphd.medium.com/is-your-brain-overloaded-how-ai-is-rescuing-us-from-the-information-tsunami-4427985db6f0.

Gustafson, Clara, and Madison Mann. "Students Reflect on Authenticity of Social Media Activism." *The Evanstonian* (Evanston Township High School), November 19, 2021. https://www.evanstonian.net/feature/2021/11/19/students-reflect-on-authenticity-of-social-media-activism/.

Kovach, Bill, and Tom Rosenstiel. *Blur: How to Know What's True in the Age of Information Overload*. Bloomsbury USA, 2010.

Li, Sophie H., Philip J. Batterham, Alexis E. Whitton, Kate Maston, Asaduzzaman Khan, Helen Christensen, and Aliza Werner-Seidler. "Cross-Sectional and Longitudinal Associations of Screen Time with Adolescent Depression and Anxiety." *British Journal of Clinical Psychology* 64, no. 4 (April 22, 2025): 873–887. https://doi.org/10.1111/bjc.12547.

Oxford University Press. "Brain Rot Added to the Oxford English Dictionary." Oxford University Press, June 26, 2024. https://corp.oup.com/news/brain-rot-added-to-the-oxford-english-dictionary/.

Rosenstiel, Tom, and Bill Kovach. *The Elements of Journalism: What Newspeople Should Know and the Public Should Expect*. Three Rivers Press, 2007.

Solid Project. "Solid for Users." Accessed December 2024. https://solidproject.org/for_users.

## Chapter 20: Teens and Truth: Connecting to Different Truths

Barrett, Lisa Feldman. *How Emotions Are Made: The Secret Life of the Brain*. Houghton Mifflin Harcourt, 2017.

Digitale, Erin. "Stanford/Packard Imaging Study Shows How Humor Activates Kids' Brain Regions." *Stanford Medicine News Center*, January 31, 2012. https://med.stanford.edu/news/all-news/2012/01/stanfordpackard-imaging-study-shows-how-humor-activates-kids-brain-regions.html.

Galloway, Scott. *The Four: The Hidden DNA of Amazon, Apple, Facebook, and Google*. Portfolio, 2017.

Haidt, Jonathan, and Greg Lukianoff. *The Coddling of the American Mind: How Good Intentions and Bad Ideas Are Setting Up a Generation for Failure*. Penguin Books, 2018.

Harris, Tristan. *How a Handful of Tech Companies Control Billions of Minds Every Day*. TED Talk, April 2017. https://www.ted.com/talks/tristan_harris_how_a_handful_of_tech_companies_control_billions_of_minds_every_day.

Harris, Tristan. Testimony before the US Senate Committee on Commerce, Science, and Transportation, June 25, 2019. https://www.commerce.senate.gov/services/files/96e3a739-dc8d-45f1-87d7-ec70a368371d.

Harris, Tristan, and Sara Frueh. "'The Complexity of Technology's Consequences Is Going Up Exponentially, but Our Wisdom and Awareness Are Not.'" *Issues in Science and Technology*, May 16, 2023. https://issues.org/tristan-harris-humane-technology-misinformation-ai-democracy/.

Hassoun, Amelia, Ian Beacock, Sunny Consolvo, Beth Goldberg, Patrick Gage Kelley, and Daniel M. Russell. "Practicing Information Sensibility: How Gen Z Engages with Online Information." In *Proceedings of the 2023 CHI Conference on Human Factors in Computing Systems*, 1–17. April 2023. https://doi.org/10.1145/3544548.3581328.

Haugen, Frances. Testimony before the US Senate Committee on Commerce, Science, and Transportation, Subcommittee on Consumer Protection, Product Safety, and Data Security, "Protecting Kids Online: Testimony from a Facebook Whistleblower," Washington, DC, October 5, 2021.

Intergovernmental Panel on Climate Change. *Climate Change 2021: The Physical Science Basis. Contribution of Working Group I to the Sixth Assessment Report of the Intergovernmental Panel on Climate Change*. Cambridge University Press, 2021.

Lanier, Jaron. *Ten Arguments for Deleting Your Social Media Accounts Right Now*. Henry Holt, 2018.

Lembke, Emma. Testimony before the US Senate Judiciary Committee, Subcommittee on Technology, Privacy, and the Law, February 14, 2023. https://www.judiciary.senate.gov/imo/media/doc/2023-02-14%20-%20Testimony%20-%20Lembke.pdf.

McKinsey & Company. "'True Gen': Generation Z and Its Implications for Companies." McKinsey & Company, November 12, 2018. https://www.mckinsey.com/industries/consumer-packaged-goods/our-insights/true-gen-generation-z-and-its-implications-for-companies.

PBS News Hour. "Students Expose Price Disparities in Low-Income Areas." September 27, 2023. https://www.pbs.org/video/price-check-1695847974/.

Qureshi, Zamaan. Testimony at the Illinois State Senate Judiciary Committee hearing on the Illinois Age-Appropriate Design Code. Design It for Us, September 20, 2023. https://designitforus.org/news/illinois-senate-hearing-on-social-medias-impact-on-children/.

SustainableMedia.Center. "Author Sherry Turkle—at SustainableMedia.Center." Sustainable Media Center. YouTube video, 11:58, December 7, 2022. https://www.youtube.com/watch?v=LdhDjwrztb4.

SustainableMedia.Center. "FULL HOUR: Unveiling the Truth Behind Facebook: Broken Code." Sustainable Media Center. YouTube video, 58:44, April 4, 2024. https://youtu.be/IcOaP2y9YYA?si=RRnbkbkF_Vanvijj.

Turkle, Sherry. *Alone Together: Why We Expect More from Technology and Less from Each Other.* Basic Books, 2011.

Turkle, Sherry. *The Empathy Diaries: A Memoir.* New York: Penguin, 2021.

Turkle, Sherry. *Reclaiming Conversation: The Power of Talk in a Digital Age.* Penguin Press, 2015.

Turkle, Sherry. "Who Do We Become When We Talk to Machines?" March 27, 2024. https://mit-genai.pubpub.org/pub/uawlth3j/release/2.

## Chapter 21: Are We Living in a Post-Truth World?

Anderson, Janna, and Lee Rainie. "The Future of Truth and Misinformation Online." *Pew Research Center.* Last modified October 19, 2017. https://www.pewresearch.org/internet/2017/10/19/the-future-of-truth-and-misinformation-online/.

Danner, Chas. "How Vance and Trump's Lies About Springfield, Ohio, Continue to Unravel." *New York Magazine (Intelligencer)*, September 18, 2024. https://nymag.com/intelligencer/article/vance-trump-pet-eating-lies-springfield-ohio-haitian-migrants.html.

Doyle, Arthur Conan. "Fairies Photographed—An Epoch-Making Event." *The Strand Magazine* 60, no. 360 (December 1920): 462–468.

Fuller, Steve. *Post-Truth: Knowledge as a Power Game.* (Key Issues in Modern Sociology). Anthem Press, 2018.

Gooding, Dan. "Trump Drops Springfield Visit as Governor Warns of 'Strain' on City." *Newsweek*, September 23, 2024. https://www.newsweek.com/springfield-ohio-trump-visit-1957958.

Halpert, Madeline. "Vance Doubles Down on False Pet-Eating Claims." *BBC News*, September 15, 2024. https://www.bbc.com/news/articles/cgj447j5711o.

Kasprak, Alex. "No Evidence Haitian Immigrants Are Eating Ducks, Geese or Pets in Springfield, Ohio." *Snopes*, September 9, 2024. https://www.snopes.com/fact-check/cats-ducks-haitians-springfield/.

Lakoff, George. *Don't Think of an Elephant! Know Your Values and Frame the Debate.* Chelsea Green Publishing, 2004.

Lynch, Michael P. *The Internet of Us: Knowing More and Understanding Less in the Age of Big Data.* Liveright, 2016.

McIntyre, Lee. *Post-Truth*. MIT Press, 2018.

Oxford Languages. "Word of the Year 2016." Accessed October 21, 2025. https://languages.oup.com/word-of-the-year/2016/.

Ramirez Uribe, Maria, and Amy Sherman. "They're Eating the Pets: Trump, Vance Earn PolitiFact's Lie of the Year for Claims About Haitians." *PolitiFact*, December 17, 2024. https://www.politifact.com/article/2024/dec/17/theyre-eating-the-pets-trump-vance-earn-politifact/.

Rosen, Jay. "If 'He Said, She Said' Journalism Is Irretrievably Lame, What's Better?" *PressThink*, September 23, 2011. https://pressthink.org/2011/09/if-he-said-she-said-journalism-is-irretrievably-lame-whats-better/.

Rosen, Jay. "If Mitt Romney Were Running a 'Post-Truth' Campaign, Would the Political Press Report It?" *PressThink*, July 12, 2012. https://pressthink.org/2012/07/if-mitt-romney-were-running-a-post-truth-campaign-would-the-political-press-report-it/.

Rosen, Jay. "Show Your Work: The New Terms for Trust in Journalism." *PressThink*, December 31, 2017. https://pressthink.org/2017/12/show-work-new-terms-trust-journalism/.

Rosen, Jay. "The View from Nowhere: Questions and Answers." *PressThink*, November 10, 2010. https://pressthink.org/2010/11/the-view-from-nowhere-questions-and-answers/.

Vance, J. D. Interview by Dana Bash. State of the Union. CNN, September 15, 2024. https://transcripts.cnn.com/show/sotu/date/2024-09-15/segment/01.

Whitehouse, John. "Misinformer of the Year: Steve Bannon's 'Flood the Zone with Shit' Approach Is Destroying American Democracy." *Media Matters for America*, December 28, 2021. https://www.mediamatters.org/steve-bannon/misinformer-year-steve-bannons-flood-zone-shit-approach-destroying-american-democracy.

### Chapter 22: The Future of Truth: Two Scenarios

Botsman, Rachel. *Who Can You Trust?: How Technology Brought Us Together and Why It Might Drive Us Apart*. PublicAffairs, 2017.

Crawford, Kate. *Atlas of AI: Power, Politics, and the Planetary Costs of Artificial Intelligence*. Yale University Press, 2021.

Frey, Thomas. "12 Famous Quotes That Will Change Your Life." Futurist Speaker: Thomas Frey (blog), February 22, 2024. https://futuristspeaker.com/futurist-thomas-frey-insights/12-famous-quotes-that-will-change-your-life/.

Frey, Thomas. *Epiphany Z: 8 Radical Visions for Transforming Your Future*. Morgan James Publishing, 2017.

Gebru, Timnit. "Race and Gender." In *The Oxford Handbook of Ethics of AI*, edited by Markus D. Dubber, Frank Pasquale, and Sunit Das, 252–269. Oxford University Press, 2020.

Khanna, Ayesha, and Parag Khanna. *Hybrid Reality: Thriving in the Emerging Human-Technology Civilization*. TED Books, 2012.

Lanier, Jaron. *You Are Not a Gadget: A Manifesto*. Alfred A. Knopf, 2010.

Leonhard, Gerd. *Technology vs. Humanity: The Coming Clash Between Man and Machine*. Futures Agency GmbH, 2019.

Medscape. "Medscape 2050: Daniel Kraft, MD." YouTube video, February 12, 2025. https://youtu.be/-OJUilLuvwU?si=0FpeIyFUpuQEaNIg.

Obama, Barack. *A Promised Land.* Crown Publishing Group, 2020.

O'Neil, Cathy. *Weapons of Math Destruction: How Big Data Increases Inequality and Threatens Democracy.* Crown, 2016.

Turkle, Sherry. *Alone Together: Why We Expect More from Technology and Less from Each Other.* Basic Books, 2011.

Zuboff, Shoshana. *The Age of Surveillance Capitalism: The Fight for a Human Future at the New Frontier of Power.* PublicAffairs, 2019.

# Index

## About the Author

Photo by Hollenderx2

Steven Rosenbaum is a pioneering media entrepreneur, Emmy-winning producer, and author who has consistently been at the forefront of storytelling and innovation. With two Emmy Awards for groundbreaking programming and two patents in video discovery and advertising technology, Steven has founded and led transformative digital media companies, including Magnify.net, Broadcast News Network, CameraPlanet, and Waywire, which he purchased from founder and US Senator Cory Booker.

As the executive director of the NYC Media Lab, Steven led a six-university consortium—including New York University, Columbia University, The New School, the City University of New York (CUNY), Pratt Institute, and Manhattan University—focused on advancing media innovation.

Today, as the founder of the Sustainable Media Center, Steven is championing a new era of ethical and impactful media. The Center is a 501(c)(3) organization with a diverse board of over 180 leaders in media, technology, and academia, including 25 Gen Z Next Gen board members. With its mission rooted in intergenerational collaboration, the Center is building a community to explore, experiment, and deploy solutions that empower young people to navigate and shape their increasingly media-centric lives with agency and well-being at the forefront.

Rosenbaum is a regular public speaker at events including TED, SXSW, The Lobby, and university conferences. He's also a writer, blogger, and podcaster. During the rise of social media, the growth of misinformation, and the emergence of AI as driver of content creation and digital overload, he spent four years at the prestigious Gallatin School of Individualized Study at NYU, searching for the historic, philosophical, and technical threads of truth. Today Rosenbaum has a master's degree in Truth, with no intention to get his PhD, though the title "Dr. Truth" is appealing.

STEVEN ROSENBAUM

OFFERS:

- PUBLIC SPEAKING
- CONSULTING
- START UP ADVISORY WORK
- GEN Z PARTNERSHIPS

TRUTH CHATS ARE ALWAYS FREE!

WWW.THEFUTUREOFTRUTH.US